IN DEFIANCE OF THE LAW

Modern American Literature
New Approaches

Yoshinobu Hakutani
General Editor

Vol. 26

PETER LANG
New York • Washington, D.C./Baltimore • Bern
Frankfurt am Main • Berlin • Brussels • Vienna • Oxford

Marisa Anne Pagnattaro

IN DEFIANCE OF THE LAW

From Anne Hutchinson
to Toni Morrison

PETER LANG
New York • Washington, D.C./Baltimore • Bern
Frankfurt am Main • Berlin • Brussels • Vienna • Oxford

Library of Congress Cataloging-in-Publication Data

Pagnattaro, Marisa Anne.
In defiance of the law: from Anne Hutchinson
to Toni Morrison / Marisa Anne Pagnattaro.
p. cm. — (Modern American literature: new approaches; vol. 26)
Includes bibliographical references and index.
1. American fiction—Women authors—History and criticism. 2. Hutchinson, Anne Marbury,
1591–1643. 3. Women and literature—United States—History. 4. Law and literature. 5. Justice
in literature. 6. Slavery in literature. 7. Afro-American women
in literature. I. Title. II. Modern American literature (New York, N.Y.); vol. 26.
PS374.W6 P34   813.009'355—dc21   00-056759
ISBN 0-8204-5115-0
ISSN 1078-0521

Die Deutsche Bibliothek-CIP-Einheitsaufnahme

Pagnattaro, Marisa Anne:
In defiance of the law: from Anne Hutchinson
to Toni Morrison / Marisa A. Pagnattaro.
−New York; Washington, D.C./Baltimore; Bern;
Frankfurt am Main; Berlin; Brussels; Vienna; Oxford: Lang.
(Modern American literature: new approaches; Vol. 26)
ISBN 0-8204-5115-0

Cover design by Dutton & Sherman Design
Cover art by Ambler Hutchinson
Typesetting by Lee Ann Pingel

© 2001 Peter Lang Publishing, Inc., New York

All rights reserved.
Reprint or reproduction, even partially, in all forms such as microfilm,
xerography, microfiche, microcard, and offset strictly prohibited.

For Simone Genovesa
so you will always remember
una brújula en la sangre

☙ CONTENTS ❧

Acknowledgments ix

List of Abbreviations xi

Introduction: In Defiance of the Law 1

PART I: TESTING THE BOUNDS OF COLONIAL LAW 7

Chapter 1: The Law of Divine Revelation 13
      Anne Hutchinson and the Antinomian
      Controversy

Chapter 2: The Law of the Great Spirit 47
      Catharine Maria Sedgwick's *Hope Leslie*

PART II: OVERCOMING SLAVE LAW 77

Chapter 3: Preemancipation Activism 83
      Harriet Beecher Stowe's *Uncle Tom's Cabin*
      and Harriet Jacobs's *Incidents in the Life of a*
      Slave Girl

Chapter 4: Perspectives after Civil Rights 115
      Sherley Anne Williams's *Dessa Rose* and
      Toni Morrison's *Beloved*

Conclusion: Beyond the Rule of Law 155

Notes 159

Bibliography 191

Index 227

❧ Acknowledgments ❧

I appreciate the critical insights of Hugh Kenner, Milner Ball, and the late Margaret Dickie, who all stimulated my thinking about literature. I am grateful to my good friends Leigh-Anne Marcellin, Mary Carney, and Janet Hurley for their valuable input during the writing process, and to Bruce Borowsky for a remark in passing that shaped the framework for this book.

I would like to acknowledge that research and writing time for this project was substantially funded by the American Association of University Women Educational Foundation. Special thanks are due to the late Blodwen Williams Zeitler and her daughter, Gwen Zeitler Brown, who made the AAUW fellowship possible through their commitment to women and education.

Special thanks are due also to Lee Ann Pingel for her careful attention to detail during the editing process and for the creative typesetting and design, as well as for her enthusiasm about this work.

I am forever indebted to my parents, Marian and Peter Pagnattaro, and my sister, Scilla Pagnattaro Gadjo, for their unceasing support and encouragement through difficult times. I also want to thank Vanita Morgan for all of her invaluable help over the last few years and Jack Beasley for his thoughts and generosity.

Most of all, my deepest thanks are to John F. Beasley, Jr., my partner in life, law, and literature, and to Simone Genovesa Beasley, my daughter, who has inspired me to look at the world with a new perspective.

⇒ List of Abbreviations ⇐

AC "The Examination of Mrs. Anne Hutchinson at the Court at Newton" in David D. Hall, ed., *The Antinomian Controversy, 1636–1638: A Documentary History*, 2nd ed. (Durham: Duke University Press, 1990).

Other documents in this collection are identified using the following abbreviations:

Hall: Commentary by David D. Hall, including the introduction.
Fast-Day: John Wheelwright, *A Fast-Day Sermon*.
Short Story: John Winthrop, *A Short Story of the Rise, reign, and ruine of the Antinomians, Familists & Libertines*
Preface: Thomas Weld, "Preface" to Winthrop's "Short Story"
Church Trial: "A Report of the Trial of Anne Hutchinson before the Church of Boston"

B Toni Morrison, *Beloved* (New York: Plume/Putnam Penguin, 1987).

DR Sherley Anne Williams, *Dessa Rose* (New York: Berkley Books, 1986).

HL Catharine Maria Sedgwick, *Hope Leslie*, 1827, ed. Mary Kelly (New Brunswick, NJ: Rutgers University Press, 1987).

I Harriet Jacobs, *Incidents in the Life of a Slave Girl: Written By Herself*, 1861, ed. Jean Fagan Yellin (Cambridge: Harvard University Press, 1987).

Key Harriet Beecher Stowe, *A Key to Uncle Tom's Cabin* (London: Thomas Bosworth, 1853).

PHS Catharine Maria Sedgwick, *The Power of Her Sympathy: The Autobiography and Journal of Catharine Maria Sedgwick*, edited by Mary Kelly (Boston: Massachusetts Historical Society, 1953).

UTC Harriet Beecher Stowe *Uncle Tom's Cabin; Or, Life Among the Lowly*, 1852 (New York: Penguin, 1986).

JW John Winthrop, *The Journal of John Winthrop, 1630–1649*, edited by Richard S. Dunn, James Savage, and Laetitia Yeandle (Cambridge: Belknap Press of Harvard University Press, 1996).

❧ Introduction ❦
In Defiance of the Law

> Do you imagine that a city can continue to exist and not be turned upside down, if the legal judgments which are pronounced in it have no force but are nullified and destroyed by private persons?
> —Plato, *Crito*

Nearly every law mediates between the desire for individual liberty and the perceived necessity for maintaining social order. As such, the "legal process has always acted as an expression of social control."[1] In practice, the law acts "to assure people that their particular consciences can be subordinated—indeed, morally must be subordinated—to the collective judgment of society."[2] Those who benefit no doubt echo Thomas Paine's celebration of the law in *Common Sense*: "in America THE LAW IS KING."[3] Individuals who are subordinated, however, should turn Paine's criticism of the British monarchy onto American law and, likewise, not necessarily assume that "the king is wiser" than the people.[4]

Literature is a powerful tool for exploring jurisprudential issues and looking critically at the American legal system. Since the publication of James Boyd White's *The Legal Imagination* in 1973, a number of scholars have attempted to define and redefine the relationship between law and literature.[5] There are four primary strands of thinking in this emerging discipline. The first, "law in literature," operates under the assumption that knowledge of the law can enhance understanding of a literary work. Scholarship in this area uses a knowledge of the law to add another dimension to interpretations of legal themes and characters in works of literature. The second, "law and literature as language," looks at the way the language of law and of literature—both a "system of signs around which we constitute ourselves as a community"—fulfill rhetorical functions in society. This very broad category encompasses divergent analyses from a variety of perspectives, including legal rhetoric, semiotics, narrative scholarship, and asceticism. The next group, known as "law as literary movement," traces the development of law in connection with the evolution of literature, philosophy, and the fine arts. This kind of scholarship treats the study of law as one of the humanities (as opposed to a social science). A final intersection considers "law and literature as ethical discourse," based on the belief that the moral lessons of literature further legal thinking about specific problems. This last perspective has a more activist stance and encompasses some of the most provocative scholarship. Much of the law-and-literature scholarship to date falls within one or more of these often overlapping* categories.[6]

These various interdisciplinary ways of looking at law and literature have developed out of the early philosophically diverse scholarship by James Boyd White, Richard Posner, Robin West,[†] Richard Weisberg, and Stanley Fish, all of whom endeavored to stake out the first law-and-literature positions by using well-known works of literature.[7] Other scholars, like Brook Thomas and Robert Ferguson, have subsequently taken a much more historical position, using legal history to shed light on literary works.[8] Within the last few years, a number of scholars have explored a variety of interests, including philosophy, theory, and the concept of narrative jurisprudence.[9] The study of law and literature has also yielded a number of collections of essays on a range of related concerns[10] and anthologies that can be used to teach law and literature classes.[11] Additionally, there is a growing body of feminist legal scholarship that uses stories to advance concern about issues related to how women are treated under the judicial system.[12]

Even the most cursory glance at the various texts reveals that there is no consensus of opinion about the relationship of law and literature and how these two disciplines can be used to advance each other.

---

* Held identifies the following additional categories of law-and-literature related work: meta-criticism, pedagogy, bibliography, anthologies, and foreign language articles.

† Robin West in *Caring for Justice* uses literature to advance her argument that women's lived experiences and perspectives should be incorporated into a theory of justice that addresses harms that women suffer disproportionately and distinctly.

Indeed, in a Phi Beta Kappa lecture, James Boyd White renewed his position that law is a subject for consideration as one of the humanities.[13] This is squarely at odds with Richard Posner's positions in his revised and enlarged edition of *Law and Literature*. Even though Posner concedes that law and literature have "significant commonalities and intersections," he continues to emphasize what he views as the essential differences between the two disciplines, because law "is a system of social control" and literature "is an art."[14] Given this dichotomy of opinion, it is little wonder that there continues to be much enthusiastic debate about this interdisciplinary scholarship.

Without attempting to uncover any grand key to the mythology surrounding the relationship between law and literature, an exploration of fictional and true-life depictions of women over a wide-ranging period in American literature provides the opportunity to explore the tension between the desire for social control—as evidenced by the law—and the effect on individuals—as depicted in art. Literary history establishes each work's place in American literature; legal history gives depth to the jurisprudential concerns raised in each character's story. Robert Cover has argued that "Legal interpretive acts signal and occasion the imposition of violence upon others: A judge articulates her understanding of a text, and as a result, somebody loses his freedom, his property, his children, even his life."[15]

By offering multiple levels of interpretation, literature highlights the effects of this violence and offers a forum for analyzing the law. Drawing on what Robin West has called "humanistic legal criticism," or the use of the humanities as a method (or set of methods) of criticizing law's authority,[16] literature can be used to "unmask the law's devices for legitimacy."[17] To the limited extent that categories can be useful, like those in the critical legal studies movement, I am interested in exploring and critiquing the "dominant vision" of law.[18] Moreover, I am philosophically aligned with those who believe that legal scholarship would benefit from exposure to narratives or stories that give an account not reflected in mainstream legal thinking.

The sentiment of John H. Wigmore (1863–1943), Dean of the Law School at Northwestern University and one of the first legal scholars to integrate literature with legal education, is instructive. He believed that a novel is a "catalogue of life's characters" and that lawyers, "whose highest problems call for a perfect understanding of human character and a skillful use of this knowledge, must expect to seek in fiction as in an encyclopedia, that learning which cannot hope to encompass his own limited experience of the humans whom chance enables him to observe at close range."[19]

Not only lawyers need to seek this learning, however. A consideration of the plight of various characters provides an understanding of the operation of social forces that become legally institutionalized, thereby creating a conflict central to each narrative and to life generally. Lawyers and non-lawyers alike can benefit from a legal-literary analysis as a valuable source of interdisciplinary knowledge about how the law informs each story and, in turn, how each story can be used to look critically at the law.

This book focuses on works that are rooted overtly in American social history, but, inasmuch as each central character breaks the law, the underpinnings of these works are also tied more subtly to legal history. American law exerts social control by reinforcing expectations about how an allegedly democratic society should operate. What follows is an exploration of the law's effect on the individual women in the selected works. Each woman acts according to her own code at odds with civil law—and thereby challenges the established order. These clashes between individual will and social order provide fertile ground for examining how the law shapes each character's life and for considering whether "justice" is found in the law or in the "lawless" act.

The law, thus, provides a new way of looking at each text and, in turn, each text can be used to look critically at the law. Part I, "Testing the Bounds of Colonial Law," explores the effects of evolving early American law. Chapter 1, "The Law of Divine Revelation: Anne Hutchinson and the Antinomian Controversy," focuses on the legal proceedings brought against Hutchinson for publicly exercising and promulgating her religious beliefs to an ever-growing group of men and women. The "examination" was designed to pressure Hutchinson to recant her beliefs and submit to the religious view of the majority. Hutchinson's mentor, John Cotton, capitulated to the colonial authorities, leaving Hutchinson alone to defend herself. She did so ably until her religious conviction overtook her advocacy skills. When she insisted that she was a direct conduit to God, Hutchinson was adjudicated as extremely dangerous to the authority of the established governmental and spiritual leaders of the colony. Fledgling colonial law was then used to banish Hutchinson from the Massachusetts Bay Colony.

INTRODUCTION

Chapter 2, "The Law of the Great Spirit: Catharine Maria Sedgwick's *Hope Leslie*," explores a similar phenomenon. Sedgwick uses this novel to give her nineteenth-century audience a window into the seventeenth-century clash between the colonists and the Pequot Indians. Early in this work, Sedgwick depicts a bloody scene in which a leader of the Pequot tribe retaliates against a colonial family. Thereafter, two Native American women of the colony are prosecuted because they are perceived as threatening to the community. Because the colonists do not understand Native American customs and fear that such cultural allegiances threaten their own values, Nelema and Magawisca are each brought before a colonial court to answer to vague accusations of wrongdoing. Nelema is condemned for using a folk remedy to save a white man's life, and Magawisca stands on the brink of conviction for her stalwart refusal to renounce her heritage in favor of colonial authority. The prosecutions of Anne Hutchinson, Nelema, and Magawisca offer a glimpse into the workings of colonial law and the country's early leaders' great concern about their ability to survive in the new world when faced with cultural and religious dissension.

Part II, "Overcoming Slave Law," examines the way federal and state law was used to entrench slavery and to prevent African Americans from enjoying the same rights as other American citizens. This section focuses on the effects of federal and selected state slave laws on female slaves, including the lack of protection against rape and sexual violence, the lack of sanction for marriage and child custody, and the fugitive slave laws. Chapter 3, "Pre-Emancipation Activism," uses Harriet Beecher Stowe's *Uncle Tom's Cabin* and Harriet Jacobs's *Incidents in the Life of a Slave Girl* to examine how these two authors argued for civil disobedience against slave law. By presenting Eliza and Linda Brent as good mothers who are unable to be "perfect" and law-abiding because of the evils of slavery, these books present a compelling case for the abolition of slavery and the recognition of African Americans as citizens under the Constitution.

Chapter 4, "Perspectives after Civil Rights " is a continuation of the legal issues raised in chapter 3, using the perspective of two twentieth-century works, Sherley Anne Williams's *Dessa Rose* and Toni Morrison's *Beloved*. By engaging with their characters' interior lives, Williams and Morrison create stories based on historical incidents that remember the past injustices perpetrated under slave law and suggest groundwork for racial healing in the present. In both novels, the protagonists lash out against an oppressive legal system and are driven to violence. Dessa Rose fights back after her lover is brutally killed by their master; as a result, she is sold to a slave trader. Later, as part of a coffle, she helps to lead an uprising that results in many injuries and in the death of several white men. In another violent reaction against oppression, Morrison's Sethe murders her daughter rather than let her be sent back into slavery. Both Williams and Morrison present these acts as understandable under the circumstances but stop short of condoning the brutality. Instead of advocating violence as a response to unjust laws, Williams and Morrison offer a model of justice worth striving for, one based on interracial cooperation and individual empowerment. Ultimately, Dessa Rose's friendship with a white female plantation owner creates a sense of sisterhood that she will carry forward throughout her life and that proves essential for moving beyond racial stereotypes. Likewise, Sethe realizes that her power as an individual is sustaining and life affirming in the face of injustice. These novels delineate the pernicious nature of slave law but then offer a basis for justice in the future.

Anne Hutchinson, Nelema, Magawisca, Eliza, Linda Brent, Dessa Rose, and Sethe all act according to a core sense of beliefs and values independent of man-made rules of law. As such, the conflict between their individual liberty and the social order offers a forum for considering the jurisprudential implications of their acts and the nature of the law. Their acts of civil disobedience make a powerful statement about the importance of defying unjust laws. Although each woman was perceived as a criminal by the authorities of her day, civil disobedience can never be equated with criminal disobedience. As Hannah Arendt writes, "There is all the difference in the world... between the criminal's avoiding the public eye and the civil disobedient's taking the law into his own hands in open defiance."[20]

Inasmuch as these women hold onto their ideals when faced with a system of justice wholly inconsistent with their own, each of them reminds us of the social and legal change that has already occurred in the past and of the necessity to continue to look critically at the effects of legal doctrine both now and in the future.

Part I

TESTING THE BOUNDS OF COLONIAL LAW

PART I

Testing the Bounds of Colonial Law

>...wee must be knitt together in this worke as one man, wee must entertaine each other in brotherly Affeccion...for wee must Consider that wee shall be as a Citty vpon a Hill, the eies of all people are vppon us.
>—John Winthrop, "A Modell of Christian Charity"

>...whether now the Lord begins not to send (as shepherds vse to doe their dogs to fetch in their stragling sheep so he) the Indians vpon his servants, to make them cleaue more close togither, and prize each other, to prevent contentions of Brethren which may proue as hard to break as Castle barres, and stop their now beginning breaches before they be as the letting out of many waters that cannot be gathered in againe.
>—John Higginson, letter to John Winthrop

When John Winthrop was on the deck of the flagship *Arabella* enroute to New England in 1630, he delivered his lay sermon, "A Modell of Christian Charity." Filled with the hope of starting a new Christian community in New England, he envisioned a society based on two rules: "Justice and Mercy."[1] With this premise he set out to lead the Puritans with a "basic model of Christian love."[2] An essential feature of Winthrop's vision was "his desire for form, unity, and stability in society,"[3] which he said would require "moderateing and restraineing" the wicked.[4] By the mid-1630s, however, that endeavor appeared to be a difficult task. Massachusetts Bay Colony was threatened by internal dissension over religious teachings and by the external threat of the Pequot Indians.

Winthrop and other colonial leaders were faced with the problem of how to maintain order and to preserve their community. When

Winthrop was re-elected Governor of Massachusetts Bay Colony in May 1637, the legal system in the colony was just beginning to be formed. A court system was established, but there was no comprehensive code of laws. Moreover, very little guidance on the matter was offered by the Massachusetts Bay Charter, which merely required that "lawes and ordinances be not contrarie or repugnant to the lawes and statutes of this our realme of England."[5] The law was, instead, literally evolving on an *ad hoc* basis to address situations as they arose. The proceedings against Anne Hutchinson and the fictionalized accounts of the trials against two Native American women in Catharine Maria Sedgwick's novel, *Hope Leslie*, offer a glimpse into this time period and the evolving and uncodified nature of colonial law. The legal action against these three women illustrate how the Puritans used the rudimentary legal system to clarify their "communal borders,"[6] thereby preserving the values of the community against the threat of dangerous individualism.

Anne Hutchinson was perceived as a menace to the social order of the state and the church. She defied Protestant orthodoxy, which held that people are saved by their faith in Christ, that ascribing Christ's virtue to an individual's account is his "justification," and that the justified person would thereafter strive to achieve a perfect Christian life, which would be his "sanctification."[7] Following the teaching of John Cotton, Hutchinson promulgated a restatement of this doctrine, concluding that good or bad conduct is irrelevant in determining who is saved. This position was considered social anathema. To the leaders of the Massachusetts Bay Colony, such beliefs could lead to the abandonment of all individual moral responsibility, to an ethical anarchy with dangerous social consequences. Hutchinson's testimony before the General Court confirmed her beliefs and, when she refused to recant her admission that she received special revelations direct from God, resulted in her expulsion from the colony and, thereafter, banishment from the Church. Vilified as a "monstrous threat" to the social order, Hutchinson epitomized dangerous individualism and represented a potential catalyst for social insurrection. Hutchinson's story serves as an example of the power of the law to reinforce a social structure deemed appropriate or necessary for the times.

A similar phenomenon is at work in Catharine Maria Sedgwick's novel *Hope Leslie*. Through this fictional but historical novel, Sedgwick analyzes the threat the Pequot Indians posed to the Massachusetts Bay Colony. Published in 1827, this novel is set in 1637, the same year that

Anne Hutchinson was ordered banished and that the colonists waged war against the Pequots. In contrast to many of the surviving historical accounts, Sedgwick endeavored to supplement the historical record with a more balanced vision of the colonists' displacement of Native Americans through the characters of Nelema and Magawisca. By illustrating the human drama in the interactions, Sedgwick presents a complicated historical picture in which the Pequots' fierce resistance and the fear that this generates helps to shape colonial policy and law. Both Nelema and Magawisca adhere to their Native American ways in the face of enormous pressure to assimilate into the community. Because the colonists do not understand Nelema's folk remedy for snake bite, she is prosecuted as a kind of a devil-inspired witch. Likewise, as the daughter of a vengeful Pequot leader, Magawisca finds herself an easy target for vague allegations of treachery, a situation exacerbated by her refusal to relinquish her Indian customs and values. Similar to Hutchinson,* when Magawisca refuses the opportunity to renounce her principles and embrace mainstream Christian beliefs, she is condemned by the court. The legal system is used as a "solution" for the problems presented by women whom the colonists fear have the power to undermine the community. Through the character of Hope Leslie, however, Sedgwick reworks the colonial system of "justice" and frees both Nelema and Magawisca, suggesting that the prosecutions were unjust.

Anne Hutchinson, Nelema, and Magawisca are defiant before the colonial legal tribunal. Each of these characters tests the bounds of colonial law and thereby prompts her community to circumscribe the legal parameters of their society. The deviant behavior of Hutchinson and of Native Americans (as represented by Nelema and Magawisca) actually helped the community "develop a tighter bond of solidarity" and fuse "together into a common sense of morality."[8] In other words, by using the legal process to reject vehemently Hutchinson's religious views and Nelema's and Magawisca's Native American values, the colonists were able to define formally their beliefs and social views. Thus, these literary works provide a forum for exploring how this developing legal system was at odds with individualism and dissension, which were perceived as destructive to the very existence of the Massachusetts Bay Colony.

---

* Fetterley suggests even that inasmuch as "supporters of Hutchinson refused to take part in the expedition against the Pequots, we might be justified in reading the trial of Magawisca as a coded representation of the trial of Anne Hutchinson" (513).

Chapter 1

The Law of Divine Revelation

Anne Hutchinson and the Antinomian Controversy

> ...a most remarkable case, in which religious freedom was wholly inconsistent with public safety, and where principles of an illiberal age indicated the very course which must have been pursued by worldly policy and enlightened wisdom.
>
> —Nathaniel Hawthorne, "Mrs. Hutchinson"

The 1630s were a precarious time in the Massachusetts Bay Colony, faced as it was with internal dissension and external threats to its existence. The colonists left England seeking political and religious freedom, yet a delicate balance needed to be struck between the rights of individuals and the preservation of the community. Anne Hutchinson presented a formidable test to the colony's willingness to entertain the promulgation of beliefs that could threaten the core of its existence. The judicial proceedings against Hutchinson reveal that there was a limit to the extent to which that freedom could be exercised. Hutchinson was perceived as threatening the social order of the community and, accordingly, undermining the colonists' efforts to be model citizens and thereby enhance their status before God. When John Winthrop, a prominent leader in the Massachusetts Bay Colony, deemed Hutchinson "this *American Jesabel*," he assigned her a pivotal role in what has become known as the Antinomian Controversy (Short Story, *AC,* 310).* All of the biblical

---

* David Hall argues that "the major figure is John Cotton" in the Antinomian Controversy (p. 4) and Battis repeatedly asserts that Anne Hutchinson was an

variations of the story of Jezebel share the same undercurrent—fear and fascination with a commanding woman—and converge at a common point of anxiety where she is made an object of reproach.* In flagrant contradiction to the teachings of mainstream ministers, Hutchinson publically espoused a Calvinist "covenant of grace," maintaining that only God's grace could save human beings from their sins and that good works could not be used to determine or secure salvation. Because this divine grace is not earned through moral behavior, Winthrop and many of the other Puritans feared that such teaching could only undermine their dream of creating an orderly society based on deep religious commitment and a sense of ethical duty.

With a characteristic degree of Puritan self-scrutiny, Winthrop and other leaders of the Massachusetts Bay Colony seemed to be captivated by the conflict generated by Hutchinson, yet feared that the extreme nature of her views threatened the existence of the community. If Hutchinson's views on the covenant of free grace prevailed, social anarchy could result. Winthrop, in an effort to defend his own leadership position and to reinforce the Puritan work ethic needed to build the community, marshaled other political and ecclesiastical leaders to utilize the full force of the law to urge Hutchinson to conform and relinquish her "dangerous" positions. Using the rudimentary legal system of the time, colonial leaders accordingly expelled the woman who so seriously endangered the authority of the established governmental and spiritual leaders of the colony and refused to recant her beliefs.†

The prosecution of Hutchinson—and others posing potential threats to the security of the colony—demonstrates the degree to which colonial law was slowly developing in response to the social needs of the community. Lacking a legal code, the colony was literally passing laws in an as-needed fashion as threats to the community arose. Moreover, even though the law established a court system that employed procedures similar to those of the time in English courts,

---

emotionally unstable woman who looked to men for guidance. Most recently, however (1996), the editors of John Winthrop's journals acknowledge that John Winthrop "certainly saw Hutchinson as his chief enemy in 1636–1638" (p. 194 n. 22).

* References to Jezebel are found in I Kings 21:5–15, II Kings 9:30–37, and Revelation 2:20–23.

† Norton and Lang both pointedly suggest that Hutchinson's gender was an important factor in the treatment she received from colonial leaders.

these provisions "provided few of the safeguards that are presently regarded as essential to the fair conduct of a criminal trial."¹

ANNE HUTCHINSON:
A LIFETIME OF INDEPENDENT THINKING

As early as October 1636, Winthrop noted the potential threat of "One Mrs. Hutchinson" in his journal, deeming her "a woman of ready wit and bold spirit" (*JW*, 192). Born in England in 1591, Hutchinson was reared on the iconoclastic teachings of her father, Francis Marbury. As a young man, Marbury was imprisoned several times for "rebellion against the status quo as he single-mindedly campaigned to raise the standards of preaching in the Church."² Marbury endeavored to chip away verbally at the church establishment with his preaching. As a headstrong twenty-three-year-old, he was called before the Ecclesiastical Court in St. Paul's Consistory in London to answer for his controversial preaching.³ Marbury's written record of the proceedings reveals the same kind of determined spunk that his daughter would display nearly sixty years later. In his verbal joust with Bishop Aylmer, Marbury is denounced as "impudent" and as an "overthwart proud Puritan knave" for steadfastly maintaining his criticism of the clergy. After he was sentenced by the bishop to the Marshalsea, a particularly loathsome prison where troublesome "Papists" were confined, Marbury retorted "I am pleased to go whither it pleaseth God, but remember God's judgments. You do me wrong. I pray God to forgive you."⁴ Following his release, Marbury married Bridget Dryden, but before their first daughter Anne was born, the ever out-spoken Marbury was "again silenced by his superiors, removed from his post, and for fifteen years thereafter" was without an official religious position.⁵

Unfortunately, the details of Anne Marbury Hutchinson's childhood are not recorded. She left no journals or letters to flesh out our understanding of the household and parenting that helped to create her great sense of confidence and strength, yet, in all likelihood, young Anne developed a deep sense of conviction from the example of her father.* It would be hard to imagine that Francis Marbury did

---

* Battis's speculation that Anne Hutchinson was "an imaginative and impressionable girl" with an "unceasing" "longing for affection" who sought her father's approval appears to be wholly unsubstantiated, as is his assertion that she was "the hapless victim of an obsessive personal insecurity" (9).

not continue to be critical of the shortcomings of the Anglican hierarchy. In 1612, a year after Anne's father's death, she married William Hutchinson, when she was twenty-one years old. She lived in Alford, Lincolnshire, with her new husband, a family friend of respectable means, who made his living as a cloth merchant. In contrast to her father, William Hutchinson apparently had a much milder temperament.* With her first child born just over nine months after her marriage, Anne Hutchinson soon learned the importance of midwifery. She became skilled in the art of delivering children and was apparently relied upon for her medical ability throughout her life—she bore fifteen children.[6]

The most significant theological event punctuating Hutchinson's life seems to be the influence of the Reverend John Cotton. While it is not known when Hutchinson first learned about Cotton's ideas, he had wide reputation in the area in England in which she lived. Probably some time in the late 1620s, Hutchinson and her husband began regularly traveling to hear him preach in the town of Boston, twenty-four miles south of Alford.[7] Cotton "warned his listeners away from the specious comfort of preparation and re-emphasized the covenant of grace as something in which God acted alone and unassisted," suggesting that "life in this world offered no evidence at all of eternal prospects."[8] Cotton believed that if God predestined his believers to salvation, he would endow them with faith and fulfill the covenant of grace.[9] In 1633, rather than appear before the archbishop in the Court of the High Commission to answer for his "Puritan leanings," Cotton fled England to join John Winthrop and the other Puritans in the Massachusetts Bay Colony.[10] Inasmuch as Hutchinson did not trust any other minister in England to preach "the Word without adulteration," Cotton's departure caused a "spiritual crisis" in Hutchinson's life.[11] Enthralled with Cotton's doctrine, Hutchinson and her family followed Cotton and arrived in Boston on September 18, 1634.[12]

After a brief controversy over her unorthodox views, the Hutchinsons became members of the Boston church where John Wilson was pastor and John Cotton a "teacher."[13] With the zeal of her father, in the summer of 1635, Hutchinson began to expound upon Cotton's sermons in weekly meetings at her home, which was located

---

* John Winthrop's unflattering portrayal asserts that William Hutchinson was "a man of very mild temper and weak parts, and wholly guided by his wife" (*JW*, 290).

across the street from John Winthrop's.[14] As an esteemed member of the community by virtue of her family ties (she was the daughter of an English minister and the wife of a respected merchant) and her own valuable work as a very capable midwife,[15] Hutchinson apparently had no difficulty attracting followers, including powerful ones like Henry Vane, the popular and well-connected young "upstart English nobleman" who unseated Winthrop from the governorship in 1636.[16] At first, only women attended her meetings, but as her popularity grew, men apparently also joined the group; at the peak of her popularity, Hutchinson was holding "double weekly lectures" attended by "fifty, sixty, or eighty" people who wanted to hear her elaborations on Cotton's ideas (Preface, *AC*, 207).

The heart of Cotton's teachings revolved around a strict Calvinist interpretation of theology. As Perry Miller so eloquently stated, "Cotton was the pure scholar who sweetened his mouth every night with a morsel of Calvin,"[17] and this led him to reject any notion of "preparation." In other words, "no man could do a thing, no matter how wonderful, to effect his own salvation."[18] Hutchinson believed in Cotton's teaching that "warned his listeners away from the specious comfort of preparation and re-emphasized the covenant of grace."[19] Armed with the covenant of grace as her guiding principle, Hutchinson began to attack the clergy as failing to adhere to Calvinist doctrine. Only Cotton and Hutchinson's brother-in-law, John Wheelwright,* who maintained their fidelity to these teachings, were spared her criticism.

The leading minister in Boston, John Wilson, was particularly under attack for "preaching that people could prepare themselves to receive the grace and be part of the elect for whom Christ died" and that they could "provide a pure vessel into which the Holy Spirit would be poured."[20] Furthermore, Hutchinson sharply objected to Wilson's suggestion that if one "led a moral, upright, and industrious life" this could be considered proof of election.[21] This antithesis to the covenant of grace is a "covenant of works," the doctrine that people could use good works to earn salvation. In Calvinist terms, this idea was blasphemy, because it undercut the role of God's divine grace. Preachers like Wilson were, in fact, walking a theological fine line by implying that works could make a divine difference, yet they could not

---

* After John Wheelwright's first wife died, he married William Hutchinson's sister, Mary (Charles Adams, *Three Episodes*, 370).

stand by and be labeled "Arminians" (those who believe that works could merit grace) because to do so would expose their patent contradiction of the Calvinist teachings upon which their sermons were supposed to be based. Hutchinson was quite clear in her belief that no works could be used for "justification" and, importantly, that "works could not be offered as 'proof'" of salvation.[22] According to Hutchinson's thought, a "true saint might consistently live in sin,"[23] a concept that was just too socially dangerous for the leaders of the Massachusetts Bay Colony to ignore, because they also believed that grace would inspire a believer to do good works.

Anne Hutchinson's vocal elaboration on the preaching of both John Cotton and John Wheelwright was particularly troubling to John Winthrop, who wanted to recoup the governorship. With Henry Vane on her side, a clear political division was developing along theological lines that pitted Hutchinson, Cotton, and Wheelwright against Winthrop and John Wilson. All of the Puritans had fled England with a similar core belief that the Church of England should be purged of its hierarchy and the traditions inherited from Rome. Puritans were required to devote themselves to seeking salvation, yet to know that Christ could utterly reject them.[24] The practical implementation, however, varied. If Hutchinson's ideas prevailed, the clergy would be stripped of their ability to encourage the colonists to live by the classic Puritan ideals that were viewed by some as necessary to maintain the community, namely an ethic "defined in terms of piety, morality, honesty, industry, sobriety, and thrift."[25] Moreover, as one historian has suggested, if all "power emanated from God, respecting no sex, rather than from male authority figures striving to interpret the Divine Word," women could no longer be kept in their place as socially and legally inferior to men.[26] Both men and women would be relegated "to the status of malleable inferiors in the hands of a higher being"—God. Because the social and spiritual ramifications of Hutchinson's teachings jeopardized the very structure of life in the Massachusetts Bay Colony, it is not surprising that she was denounced as "Antinomian,"* a sixteenth-century pejorative label applied to those who "maintain that the moral law is not binding upon Christians" (*JW*, 206 n. 57).[27]

---

* During the "Antinomian Crisis" virtually no one referred to the events as such; the phrase became popular after John Winthrop published his version of the events in *A Short Story of the Rise, reign, and ruine of the Antinomians, Familists & Libertines, that infected the Church of New England* in 1644.

With this background in mind, Winthrop's 21 October 1636 journal entry about Anne Hutchinson takes on a much larger meaning by implicitly recognizing her as a worthy political adversary. He charges Hutchinson with "dangerous errors," namely: "1. That the person of the Holy Ghost dwells in a justified person. 2. That no sanctification can help to evidence to us our justification" (*JW*, 193). Noting that her brother-in-law John Wheelwright, "a silenced minister sometimes in England," joined with her in these opinions, Winthrop next records that upon hearing about "these things" the other ministers of the colony came to Boston at the time of the general court, and entered conference in private with them to determine if any action needed to be taken (*JW*, 194). Reverend Cotton was also called to join in the meeting, as there was some concern about his sermons. While it is not clear just what transpired in the meeting, Winthrop reports that Cotton and Wheelwright "gave satisfaction" to the church leaders "in the point of sanctification" (*JW*, 194-95). Anne Hutchinson apparently persisted in her views.

Undaunted by the conference and thoroughly disenchanted with Wilson, Hutchinson sought to have Wheelwright installed as a teacher in the church. This was an undisguised attempt to buttress Cotton's teaching and to muster support for Cotton eventually to replace Wilson. Winthrop vehemently opposed the appointment and led a successful resistance effort that resulted in Wheelwright's removal (*JW*, 195-96).[28] Apparently when Cotton "saw the zeal with which John Winthrop" opposed the plan by arguing the sufficiency of the existing ministry and the disputatiousness of certain of Wheelwright's opinions, he publicly counseled that it would be best if Wheelwright did not take office but was dismissed to officiate over the Mount Wollaston church.[29] The Wheelwright controversy, however, was far from over. On 20 January 1637, when a general fast was to be kept in all the churches in hopes of finding a solution to, among other things, the "dissensions in our churches," Wheelwright gave his infamous "Fast-Day Sermon" (*JW*, 209-11). The sermon is largely innocuous, yet it is punctuated with denouncements of those who preached a covenant of works, a theological misstep. Wheelwright rallied his followers by asserting that "we must all of us prepare for battell and come out against the enimyes of the Lord, and if we do not strive, those under a covenant of works will prevaile" (Fast-Day, *AC*, 158). This kind of preaching, coupled with the egregious suggestion that the Boston church was like Jesus faced with Herod and Pontius Pilot (the rest of Massachusetts), was sufficiently inflammatory to his audience to have him adjudicated guilty of "contempt & sedition"[30] by the General Court the following March (Fast-Day, *AC*, 159). The basis for the crime seems to be the fact that the fast was intended "as a means of reconciliation of the differences" and Wheelwright "purposely set himself to kindle and increase them" (*JW*, 210–11).

Foreshadowing what was to come with Hutchinson, Wheelwright was sentenced to be banished from the colony. His departure, however, was not without protest. In March 1637, friends of Wheelwright presented a petition defending his action and "sixty persons signed a 'remonstrance' protesting his conviction" (Hall, *AC*, 153). Presumably Anne Hutchinson was on the organizing end of things, although she was not able to petition the court by virtue of her gender. The effort was not successful, and Wheelwright left Massachusetts in November. During this same time, Winthrop was able further to coalesce his power formally by defeating Henry Vane in the May gubernatorial election. By Winthrop's own estimation, there "was a great danger of a tumult that day; for those of that side grew into fierce speeches, and some laid hands on others" as the Vane/Hutchinson supporters vied for power against the Winthrop/Wilson camp (*JW*, 215). Thus, by mid-year, "the colony was divided into two hostile camps, one centering in Boston, the other spread out around it, constantly sniping at each other."[31]

THE LEGAL CONTEXT

The legal history of the Massachusetts Bay Colony in New England formally begins with the charter of incorporation, which was issued on 4 March 1629.[32] In terms of government, the charter provided that there shall be one Governor, one Deputy Governor, and eighteen Assistants, all elected officials, who shall or may once every month, or "oftener at their pleasures, assemble, and houlde, and keepe a Courte or Assemblie of themselves, for the better ordering and directing of their affaires."[33] Four Great and General Courts were likewise to be assembled and empowered to make, ordain, and establish all manner of wholesome orders, laws, statutes, ordinances, directions, and instructions not contrary to the laws and statutes of England.[34] As Peter Hoffer points out, however, the "charter, with its royal seal, was a corporeal embodiment of a covenant, but no sooner did the Puritans set foot on the New England shore than the leaders of the colony discovered how difficult it was to impose the covenant ideal of law upon all the settlers."[35] The dissension by John Wheelwright and Anne Hutchinson certainly compounded this problem.

In the period surrounding the Antinomian crisis, from 1636–1638, legislation of the General Court established the judicial system.[36] At the lowest rank were the Commissioners' Courts, presided over by an assistant with civil and criminal jurisdiction over primarily "small causes."[37] Four County Courts were established in 1636 in Boston, Newton (Cambridge), Ipswich, and Salem with general civil jurisdiction and jurisdiction in criminal matters of lesser gravity.[38] The Court of Assistants, which generally sat in Boston, exercised appellate jurisdiction over the County Courts and also had original jurisdiction over criminal cases in which the penalty was "banishment or loss of a member or of life."[39] The most sweeping power seems to have been exercised by the General Court, which assembled only rarely prior to 1634, when the jurisdiction of the court system began to be more defined.[40] Thereafter, records indicate that it heard both civil and criminal cases, some in the first instance and others on appeal from the lower courts. The proceeding against Anne Hutchinson took place before the General Court at Newtown.

In terms of specific penal laws, the newly elected and politically savvy Winthrop took immediate action in 1637 to limit both internal and external threats to Massachusetts Bay. He was well aware that, even though he was respected as the first governor of the colony (elected in 1630), he could be ousted again by the same capricious electorate that had preferred Henry Vane and Thomas Dudley at elections in the past. Therefore, shortly after his re-election, the General Court enacted laws in preparation for war with the Pequots* and the following statute aimed at matters within the colony: "It is ordered, that no towne or pson shall receive any stranger, resorting hither wth intent to reside in this jurisdiction, nor alow any lot or habitation to any, or intertaine any such above three weeks."[41] This law was designed "to keep out such persons as might be dangerous to the commonwealth" (*JW*, 219). In practice, this "alien law" was "intended to exclude from the colony all those whose opinions did not meet the approval of the magistrates."[42] Not surprisingly, friends of Wheelwright and Hutchinson made "strenuous protests" against the

---
* Laws regarding trade and arms restrictions regarding the Indians are discussed in the next chapter.

order.⁴³ Thereafter, Winthrop wrote "A Declaration in Defense of an Order of Court in May, 1637" for the purpose of "clearing of such scruples as have arisen about this order."⁴⁴ Claiming that he was acting in the interest of the colony as a whole, Winthrop argued that "If we are bound to keepe off whatsoever appears to tend to our ruine or damage, then we may lawfully refuse to receive such whose dispositions suite not with our and whose society (we know) will be harmfull to us, and therefore it is lawful to take knowledge of all men before we receive them."⁴⁵

Using this new exclusionary law, Winthrop continued to exert his influence over any potential Hutchinson sympathizers during the summer of 1637. In July, when Samuel Hutchinson (Anne Hutchinson's brother-in-law) and some of Wheelwright's friends arrived in the colony from England, Winthrop decided that they were "not fit" to remain (*JW*, 226). He "allowed them four months" to remain in the colony, "to save others from the danger of the law in receiving them" (*JW*, 226). Of course, the four months was designed merely to give the illusion of an adequate trial period. This tyrannical decision rekindled old hostilities and, as Winthrop observed, "was taken very ill by those of the other party [the Hutchinsonians], and many hot speeches given forth about it, and about their removal, etc." (*JW*, 226).

With the exception of this exclusionary act and a handful of miscellaneous laws, statutory law was largely undefined in the Massachusetts Bay Colony. Colony records reveal that the prosecutions just prior to the Hutchinson proceedings were involving fairly routine kinds of crimes, such as murder, adultery, drunkenness.⁴⁶ In general, the "Puritan leaders regarded themselves as instruments in the divine hand for carrying out a great religious mission, and there was nothing democratic in their political theory."⁴⁷ In practice, this meant that the court magistrates and judges were viewed as "God's deputies" and, with the Bible as their guide, were afforded a great deal of discretionary power.⁴⁸

As can be seen in the prosecution of Anne Hutchinson, "law was viewed as a restraint on individual action in the interest of the order of the whole group" and "was designed to further effective organization and good order of the community."⁴⁹ The men of the colony who controlled the affairs determined that the churches and government "should be strictly based upon the teachings of the Bible."⁵⁰ By 1635, efforts were underway to compile a body of fundamental laws.⁵¹ The colonists desired to broaden the base of their new government, yet wanted some "security against arbitrary power of their leaders."[52] Winthrop, too, on 6 May 1635, expressed the concern of the deputies who "conceived great danger to our state in regarde" that our magistrates "for want of positiue Lawes in many Cases...might proceed accordinge to their discreations" (*JW*, 146).[53] He continues stating that it was agreed that "some men should be appointed to frame" a body of laws in resemblance to the Magna Carta. Winthrop was among those selected to draft the laws (*JW*, 146 and n. 1). In October 1636, when the Hutchinson/Wheelwright controversy was just beginning, John Cotton was requested by the general court to assist the magistrates in compiling laws "agreeable with the word of God."[54] He drew up a code known as "How far Moses Judicialls bind Massachusetts," which was never adopted.[55] In any event, by March 1638 there still were no "fundamental laws" in place and another committee was appointed (*JW*, 195, 248).

Still no action was taken, and in May 1640 Cotton and Nathaniel Ward were each directed to frame a model of laws. Ward's draft was preferred to Cotton's and, known as the Body of Liberties, it was eventually approved as a formal code in 1641 for a three-year provisional period.[56] Any clauses not repealed during this time were to become the law of the colony and, accordingly, in 1641, the Body of Liberties, which consisted of about one hundred civil and criminal laws, was voted to stand in force.[57] Cotton's judicial code, which was published in England in 1641 as *An Abstract; or, the Lawes of New England*, was not adopted as the law in Massachusetts. Ward's code remained in place until the arrival of the Province charter in 1692.[58] Accordingly, due to the absence of codified law, when Anne Hutchinson was prosecuted in 1637, local law and custom seemed to prevail.[59]

THE MEETING OF THE SYNOD: 30 AUGUST TO 22 SEPTEMBER 1637

The legal action that was ultimately to be taken against Hutchinson began with the meeting of the senior church officials, or the "synod," in the late summer of 1637. Sensing that the time was appropriate to "solidify their rapidly improving position," the colony leaders agreed that a synod of the churches was appropriate to assert pressure on Cotton to "signal his acceptance of their insistence that sanctification could be used as evidence of justification, and that the Holy Spirit does not dwell within the believer."[60] Preparation for the synod "chiefly consisted of gathering up for public refutation all of the offensive opinions which had been vented, and in extracting from Cotton's sermons and conferences those things which were distrusted."[61] The idea was to nudge Cotton into "clarifying" his opinions in a way that would make them consistent with those of other church leaders, such as Wilson. As Perry Miller notes, this conception had "social bearings"—people who undertake "the work of preparation, in the hope that it may be followed by the successive works, will endeavor to perfect external behavior."[62] More simply stated, to the extent that the colonists were striving to present themselves as perfect citizens in God's eyes, the social order of the community as a whole would be enhanced.

To advance this view, Winthrop assembled a catalog of eighty-two erroneous Antinomian opinions, with the ministers' refutation of each error. Even though Cotton was publically called to address formally the errors, they were implicitly directed at Hutchinson, too. As one critic observes, "[q]uite a few of these alleged errors could be safely laid at her door."[63] For example:

Error 18:	The Spirit doth worke in Hypocrites, by gifts and graces, but in Gods children immediately;
Error 23:	We must not pray for gifts and graces, but onely for Christ;
Error 40:	There is a testimony of the Spirit, and voyce unto the Soule, meerely immediate, without any respect unto, or concurrence with the word;
Error 67:	A man cannot evidence his justification by sanctification; and
Error 71:	The immediate revelation of my good estate, without any respect to the Scriptures, is as cleare to me, as the voyce of God in Heaven to Paul.[64]

Each of these "errors" goes to the roots of Hutchinson's teaching under the influence of Cotton; like her mentor, she "would have found it difficult to abandon her conviction that once God's children had been sealed in His love, the seal could not be removed."[65]

By the end of the synod, the ministers agreed to condemn the errors and, in a "private meeting," the ministers persuaded Cotton and Wilson to "drop the grievances each had against the other" (Hall, *AC*, 173). As Winthrop notes in his journal, even after the condemnation of the errors, "five points" remained in question, "which were after reduced to three" (*JW*, 233). Cotton's answers were published in 1646 as *A Conference Mr. John Cotton Held at Boston With the Elders of New-England* (*AC*, 175–98). The answers reveal that whereas Cotton was persuaded to tame his views to a palatable degree, questions still were open about Hutchinson. Indeed, on the "last day of the assembly" it was decided that "though women might meet (some few together) to pray and edify one another; yet such a set assembly, (as was then the practice in Boston,) where sixty or more did meet every week, and one woman [Anne Hutchinson] (in a prophetical way, by resolving questions of doctrine, and expounding scripture) took upon her the whole exercise, was agreed disorderly and without rule" (*JW*, 234). In other words, Hutchinson presented a threat to the social order and to male privilege.

THE EXAMINATION OF ANNE HUTCHINSON BEFORE THE GENERAL COURT

Even though Governor Winthrop believed there "was great hope" that the preceding actions would have a "good effect in pacifying the troubles and dissensions about matters of religion," Wheelwright and, presumably, Hutchinson "persisted in their opinions, and were as busy in nourishing contentions (the principle of them) as before" (*JW*, 239). Given the growing enthusiasm of her followers, it was beginning to appear that she might have the power to undermine the kind of cohesive community that Winthrop spoke so passionately about in his "Model of Christian Charity" while crossing the Atlantic on the *Arabella*. There was a sense of urgency that some action needed to be undertaken; when the General Court was assembled on 2 November 1637 it called Hutchinson to appear.

Remarkably, the trial transcript of the actual proceeding against Anne Hutchinson exists. The examination first appeared as an appendix in the *History of the Colony and Province of Massachusetts Bay* (1767) by Thomas Hutchinson (Anne's great-great grandson); it is believed that the original manuscript "may have disappeared in the sacking of Hutchinson's house during the Stamp Act riots of 1765" (Hall, *AC*, 311). Because the transcript has been readily available, the trial and the entire antinomian affair have been scrutinized for well over three centuries, generating a wide range of opinions about Hutchinson's defiant stance.

Feeling compelled to lay "downe the order and sense of the story," colonist Thomas Weld was one of the first commentators; he added a preface to Winthrop's own version, *A Short Story of the Rise, reign, and ruine of the Antinomians, Familists & Libertines*, which was published in 1644. Weld's observations express concern about Hutchinson's religious opinions and, importantly, are filled with such editorializing words and phrases as "mischievous opinions," "Seducers," and "audaciously insolent, and high-flowne in spirit and speech"—all insinuating that Hutchinson's preaching was outrageously unacceptable (Preface, *AC*, 207, 208, 211). Hutchinson's nineteenth-century critics characterized Hutchinson's behavior as inappropriate for a woman: John Stetson Barry asserts that "Mrs. Hutchinson was so far seduced by the popularity she enjoyed, as to transgress the bounds of decorum and propriety," and Charles Francis Adams states that when "Mistress Hutchinson claimed, through a process of introspection, to evolve a knowledge of the divine will from her own inner consciousness...she did so through the assertion of a most impudent and irritating superiority."[66] Such language clearly illustrates that Anne Hutchinson's "unwomanly" behavior was as much of an affront as her message.

In contrast, most twentieth-century assessments show great respect for Hutchinson's dazzling ability to defend herself before the tribunal. The passage of time has favored Hutchinson and created an environment in which her impassioned commitment to an alternative theology is appreciated. A sampling of the works reveals admiration for Hutchinson's intellectual luminescence: "Hutchinson was [Winthrop's] intellectual superior in everything except political judgment...in nearly every exchange of words, she defeated him," and the records of the court reveal a "[p]roud, brilliant woman put down by men who had judged her in advance";[67] Hutchinson was characterized as having a "brilliant mind, and rapier-like wit";[68] and "Hutchinson parried the accusations of her examiners with a wit and verve that reduced them to confusion" (Hall, *AC*, 311). Most recently, critics have focused on Hutchinson as an early feminist, speaking out against the patriarchal values that denied her a full role in Puritan society and religious matters.[69] There have also been numerous fictional depictions of Anne Hutchinson,[70] yet none is as compelling as Nathaniel Hawthorne's 1830 sketch, "Mrs. Hutchinson," in which he breaks from the other nineteenth-century voices to deem her "a woman of extraordinary talent and strong imagination."* Thus, Hutchinson has been both vilified and glorified for her outspoken public stance.† Despite all of this writing,[71] however, few have analyzed the legal implications of the trial, and most merely present a cursory glance at the issues.[72]

Day One of the Examination: 2 November 1637

Nathaniel Hawthorne transports readers into the seventeenth century through his detailed, albeit fictional, "description" of the chill of that November day and the courtroom scene:

> The floor of the low and narrow hall is laid with planks hewn by the axe—the beams of the roof still wear the rugged bark with which they grew up in the forest, and the hearth is formed of one broad unhammered stone, heaped with logs that roll their blaze and smoke up a chimney of wood and clay. A sleety shower beats fitfully against the windows, driven by the November blast...In the highest place sits Winthrop...the next is Endicott...In the midst, and in the centre of all eyes, we see the Woman.[73]

Hawthorne describes Hutchinson as standing "loftily before her judges, with a determined brow, and, unknown to herself, there is a flash of carnal pride half hidden in her eye, as she surveys the many learned and famous men whom her doctrines have put in fear."[74] Indeed, Hutchinson probably did stand before her accusers with the steely determination envisioned by Hawthorne, as the trial transcripts likewise attest to her defiant and brilliant mind.

The most striking aspect of the proceeding is that Hutchinson was apparently called before the court for a fact-finding "examination"—as opposed to a trial following an indictment—yet, through jurisprudential wrangling Hutchinson was essentially convicted of a crime and punished by expulsion from the colony. The examination of Hutchinson became a proceeding designed "to frighten other would-be offenders into submission."[75] In many ways, instead of being "trials

---

* Lang observes that Hawthorne's treatment of the Hutchinson matter as "social rather than theological" broadens its "relevance" (11–13).

† Other criticism on the proceedings against Anne Hutchinson is varied and covers a range of different perspectives, including historical, feminist, linguistic, and sociological, all of which are generally favorable to Hutchinson, as a "woman greatly misunderstood, misjudged and mistreated" (Bolton, ix). These should be compared with Battis's analysis of Hutchinson as a neurotic woman whose behavior "can be explained largely in terms of menopausal symptoms" (248 n. 49).

in the proper sense of the word," the Hutchinson and Wheelwright prosecutions amounted to "relentless inquisitions used by the government for the purpose of crushing the opposition."[76] The inquiry into Hutchinson's acts and beliefs was not, by any stretch of the imagination, before a fair and impartial trier of fact. On the contrary, throughout the trial, "the court made no effort to conceal its prejudice against the accused."[77]

The lack of a jury is unsettling by twentieth-century standards, yet it was not unusual prior to the enactment of the Body of Liberties in 1641. One of the few laws in place when Hutchinson was tried stated: "it is agreed, that noe tryall shall passe vpon any, for life or banishment, but by a jury soe sumoned, or by the Genall Courte."* Passed on 14 May 1634, this law did not give the accused the option, but rather gave the government the power to try Hutchinson without a jury. Pursuant to the charter, colonial law in Massachusetts Bay was intended to encompass the essential features of English law, which were quite restrictive in matters of felonies and treason. Seventeenth-century English law "provided few of the safeguards that are presently regarded as essential to the fair conduct of a criminal trial."[78]

In any event, given the seriousness of the accusations levied against Hutchinson, it is surprising that the court did not make more of an effort to give the appearance of fairness. Because there was no jury, "Winthrop should have disqualified himself as partisan in the cause."[79] In effect, Winthrop initially undertook the role of chief prosecutor and lead judge in opposition to Hutchinson, who was potentially leading a revolt against the established governmental and ecclesiastical authorities. His bias against Hutchinson is readily apparent in Winthrop's own description in his *Short Story*. Here Winthrop deemed Hutchinson "the head of all this faction," the "*Dux foemina facti*" (from the *Aeneid*, Book 1, line 364: "a woman was their leader") and described her as "a woman of a haughty and fierce carriage, of a nimble wit and active spirit, and a very voluble tongue, more bold than a man, though in understanding and judgment, inferiour to many women" (Short Story, *AC*, 262–63).

However, Winthrop could not take the lead in the interrogation of this "haughty" woman and also be an impartial trier of fact. The two roles are inherently in conflict. Winthrop studied law in England,

---

* The *Mass. Bay Records* note that the "last five words are in the handwriting of Mr. Nowell," and it is unclear when they were added (Shurtleff, 118).

THE LAW OF DIVINE REVELATION

where he served as an attorney in an English court,[80] and must have been aware of this problematic ethical dynamic.

One can only speculate that perhaps Winthrop felt that because Hutchinson was not under indictment, the proceedings were not a trial per se and, therefore, he could act in both roles. The purpose of an indictment is to ensure that a defendant is apprized in writing of the charges levied. Hutchinson was called to appear without knowing the exact charges against her, and she was unrepresented by counsel. Because there were no practicing lawyers in the colony, she represented herself pro se before the most powerful political and religious leaders in the Massachusetts Bay Colony. Despite the readily apparent power differential, she had no right to counsel by law, and the court never inquired about the appropriateness of representation. Thus, the examination of Hutchinson is framed in broad terms, summoning her to answer to general allegations of criminal wrongdoing in which she is expected to testify before the court, yet without formal charges in place.

The transcript begins with Governor Winthrop's pointed opening statement in which he attempts to articulate, rather inartfully, that which is the apparently non-statutory basis of her prosecution. He asserts,

> Mrs. Hutchinson, you are called here as one of those that have troubled the peace of the commonwealth and the churches here; you are known to be a woman that hath had a great share in promoting and divulging of those opinions that are causes of this trouble, and to be nearly joined not only in affinity and affection with some of those the court had taken notice of and passed censure upon, but you have spoken divers things as we have been informed very prejudicial to the honour of the churches and ministers thereof. (*AC*, 312)

These initial words about the charge suggest guilt by association with John Wheelwright. Recall that Hutchinson was among those who sought to have Wheelwright installed as a teacher in the church before he was convicted for his seditious acts. Furthermore, Hutchinson was undoubtably involved in the preparation of the postconviction petition on Wheelwright's behalf. However, inasmuch as she could not, as a woman, sign the petition, she could not be charged with direct involvement.

Winthrop continues his introductory remarks, claiming that Hutchinson "maintained a meeting and an assembly" in her "house that hath been condemned by the general assembly as a thing *not tolerable nor comely* in the sight of God *nor fitting for your sex*" (Hall, *AC*, 312) (emphasis added). His outrage at Hutchinson's departure from her expected role is unmistakable. This is not entirely surprising, given Winthrop's response to one Edward Hopkins, who sought advice about how to deal with his wife, Ann Yale Hopkins, as she was reportedly losing her "understanding and reason" after she had given herself "wholly to reading & writinge, & [had] written many books": "if she had attended her household affaires, & suche thinges as belong to women, & not gone out of her waye and callinge, to meddle in suche things as are proper for men, whose mindes are stronger&c: she might have kept her wittes, & might have improved them vsefully & honorably in the place God had sett her" (*JW*, 570). Hutchinson's rebellion must have been viewed by Winthrop as no less unnatural for a woman. Certainly harassed by the fact that Hutchinson persisted in her opinions even after "that was cried down," Winthrop admits that Hutchinson was called before the General Assembly so that they could make her "understand how things are," and to be "reduced" so that she "may become a profitable member" of the community (*AC*, 312). Winthrop even goes so far as to threaten Hutchinson, warning that if she "be obstinate" in her "course," then the court "may take such course" to ensure that she "may trouble us no further" (*AC*, 312). Undaunted by Winthrop's vague assertions and intimidation tactics, Hutchinson immediately challenges the accusation: "I am called here to answer before you but I hear no things laid to my charge" (*AC*, 312).

Hutchinson's demand that she be informed as to the nature and cause of the offense was reasonable and, in fact, later became a threshold for a proceeding to be constitutional under the Sixth Amendment. The articulation of the charges remained less than clear; unlike Wheelwright, the trial transcript reveals that she was never accused outright of sedition.* The alleged criminal acts, however, fall generally into three categories: political speech, assembly, and religious beliefs. Of course, such behaviors became legal after the passage of the Constitution and the First Amendment guarantee of freedom of religion, speech, and assembly. Fearing the disintegration of the community, issue was taken with Hutchinson's sermons because community members were actively listening to a woman who was speaking out in contradiction of the beliefs promulgated by Winthrop and Wilson.

---

* Cf. John Winthrop's *Short Story*, in which he accuses Hutchinson of "sowing seditions" (*AC*, 266).

☞ THE LAW OF DIVINE REVELATION

The undercurrent making each of these "offenses" particularly egregious is that Hutchinson engaged in inappropriate behavior for a woman. When Hutchinson states that the reasons for her actions are a "matter of conscience," Winthrop snaps back authoritatively: "Your conscience you must keep or it will be kept for you" (*AC*, 312). This exchange certainly lacks the air of an impartial judicial proceeding, yet the issue still remains: What is the charge? In an attempt to clarify the crime, Winthrop employs an analogy:

> Say that one brother should commit a felony or treason and come to his other brother's house, if he knows him guilty and conceals him he is guilty of the same. It is his conscience to entertain him, but if his conscience comes into act in giving countenance and entertainment to him that hath broken the law he is guilty too. So if you do countenance those that are transgressors of the law you are in the same fact. (*AC*, 313)

Specifically, he wanted to know whether Hutchinson was in agreement with Wheelwright's "sermon and the petition." Winthrop had apparently adopted a "zero tolerance" position regarding political and religious dissenting speech. Unpersuaded, Hutchinson once again seeks to determine the actual law that she has allegedly transgressed. Lacking a statutory criminal code, Winthrop relies on the "law of God and that of the state." Pending the adoption of fundamental laws in a code, in May 1636, a general catch-all statute was enacted stating that "the magistrates & their assosiates shall proceed in the courts to hear & determine all causes according to the lawes nowe established, & where there is noe law, then as neere the lawe of God as they can."[81] When pressed by Hutchinson for particulars, Winthrop fell back on the Fifth Commandment, claiming that Hutchinson failed to "honour thy father and thy mother" because she "countenanced" Wheelwright after he preached the offending Fast-Day sermon, and "joined with them in the faction" (*AC*, 313). Hutchinson, however, is a step ahead of Winthrop. When he accuses her of joining with Wheelwright's supporters in presenting the petition, she reminds him that she "had not [her] hand to the petition." Winthrop then attempts to attach criminal liability to Hutchinson for "entertaining" the petitioners, thereby breaching the "law" by "dishonoring parents"—the "fathers of the commonwealth" (*AC*, 313–14). Hutchinson's political speech is deemed illegal because it dishonored those to whom Winthrop refers as "us," the leaders of the colony, including himself.

The second "offence" centers around the assemblies at Hutchinson's home. Winthrop asks: "Why do you keep such a meeting at your house as you do every week upon a set day?" When Hutchinson asserts that her meetings have been "lawful," Winthrop reveals the rub: "I will say that there was no meeting of women alone, but your meeting is of another sort for there are sometimes men among you" (*AC,* 314). Hutchinson denies the presence of men and justifies her assemblies under the "clear rule in Titus, that the elder women should instruct the younger." Titus provides that the older women are charged with the responsibility of teaching what is good, and acting so that no one would malign the word of God.[82] When pressed as to whether she would instruct a man, Hutchinson acknowledges that this "would cross a rule." Turning the questions on to Winthrop, Hutchinson inquires, "Do you think it not unlawful for me to teach women and why do you call me to teach the court?" (*AC,* 315). Hutchinson forces Winthrop to agree that it is lawful for her to instruct women and questions Winthrop's motives for calling her to instruct the court—consisting of all men—if it is unlawful for her to do so. Winthrop's response, that she was called not to "teach the court" but rather to "lay open" herself sounds suspiciously like an invitation for Hutchinson to incriminate herself.

Lacking evidence early in the proceeding, Winthrop begins to rely on the defendant to come forth with damaging testimony. Because he has no direct rejoinder, Winthrop attempts to invoke the rule in Corinthians, that it is disgraceful for a woman to speak in the churches.[83] Of course, Hutchinson was speaking at her home, not in the churches. Trapped in his own attempts to articulate the charges against Hutchinson, Winthrop is reduced to bullying his witness and invoking the court's authority: "we see how it is we must therefore put it away from you, or restrain you from maintaining this course" (*AC,* 316). The beleaguered Winthrop is then relieved by two other members of the court, Simon Bradstreet and Deputy Governor Thomas Dudley (Anne Bradstreet's husband and father, respectively) who join in the questioning and spare Winthrop from rapidly losing any more intellectual ground. When questioned further by Dudley about the presence of men, Hutchinson admitted that she held two weekly meetings at her house, one for men and women and another only for women (*AC,* 317). On this key point, Hutchinson continued to maintain that she never "heard" women instructing the men.

THE LAW OF DIVINE REVELATION

The subject of the third transgression is Hutchinson's religious beliefs, including the allegation that she accused the "ministers in the land" of preaching "a covenant of works, and only Mr. Cotton a covenant of grace" (*AC*, 318). The actual law violated is never clear; Hutchinson seems to be under attack for holding meetings and speaking about religious opinions that are contrary to those of many of the ministers in the colony. With Winthrop's prosecutorial skill in doubt, Dudley begins to take a more active role in the questioning, attempting to entice Hutchinson into an admission. After referencing the fact that "Cotton hath cleared himself that he was not of that mind," he acknowledges that Hutchinson "hath a potent party in the country" (*AC*, 318). Facing the brunt of ecclesiastical authority, by this time Cotton had significantly backed off of his public preaching about the covenant of grace.

However, unlike Cotton, Hutchinson did not cave in to the leaders of the colony. Now, when pressed about the issue, the formidable Hutchinson, who was likely aware that no credible evidence of criminal behavior had yet been proved, astutely issued her directive: "I pray Sir prove it that I said they preached nothing but a covenant of works" (*AC*, 318). Fully understanding the heresy associated with accusing the ministers of preaching a covenant of works, Hutchinson carefully defines her position by stating that "one may preach a covenant of grace more clearly than another" (*AC*, 318). The exchange that follows illustrates the brilliance of Hutchinson's articulative powers:

Mrs. H.	Prove this then Sir that you say I did.
Dep. Gov.	When they do preach a covenant of works do they preach truth?
Mrs. H.	Yes, Sir, but when they preach a covenant of works for salvation, that is not truth.
D. Gov.	I do but ask you this, when the ministers do preach a covenant of works do they preach a way of salvation?
Mrs. H.	I did not come hither to answer to questions of that sort.
D. Gov.	Because you will deny the thing.
Mrs. H.	Ey, but that is to be proved first. (*AC*, 318)

At this early point in the proceedings, Hutchinson does not fall into the trap of self-incrimination, specifically, of instructing the men of the court about religious matters. She merely steadfastly holds her accusers to a burden of proof. An exasperated Dudley announces that he will "prove" that Hutchinson "said the gospel in the letter and words holds forth nothing but a covenant of works and that all that do not hold as you do are in a covenant of works." Still maintaining her privilege not to speak, Hutchinson states "I deny this for if I should so say I should speak against my own judgment." Clearly agitated by Hutchinson's ability to hold her own and his own relegation to the sidelines of the interrogation, Winthrop interjects "I would add this. It is well discerned to the court that Mrs. Hutchinson can tell when to speak and when to hold her tongue. Upon the answering of a question which we desire her to tell her thoughts if she desires to be pardoned" (*AC*, 318). Thus, well into the trial, no evidence exists with which to convict Hutchinson.

As if on cue, in an attempt to rescue the viability of the proceedings, the other members of the court begin to testify against Hutchinson. Six ministers give unsworn testimony to "prove" the two points at issue: that Hutchinson said they preached a covenant of works and were not able ministers of the New Testament. Hugh Peter, minister at Salem, begins his long statement claiming that he is merely presenting a "brief account" for the country and posterity by stating that those who speak are not "informers against the gentlewoman" (*AC*, 319). The information that is presented to the court belies this assertion. Peter first places Hutchinson's character at issue by testifying that "she was a woman not only difficult in her opinions, but also of an intemperate spirit" (*AC*, 320). He continues to describe a meeting to which Hutchinson was summoned along with several ministers to explain her religious positions and answer to the charge that she had spoken out against a covenant of works. After initially presenting herself in the meeting as "very tender," Hutchinson apparently said, "The fear of man is a snare why should I be afraid." Quoting Proverbs 29.25— "Fear of man will prove to be a snare, but whoever trusts in the Lord is kept safe"—Hutchinson invoked God to her side when challenged by the ministers. Peter incredulously tells the court, "*These were her words*" (emphasis added), as if to make sure that they are aware of the degree of the affront (*AC*, 320). Continuing his testimony, Peter alleges that Hutchinson said "there was a wide and broad difference between our brother Mr. Cotton and our selves...that he preaches the covenant of grace and you the covenant of works, and that you are not able ministers of the new testament and know no more than the apostles did before the resurrection of Christ...that she did conceive that we were not able ministers of the gospel" (*AC*, 320–21). Neither admitting nor denying the allegations, Hutchinson coolly continues to advocate on her behalf, suggesting that Peter's testimony is not truthful and that if "our pastor would shew his writings you should see what I said, and that many things are not so as it is reported" (*AC,* 321). Wilson, the pastor of the Boston church, is quick to deny the existence of any such writings, leaving Peter's testimony uncorroborated by written documentation.

Determined to prove the case against Hutchinson, Dudley calls upon the other ministers to come forth and "say what Mr. Peters hath said." Of course, the rules of criminal procedure eventually enacted in the American criminal justice system prohibit witnesses from listening to the testimony of other witnesses in a trial. Inasmuch as all of the other ministers who are about to testify have already listened to Peter's statements, their own testimony and recollections are potentially tainted. Not surprisingly, each of the following ministers' testimony about Hutchinson's statements is remarkably similar:

Mr. Weld	...that which our brother Peters hath spoken was the truth and things were spoken as he hath related...that Mr. Cotton did preach a covenant of grace and we a covenant of works. And this I remember she said we could not preach a covenant of grace because we were not sealed, and we were not able ministers of the new testament no more than were the disciples before the resurrection of Christ.
Mr. Phillips	...at length she said there was a great deal of difference between Mr. Cotton and we...Being asked of the particulars, she did instance in Mr. Shephard that he did not preach a covenant of grace clearly, and she instanced our brother Weld...She likewise said that we were not able ministers of the new testament and her reason was because we were not sealed...
Mr. Shephard	...Now I remember that she said that we were not able ministers of the new testament. I followed her with particulars, she instanced myself as being at the lecture and hearing me preach when I gave some means whereby a christian might come to the assurance of God's love. She instanced that I was not sealed. I said why did she say so. She said because you put love for an evidence. (*AC,* 321–24)

Hutchinson apparently believed that some ministers, such as Cotton, had the "seal of the spirit" in that they had "the full assurance of God's favour by the holy ghost" (*AC,* 335). This belief was grounded in

Ephesians 1:13–14: "And you also were included in Christ when you heard the word of truth, the gospel of your salvation. Having believed, you were marked in him with a seal, the promised Holy Spirit, who is a deposit guaranteeing our inheritance until the redemption of those who are God's possession—to the praise of his glory." Thus, an accusation that some of the ministers were not under such a seal was an affront that went to the core of their prerogative to preach.

In an attempt to buttress the testimony of his fellow ministers, John Eliot, minister of Roxbury, claimed that he "did write the substance of what hath been here spoken," that he had it "in writing" (*AC*, 324). In addition to these allegations, Zechariah Symmes, minister of Charlestown, also testified that he knew of Hutchinson from their voyage from England where they "were in the great cabin together" and that he "took notice of what was the corruptness and narrowness of her opinions" (*AC*, 322). Significantly, each of these witnesses testified to matters involving religious opinions and beliefs—the criminal significance of Hutchinson's speech is never defined. Her only "crime" at this juncture seems to be holding and disseminating beliefs to a growing group of followers that were contrary to those of the colony leaders.

Faced with these witnesses against her, Hutchinson maintained her innocence, admitting only that she used "the words of the apostle to the Corinthians" to Nathaniel Ward, minister at Ipswich, "that they that were ministers of the letter and not the spirit did preach a covenant of works. Upon his saying there was no such scripture, then I fetched the Bible and shewed him this place II Cor 3:6. He said that was the letter of the law. No said I it is the letter of the gospel" (*AC*, 326). Ever well-versed in the Bible, Hutchinson used the message in Corinthians—that able ministers of the new testament are true to the spirit, not the letter, "for the letter killeth, but the spirit giveth life"—to suggest that the ministers were "legalists," or those who believed that people could earn salvation and that the process could be mapped. This suggestion was certain to inflame her prosecutors.

Winthrop's only response at the end of the first day of the trial was that "the court hath labored to bring you to acknowledge the error of your way that so you might be reduced" and, because the "time now grows late, we shall therefore give you a little more time to consider it" until court reconvened the next morning (*AC*, 326). The import of his remarks is that the court was giving Hutchinson some time to reconsider her position. Should she recant, they probably would take no further action. Because she persisted in her refusal to foreswear the opinions attributed to her, however, the proceeding continued in an effort to force Hutchinson to give them assurances that her beliefs were consistent with those of the ministers who testified against her.

Day Two of the Examination: 3 November 1637

The next morning the court reconvened with Winthrop presiding; he was careful to open the proceedings with his slant on the status of the evidence, stating that there "were divers things laid to her charge, her ordinary meetings about religious exercises, her speeches in derogation of the ministers among us, and the weaking of the hands and hearts of the people towards them" (*AC*, 326). Asserting that "sufficient proof" existed in the record regarding the accusations about the ministers' ability and the substance of their preaching, he then opened the proceedings for "anything else that the court hath to say." Winthrop strategically attempted to reassert his authority by assuming that adequate evidence had already been presented to convict Hutchinson and carried on as if the previous day had finished up in the court's favor.

Hutchinson had her own agenda as she continued her defense by attacking the "evidence" which was before the court. Noting that the "ministers come in their own cause"—that of self-interest—she asked the court to make them testify under oath. Using scripture as the basis of her request, Hutchinson reminded the court that "the Lord hath said that an oath is the end to all controversy." Hutchinson skillfully turned "a ritual into a real evidentiary hearing."[84] This was a particularly sensitive issue for the Puritans, who were very serious about the import of the third commandment, which prohibits using the name of God for vain purposes. The Westminster Confession of faith provided that "Whosoever taketh an Oath ought to consider the weightiness of so solemn an act, and therein to avouch nothing but what he is fully perswaded is the truth" (Hall, *AC*, 328 n. 22). Claiming that she "perused some notes out of what Mr. Wilson did then write" and that she found "things not to be as hath been alleged," Hutchinson was very persistent about the oath issue. The comments by both Winthrop and Bradstreet suggesting that testimony under oath was not necessary did not dissuade her from the cause. Addressing the gravity of taking an oath, Richard Brown, a deputy to the General Court, interjected his own apprehension about giving sworn testimony: "If I mistake not an oath is of a high nature, and it is not to be taken but in a controversy, and for my part I am afraid of an oath and fear that we shall take God's name in vain, for we may take the witness of these men without an oath" (*AC,* 328).

The ministers presumably were reluctant to testify under oath because of the fallibility of human memory; they felt the need to be very sure of the facts before giving sworn testimony. As Winthrop himself acknowledged, the "elders do know what an oath is and as it is an ordinance of God so it should be used" (*AC,* 332). In other words, unless the ministers were very sure about exactly what was said, they should not swear to their recollections before God. The ensuing controversy about whether the ministers should be required to take an oath or not illustrates the moral pocket in which the court found itself. If the testimony is truthful, then the ministers should not object to taking an oath; if the ministers are not sure enough to take an oath, then the testimony should not be sufficient evidence with which to convict Hutchinson.

In an apparent attempt to dodge this unresolved, very problematic issue, Winthrop turned to John Cotton to change the course of the proceeding. By this time, Cotton had adopted a position that the colony and church leaders no longer thought was problematic. John Eliot had "gone to great pains to translate Cotton's doctrine into one more palatable to himself and suitable for his Roxbury congregation."[85] Reluctant to speak out on behalf of or against Hutchinson, Cotton initially adopted the stance that because his testimony was unanticipated, he "did not labour to call to remembrance what was done" in the conference in question between Hutchinson and the ministers (*AC,* 333). He endeavored to "allow her to argue her case, as indeed she must, but to reason with her about her error should any appear and to temper her less judicious statements."[86]

Ironically, it is ultimately Hutchinson's own testimony about her fervent religious beliefs that the court uses as the basis for her banishment. Nearly interrupting Cotton's testimony, Hutchinson suddenly began to speak out. The decision to speak or not must have presented a formidable dilemma: "[s]ilence, which might have saved her and embarrassed her prosecutors, would have implied acceptance of the policy that women had no role in formulating doctrine or in governing the church. Speaking her mind, on the other hand, would give the state the legal justification needed to banish her."[87] Thus, when

THE LAW OF DIVINE REVELATION

Hutchinson offered the source of her beliefs, she was *in flagrante delicto* of Puritan beliefs. Her decision to speak can be viewed either as a proclamation of her beliefs based on great faith in the power of God, or as a strategic misstep in what had been a very able defense. Given Hutchinson's nimble wit and force of spirit, it seems more likely than not that Hutchinson found it more palatable to maintain her beliefs publically rather than be bullied into submission like her mentor, John Cotton. Arguably, "Hutchinson's decision to abandon the law may have been a conscious affirmation of the triviality of all men's endeavors...a conscious decision to transform a hollow, foreordained legal ritual into a kind of personal theater: Hutchinson, after dominating the legal stage, realized herself through an act at once politically defiant and religiously satisfying."[88]

The damning testimony begins with her admission that "he hath let me to distinguish between the voice of my beloved and the voice of Moses, the voice of John the Baptist and the voice of antichrist" (*AC*, 339-37). By acknowledging that she knew that it was the spirit by "immediate revelation," she not only protected Cotton from being liable as the source of her position, but also violated sacred beliefs. Hutchinson "convicted herself of blasphemy, since the orthodoxy constructed by the clergy denied the possibility of direct communication from God."[89] Because divine revelation "creates a direct, personal and intimate relationship between God and the soul," it "reinforces the character and power of the individual believer" completely apart from the "church, society, or state."[90] Thus, such an independent stance positioned Hutchinson outside of the authority structures that governed the Massachusetts Bay Colony.

Matters were further exacerbated when Hutchinson made it unequivocally clear that she defied colonial law, stating, "You have power over my body but the Lord Jesus hath power over my body and soul" (*AC*, 338). She then proceeded to compare her experience to that of Daniel, claiming that God desired her to "see this scripture fulfilled" (*AC*, 338). Quick to recall that "Daniel was delivered by miracle," Winthrop put the key question to Hutchinson: "do you think to be deliver'd so too?" (*AC*, 338). No holds barred, Hutchinson is completely candid, replying "I do here speak it before the court" (*AC*, 338). This ultimately pitted Hutchinson against Cotton, who implicitly "drew a line and turned against her."[91] By asking Cotton to tell the court whether he approved of "Mrs. Hutchinson's revelations as she hath laid them down" (*AC*, 341), Deputy Governor Dudley seized upon the opportunity both to condemn Hutchinson and to put Cotton's loyalty to the test. Cotton's feigned lack of understanding soon gave way to his careful exercise of semantics with the final admission that if Hutchinson's revelations "be by way of miracle then [he] would suspect it" (*AC*, 341). His later weak attempt to rescue Hutchinson by maintaining that he dared "not bear witness against it" and that such "revelations broach new matters of faith and doctrine" only served to fuel the prosecution and feed Winthrop's fear that Hutchinson's assertions "may breed more if they be let alone" (*AC*, 342); she was a persuasive speaker professing religious beliefs with dangerous social consequences.

Characterizing Hutchinson's testimony as some sort of fantastic illusion, Dudley denounced her: "I am fully persuaded that Mrs. Hutchinson is deluded by the devil, because the spirit of God speaks truth in all his servants" (*AC*, 343). When the proceeding was nearly finished, but before any censure was issued by the court, William Coddington, a deputy to the General Court from Boston, finally spoke out on Hutchinson's behalf: "Now I do not see any clear witness against her, and you know it is a rule of the court that no man may be a judge and an accuser too. I do not mean to speak to disparage our elders and their callings, but I do not see any thing that they accuse her of witnessed against her, and therefore I do not see how she should be censured for that" (*AC*, 344).

He continued, imploring Winthrop to not "force things along" because he did not see "any equity in the court." Coddington even went so far as to maintain that there was "no law of God that she hath broken nor any law of the country that she hath broke, and therefore deserves no censure." That is, no evidence was presented from individuals who claimed to have heard Hutchinson speaking in public at her weekly meetings. Ostensibly, inasmuch as the only evidence presented against Hutchinson involved statements made to the ministers in private, they should not be actionable. Coddington took the position that even "if she say that the elders preach as the apostles did, why they preached a covenant of grace and what is that to them, for it is without question that the apostles did preach a covenant of grace," Hutchinson still did not break any "law of God or man" (*AC*, 345). When it became clear that the court was about to censure her, Israel Stoughton of Dorchester also spoke out, noting the procedural deficiencies: "because she desires witness and there is none in a way of witness therefore I shall desire that no offence be taken...because she hath not been formally convicted as others are by witnesses upon oath" (*AC*, 345). Concurring in this position, Coddington added, "because Solomon saith, every man is partial in his own cause, and here is none that accuses her but the elders" (*AC*, 345-36).

With this dissension, Weld and Eliot were chosen and agreed to testify under oath. Eliot first testified that "Mr. Cotton did preach a covenant of grace and we of works and she gave this reason—to put a work in point of evidence is a revealing upon a work. We did labor then to convince her that our doctrine was the same with Mr. Cotton's: She said no, for we were not sealed...she said we were not able ministers of the gospel because we were but like the apostles before the ascension" (*AC*, 346-47). Weld added that he clearly remembered that Hutchinson told the ministers that they "were not able ministers of the new testament" and that they "were not clear" in their experience because they "were not sealed" (*AC*, 347). This was enough testimony to satisfy Stoughton, who was quick to say that "this testimony doth convince me in the thing, and I am fully satisfied the words were pernicious, and the frame of her spirit doth hold forth the same" (*AC*, 347).

Wasting no time, Winthrop denounced Hutchinson for the "troublesomeness" of her spirit and "the danger of [her] course amongst us." Lacking any legal express authority, Winthrop then couches the "charges" against Hutchinson in social terms; because "these things that appear before us is unfit for our society" (*AC*, 347), a vote was to be taken. All but three decided that Hutchinson should be imprisoned until she could be banished. Only Coddington and William Colburn, a deputy from Boston who had signed the remonstrance protesting the court's action against Wheelwright, voted in favor of acquittal; William Jennison abstained (*AC*, 331 n.25, 348). With no further proceedings, Winthrop pronounced the sentence, banishing her from the jurisdiction "as being a woman not fit for our society" (*AC*, 348).

The proceedings against Hutchinson may have commenced as a mere examination, but by the end of the second day, Hutchinson was subjected to the punishment of banishment. She was never indicted; there was no real trial, yet she was harshly punished. Moreover, there was no appellate procedure for further redress. As Edmund Morgan observes, even though the "purpose of the trial was doubtless to make her conviction seem to follow due process of law...it might have been better for the reputation of her judges if they had simply banished her unheard."[92]

THE REPERCUSSIONS

Anne Hutchinson's failure to recant, to submit to the authority of the General Court, was not without repercussion. Hutchinson and Wheelwright threatened the very heart of the ecclesiastical and political institutions at Massachusetts Bay. Accordingly, great effort was made to ensure there was no such similar rebellion in the near future.

THE EXERCISE OF STATE POWER

Fearing a repeat of the Hutchinson affair, the colony took the following action on 20 November 1637 to disarm certain citizens and thereby thwart any similar potential uprisings:

> Whereas the opinions & revelations of Mr. Wheelwright & Mrs. Hutchinson have seduced and led into dangerous errors many of the people heere in Newe England, insomuch as there is iust cause of suspition that they, as others in Germany, in former times, may, vpon some revelation, make some suddaine irruption vpon those that differ from them in judgment, for prevention whereof it is ordered, that all those whose names are vnderwritten shall...deliver...all such guns, pistons, swords, powder, shot, & match as they shalbee owners of, or have in their custody.[93]

Among those listed were Hutchinson's relatives: William, Richard, and Edward Hutchinson. This law aimed at disarming Hutchinson's followers and sympathizers was yet another step in thwarting dissension. On that same date, the court, "being sensible of the great disorders growing" in the commonwealth,

> doth order & decree, that whosoever shall hereafter openly or willingly defame any court of iustice, or the sentences proceedings of the same, or any of the magistrats or other iudges of any such court, in respect of any act or sentence therin passed, & being thereof lawfully convict in any Generall Court, or Court of Assistants, shalbee punished for the same by fine, inprisonment, or disfranchizement, or banishment, as the quality & measure of the offence shall deserve.[94]

Suggesting that the action taken against Hutchinson may have lacked substantive and procedural safeguards, the court also found that "it may fall out sometimes that some of the magistrats, or other judges, or members of the Courts, may transgresse the limits of their liberty & authority" and "therefore ordered, that if any magistrate, or other member, of any Court shall vse any reproachful or vnbeseeming speaches, or behaviour" toward any members of the court, he shall be subject to reprimand and possibly further censure, including fine or imprisonment.[95]

The Ecclesiastical Trial: The Boston Congregation

Because Hutchinson's sentence was levied in November, she was imprisoned in the home of Joseph Weld (Thomas Weld's brother) in Roxbury during the winter. Then, in March 1638, the Boston Church again tried Anne Hutchinson. Putting her membership in the church at issue, the proceeding "was meant to inspire repentance, and a genuine act of repentance could lead to the restoration of church membership" (Church Trial, *AC*, 350). Sixteen charges were formally pressed against her, "but only the first four were pressed at her examination."[96] Impassioned about her beliefs, Hutchinson failed to confess her errors and was cast out of the church. Lest there be any doubt about the reason, Hugh Peter effectively summarized the collective outrage at Hutchinson's failure to adhere to her proper role: "I would commend this to your Consideration that you have stept out of your place, *you have rather bine a Husband than a Wife and a Preacher than a Hearer; and a Magistrate than a Subject*" ("Church Trial," *AC*, 383). Hutchinson was duly punished for attempting to take a leadership role and promulgating beliefs that were considered manifestly dangerous to the order of the Massachusetts Bay Colony community.

More Evidence of Unfitness: The Case of Mary Dyer

Just after Hutchinson had left Massachusetts, Winthrop learned about her involvement with the stillborn daughter of one of her most ardent followers, Mary Dyer. In what was perhaps her most controversial act of midwifery, Hutchinson was called five months earlier on October 17th to help deal with the premature birth of the severely malformed child. Mindful that the Puritans would likely condemn this tragedy "steeped in Biblical metaphors" with the fear that an "angry God" had acted in "divine opprobrium," Hutchinson sought the counsel of John Cotton who advised her to "conceal the birth."[97]

Upon learning about the event, Winthrop sent for the other midwife in attendance, Jane Hawkins, to interrogate her about the birth. Hawkins confessed that the birth had been breach, allegedly giving the following description:

> it had a face, but no head, and the ears stood upon the shoulders and were like an ape's; it had no forehead, but over the eyes four horns, hard and sharp; two of them were above one inch long, the other two shorter; the eyes standing out, and the mouth also; the nose hooked upward; all over the breast and back full of sharp pricks and scales, like a thornback; the navel and all the belly, with the distinction of the sex, were where the belly should have been; behind, between the shoulders, it had two mouths, and in each of them a piece of flesh sticking out; it had arms and legs as other children; but, instead of toes, it had on each foot three claws, like a young fowl, with sharp talons. (*JW*, 254)

Winthrop ordered the body to be exhumed and then confirmed the existence of "horns and claws" in the "much corrupted" corpse (*JW*, 255). Using "monstrous birth" as "proof positive that God had turned against the Antinomians," Winthrop expressed vindication about his crusade against Hutchinson and her followers (*JW*, 254 n. 24).

Conclusion: Life in Exile

Excommunicated from the church and banished from the colony, on 28 March 1638, Hutchinson moved to Rhode Island, joining her husband.[98] Here, Hutchinson experienced her own personal tragedy in childbirth. In July or early August, Hutchinson gave birth to what was described as about twenty-seven lumps of flesh that lacked differentiation.[99] Along with Mary Dyer's child, this unfortunate fact was cited as further evidence that "she vented misshapen opinions, so she must bring forth deformed monsters" (Preface, *AC*, 214). Ann Kibbey comments that by "associating childbirth with antinomianism so closely, Winthrop and Weld emphasized their association of the female gender with antinomianism, implying that Puritan women were potentially a threat to the social and natural order simply because they were women."[100] Such an association with gender, however, underestimates the actual threat Hutchinson presented as an effective and persuasive speaker who had already demonstrated her power to rally both men and women. Weld's comments illustrate that, even with her in exile, Hutchinson's opponents felt compelled to assert justifications for their actions.

Following her husband's death in 1642, Hutchinson left Rhode Island and moved to the New Netherlands. Settling on Long Island Sound, near what is now on the outskirts of New York City, Hutchinson and five of her children were massacred by Indians the following year.[101] In the ultimate justification for the legal, social, and ecclesiastical action taken against Hutchinson, in his preface to Winthrop's *Short Story,* Thomas Weld decreed that "Gods hand" selected "this wofull woman, to make her and those belonging to her, an unheard of heavie example of their cruelty above al others. Thus the Lord heard our groanes to heaven, and freed us from this great and sore affliction" (Preface, Short Story, *AC,* 218). Via the legal system, colonial social control prevailed. Even though Anne Hutchinson paid the highest price for adhering to her own sense of religious beliefs in the face of enormous pressure to conform, the spirit of her teachings ultimately was vindicated well over a century later when the First Amendment was passed and all persons were assured the right to freedom of assembly, speech, and religion.

Chapter 2

The Law of the Great Spirit

Catharine Maria Sedgwick's
Hope Leslie

> "I know," she replied, "that it contains thy rule, and it may be needful for thy mixed race; but the Great Spirit hath written his laws on the hearts of his original children, and we need it not."
> —Magawisca in *Hope Leslie*

Just after John Winthrop's re-election in May 1637, between the initial concerns about Anne Hutchinson's meetings and her subsequent prosecution, the colonists waged war against the Pequot Indians.* Believing that their beneficent God approved of the massacre, colonial leaders celebrated their victory over this indigenous population that violently disrupted their efforts to settle in New England. As we will see, contemporaneous accounts of the events that transpired suggest that the siege was justified, yet there appears to be no surviving Native American version of the facts in the historical record. In 1827, however, Catharine Maria Sedgwick undertook to revisit this brief segment of history to present a more balanced portrait. In her historical novel, *Hope Leslie; Or Early Times in the Massachusetts*, Sedgwick incorporates a fictionalized Native American perspective to explore the clash that resulted between the Pequot Indians' insistence on undisturbed liberty and the colonists' efforts to settle New England.

The question remains to be answered as to why Sedgwick chose to create female characters "endowed with heroic capabilities

---

* Sedgwick and many early historians refer to these people as the "Pequod" tribe. For unknown reasons, later historians changed the spelling to "Pequot."

unrestrained by probabilities"[1] of colonial America to illustrate "the character of the times" for her nineteenth-century audience (Sedgwick, Preface to *HL*, 5). There is general agreement that Sedgwick intentionally sought to rewrite history, but speculation about her motive varies from the desire "to portray the state the Puritans founded as one that exterminated Indians and oppressed women,"* to "subversive commentary on the patriarchal assumptions of both Puritans and her contemporary male audience,"[2] to asserting "that the female conscience is as valid a source of social authority† as is the legal power held by men."[3] Most recently, Philip Gould has asserted that *Hope Leslie* is "an exercise in contemporary cultural criticism," in which "Sedgwick thematizes the incompatibility of gendered forms of 'republican' virtue" in her revisionist history of the Pequot war.[4] Sedgwick's preface to *Hope Leslie* suggests that she is, indeed, engaging in a kind of cultural criticism, yet it may be more straightforward than many critics acknowledge:

> The liberal philanthropist will not be offended by a representation which supposes that the human elements of virtue and intellect are not withheld from any branch of the human family; and the enlightened and accurate observer of human nature, will admit that the difference of character among the various races of the earth, arises mainly from the difference of condition. (Preface to *HL*, 6)

The most striking and problematic "difference of condition" in the nineteenth century was between white and black Americans. Sedgwick's critique of the Puritans' views of the Pequot Indians may have been prompted by continuing discussions about slavery in the aftermath of the ratification of the Constitution and by her belief that slavery was incompatible with "the demonstration of the truth" on which the Declaration of Independence is based.[5] Moreover, *Hope Leslie* may be a subtle way of asking readers to reevaluate, by analogy, the way in which they view black Americans and the justifications for slavery. By incorporating thinly veiled references to the life of

---

* Bardes and Gossett assert that *Hope Leslie* "is inherently seditious in meaning, since it sets conscience, innocence, and individual liberty against the needs of the community or the state" (23).

† Bauermeister even goes so far as to say that "*Hope Leslie* presents a world where rebellion and independence are applauded and the strict dictates of religion are questioned" (19). Bauermeister here builds on the work of Christopher Castiglia, who considers the "indictment of religion" in *Hope Leslie* (6–14).

Elizabeth Freeman, the former slave who worked for the Sedgwick family, Sedgwick broaches the subject of contemporary treatment of enslaved Americans. Sedgwick clearly respected the personal strength and determination of Freeman (affectionately known as "Mumbet"*), who believed that the Declaration of Independence applied to all Americans and, accordingly, sought to legally assert her right to freedom. On the eve of Freeman's death, Sedgwick wrote in her journal that she admired her "strong love of justice" (*Power*, 125). Years later, in "Slavery in New England," Sedgwick extolled Freeman's great courage in seeking liberation.[6] Like the outspoken heroines in *Hope Leslie*, Freeman was guided by her own sense of integrity and successfully asserted her rights in opposition to prevailing prejudice and legal theories.

This is not to say that Sedgwick equated the condition of slaves with that of colonial Native Americans. To the contrary, she is quite pointed in her observation that the "Indians of North America are, perhaps, the only race of men whom it may be said, that though conquered, they were never enslaved" (Preface to *HL*, 6). It is, however, Sedgwick's sense of enlightened observation that broadens her perspective about colonial history. Using two fictional Native American women, Nelema and Magawisca, Sedgwick recreates the Puritan-Pequot conflict to advance a new narrative about the treatment of fellow human beings and justice. Sedgwick's dramatic depiction of the criminal prosecutions of Nelema and Magawisca reveals the extent to which colonial fear of cultural and racial differences created an institutionalized air of distrust. Because Nelema and Magawisca denounce the military action that took place against the Pequots, they become vulnerable as prosecutorial targets.

Like Anne Hutchinson, who was called before the General Court to answer for beliefs that were perceived as having the ability to undermine the community, here colonial leaders attempt to use the law to subdue any potential threat that Nelema and Magawisca represent as Native Americans. This action is presented as somewhat understandable in light of the Pequots' retaliatory slaughter of the Fletcher family. Ironically, though, both women are fated in connection with "crimes" that actually involve beneficent acts on behalf of white individuals: Nelema is condemned for curing a deadly snake

---

* The spelling of Freeman's nickname varies: in Sedgwick's "Slavery in New England" she refers to Freeman as "Mum-Bett" (418).

bite, and Magawisca is held liable for treachery as a result of facilitating Hope Leslie's reunion with her sister. Hailed as heathens, in an atmosphere of fear and suspicion, the two are adjudicated "guilty" for their loyalty to their heritage and defiance of colonial authority. Moreover, using this scenario, Sedgwick offers her own version of justice through Hope Leslie, a young English woman who also refuses to submit to colonial authority. Nelema's and Magawisca's defiance is recast into what Sedgwick has called "high-souled courage and patriotism" (Preface to *HL,* 6). When Hope Leslie comes to the aid of each, she becomes an iconoclastic statement about justice and the never achieved possibility of peaceful coexistence. By publishing this story, Sedgwick "participates in the public life of the nation,"[7] asking her readers to reconsider the past and, implicitly, to consider the treatment of fellow human beings in the present as well.

SEDGWICK'S LIFE:
A FAMILY OF LAWYERS AND INDEPENDENT THINKERS

The activism in *Hope Leslie* has its roots in Catharine Maria Sedgwick's early exposure to the law and her thoughtful scrutiny of her family's values.[8] Born in 1789, as the third daughter and sixth child in her family, Sedgwick began with a greater potential to be free from those psychological constraints that often fetter the eldest to convention. Sedgwick's family occupied a distinguished social and political place in the colonial aristocracy of New England. Her mother, Pamela Dwight Sedgwick, was descended from the "old established gentry of Western Massachusetts, connected by blood and friendship with the families of the 'River-gods,' as the Hawleys, Worthingtons, and Dwights of Connecticut River were then designated" (*Power,* 78).*
These ancestors wielded immense power over colonial affairs, and "maintained their social and political dominance throughout the next century" (*Power,* 78 n. 39).[9] The Dwight family initially objected to Sedgwick's father, Theodore Sedgwick, "on the score of family, they priding themselves on their gentle blood."[10] Despite his less than genteel beginnings, Sedgwick's father became a self-made, powerful, and influential leader in the Berkshires.[11]

---

* Note that within *The Power of Her Sympathy,* pages 45–111 are Sedgwick's autobiography and pages 112–58 are her journal.

Sedgwick's desire to make a public contribution was influenced by the level of her father's achievement in the legislative and judicial systems. She admired the fact that her father's "kind, courteous, considerate manners were said by his contemporaries to have produced an entire revolution" (*Power*, 79). Admitted to the Massachusetts bar in 1766, he was active in the Revolutionary War and, as a believer in the need for a strong federal government, became a member of the Provincial Congress.[12] Repeatedly a member of the United States Senate and House of Representatives, he counted George Washington, John Jay, Henry Knox, and Alexander Hamilton among his friends. As a prominent leader in the movement to ratify the Federal Constitution, Theodore Sedgwick reached the peak of his political career when he was chosen to be the Speaker of the House of Representatives.[13] His legal career was no less distinguished. Although he was passed over (presumably for his Federalist political views) as the choice for the Chief Justice of Massachusetts, he served on the Massachusetts Supreme Court as a respected justice.[14] All of the Sedgwick sons followed their father and became lawyers.

Sedgwick apparently thrived intellectually in the company of her legally minded father and brothers. Describing her household as "an atmosphere of high intelligence," Sedgwick noted her father's "uncommon mental vigor" and her "kindred taste" for her brothers' intellectual "daily habits, and pursuits, and pleasures."[15] The educational expectations for Sedgwick, however, were much more traditional.[16] Her formal education was the best offered for young women of her time, yet typically meager. Attending Mrs. Bell's school in Albany and Mr. Payne's in Boston, Sedgwick complained that she was taught little French and that her studies "left her much time to charm the Bostonians."[17] Later, Sedgwick harshly dismissed her "school life" as a "waste," bluntly asserting that her "home life" was her "only education" (*Power*, 84). Fortunately, Sedgwick received her literary education from her father who, "whenever he was at home," kept her "at his side till nine o'clock in the evening, to listen to him while he read" passages from Hume, Shakespeare, and Cervantes.[18] Interestingly, Samuel Butler's satirical poem *Hudibras*—a burlesque attack on Puritan fanaticism and hypocrisy—was also on their regular reading list (*Power*, 74). Even though Sedgwick claims that she "did not understand them," this reading experience inspired her: "some glances of celestial light reached my soul, and I caught from his magnetic sympathy some elevation of feeling, and that love of reading which has been to me 'education'" (*Power*, 74). Sedgwick's father also expressed his hope that she would "find it in [her] power to devote [her] mornings to reading," reminding her that "there are few who can make such improvements by it and it would be lamented if this precious time should be lost."[19]

Sedgwick's informal intellectual upbringing was coupled with a strong moral sense, including the legacy of her father's representation of Elizabeth Freeman. Acting on a constitutional principle, Theodore Sedgwick challenged the legality of slavery in Massachusetts. Freeman, a slave owned by the politically influential Colonel John Ashley, sought out Theodore Sedgwick for protection after she was "struck violently with a shovel by Ashley's wife."[20] After Freeman questioned, "If all are free and equal" under the Declaration of Independence, then "why are we all slaves?" Sedgwick's father commenced a suit on her behalf in 1781 (*Power*, 125).* Using the recently enacted Massachusetts Declaration of Rights, he successfully argued that "slavery had never received specific legal sanction," obtained Freeman's release, and "the blacks of the Commonwealth were restored to their natural rights—declared free."[21] Although the precedential value of the case, known as *Brom and Bett v. Ashley*, is unclear,[22] it was certainly a legal landmark in Massachusetts.†

Following the trial, Freeman became a valued member of the Sedgwick household. Because Sedgwick's mother was in frail health, frequently incapacitated, and then died when Sedgwick was a teenager, Sedgwick thought of her as a surrogate mother and a "faithful friend" (*Power*, 124–25). Importantly, Freeman's example provided Sedgwick

---

* It should be noted, however, that even though Theodore Sedgwick represented Freeman and was a member of Franklin's Abolition Society of Pennsylvania from 1792 until his death, he also "virtually authored the first Fugitive Slave Law" in 1791. His biographer, Richard Welch, observes that even though "Sedgwick was no friend of Slavery," he "was prepared to respect and obey" the Constitutional protections of that institution (*Theodore Sedgwick*, 102). Theodore Sedgwick also reportedly declared in Congress that "to propose an abolition of slavery in this country would be the height of madness" (Edward Foster, *Catharine Maria Sedgwick*, 29–30, quoting William Cullen Bryant and Sydney Howard Gray, *A Popular History of the United States* [New York, 1881] IV, 261).

† Just prior to the verdict in Freeman's case, the Massachusetts Supreme Court ruled in *Caldwell v. Jennison* that slavery was unconstitutional in Massachusetts. Arthur Zilversmit speculates that this may have persuaded Col. Ashley not to pursue his appeal.

with yet another moral anchor. Just a month before Freeman's death, Sedgwick wrote a moving tribute in her journal describing her as having "a life...more perfect than I have ever known. Her talents were not small nor limited: a clear mind—strong judgment—a quick and firm decision—an iron resolution—an incorruptible integrity—an integrity that never for a moment parleyed with temptation—a truth that never varied from the straight line" (*Power*, 125). Sedgwick's father's advocacy and Freeman's strong moral imperative clearly made an indelible impression on Sedgwick.

Despite the vocational limitations on Sedgwick's ability to act on moral issues and questions in the public sphere, she broke free from many conventional attitudes in her personal life. In several notable realms—politics, religion, and marriage—Sedgwick proved herself to be an independent thinker. The political climate in the Sedgwick household was clearly defined. As a staunch Federalist, Theodore Sedgwick "seldom tolerated opinions which conflicted with his own."[23] He once called Thomas Jefferson "the greatest rascal and traitor in the United States"[24] and "spoke politically of the people as 'Jacobins,' 'sans-coulottes,' and 'miscreants'" (*Power*, 64). As a child Sedgwick recalled "looking upon a Democrat as an enemy to his country," and she "thought every Democrat was grasping, dishonest, and vulgar" (*Power*, 63 and 81). She later reflected that the Federalists' "misfortune...was a thorough distrust of the 'people'" (*Power*, 64). After her father's death in 1813, however, Sedgwick gradually became a Jacksonian democrat, freeing herself of the prejudices of the aristocratic tendency of her family.*

Sedgwick also rejected her Calvinist upbringing and embraced Unitarian teachings. Reared in one of the "last bulwarks of Calvinism in New England," Sedgwick heard many sermons by Reverend Stephen West, the Stockbridge minister who was Jonathan Edwards' successor.[25] Continuing with her family's beliefs, Sedgwick joined a Calvinist church in New York when she was twenty, but "increasingly offended by what seemed to her to be the uncharitable hypocrisy of Calvinism, she went over to Unitarianism in 1821."[26] This decision, however, was not without precedent in her family. On his deathbed,

---

* The reason for this change is unclear. Michael Bell suggests that the shift in Sedgwick's political and religious views parallels that of the "conventional nineteenth century attitude toward history, a belief in 'progress'" or a movement from the "artificial" to the "natural" (214).

Theodore Sedgwick broke with Calvinist orthodoxy when he asked that the liberal Boston minister, William Ellery Channing, administer the sacraments.[27] Thus, even though conversion was a way of professing religious allegiance with her father, Sedgwick's decision to leave the Congregational Church created "spiritual solitude in the midst of Berkshire orthodoxy."[28] As Edward Halsey Foster notes, Sedgwick "turned to Unitarianism" rather "than accept the Calvinist picture of a merciless God who ruled men of essentially corrupt and sinful natures."[29]

In the social realm, too, Sedgwick maintained her independent thinking. Never marrying, Sedgwick escaped the troubling institution that created an unhappy state for many of those around her. In 1847, she wrote to her niece, "so many I have loved have made shipwreck of happiness in marriage or have found it a dreary joyless condition."[30] Sedgwick watched her mother struggle with fragile health and a difficult life tending to many children during her husband's frequent absences. Her sisters' experiences likewise were consistent with this observation. Her eldest sister, Frances, was trapped in a miserable relationship in which she was subjected to what Sedgwick described as the "brutal" conduct of her husband.[31] Even though her sister Eliza's marriage was a loving one, it was still filled with the hardship of "the painful drudgery of bearing and nurturing twelve children."[32] With the help of her brothers who all "welcomed her into their households" and offered her "care, affection, and companionship,"[33] Sedgwick opted against marriage and for the freedom that allowed her to write.

Stimulated by her home life and her brothers' encouragement, Sedgwick found an outlet for her own creativity in her literary career. Sedgwick's careful reflection about her own values and the way she chose to live her life are reflected in the deliberate social critique that is the heart of *Hope Leslie*. Through Nelema and Magawisca, Sedgwick did not hesitate to utilize the law to emphasize the level of institutionalized distrust of the Pequot Indians and to take a firm moral stance to redress the injustice.

THE PEQUOT WAR: THE LEGAL AND HISTORICAL CONTEXT

By March of 1636, tension was running high between the Massachusetts Bay colonists and the Pequot Indians. The colonists received a warning (although the authenticity is unclear) that the

Pequots' mistrust of the English was about to prompt them into acts of aggression.³⁴ Then in July, fur trader John Oldham was found murdered, allegedly as the result of a dispute between the Pequots and the Naragansetts.* John Winthrop reported the gruesome scene: "they found John Oldham under an old seine, stark naked, his head cleft to the brains, and his hand and legs cut as if they had been cutting them off, and yet warm."³⁵

Despite the fact that Oldham had troubled dealings with the colonists, his murder solidified the animosity with the Pequots. In December 1636, at the meeting of the General Court in Boston, the Court made a motion to entreat the Governor and council to consider waging war against the Pequots and Block Island (where Oldham was killed).³⁶ In March, because there had been so many complaints about safety, it was recognized that it was a "time of so much great danger" because of the threat of Indian attack, and it was ordered that military officers should keep watch in every town.³⁷ The next month the General Court met "for the speciall occasion of psecuting the warr against the Pecoits."³⁸ At this special session, it was agreed and ordered that the wars were about to be undertaken upon "just grounds" and, accordingly, specified the number of soldiers who were to take part and other logistical information.³⁹

John Winthrop was reelected Governor of Massachusetts Bay just before the war began. The same colony record dated 17 May 1637 that notes his victory also set forth the comprehensive new law that prohibited any dealings with Indians regarding arms: "It is ordered, that no man wthin this jurisdiction shall, directly or indirectly, amend, repair, or cause to bee amended or repaired, any gun, small or greate, belonging to any Indian, nor shall endevour the same, nor shall sell or give to any Indian, directly or indirectly, any such gun, or any gunpowder, or shott, or leade, or shot moulde, or any military weopons, or armour."⁴⁰

The law also provided punishment for offenders: "ten pound fine for evry offence" and gave the Court of Assistants discretionary power to "increase the fine or to impose corporall punishment."⁴¹ The arms law was further reinforced by a general trade restriction which ordered that no person in the jurisdiction "shall trade out of the limits

---

* Historical accounts as to the identity of the perpetrators vary: Jennings reports that Oldham was murdered by the Naragansett Indians (206); Moseley states that members of the Naragansetts killed Oldham for trading with their enemies, the Pequots (77); Ziff lays blame on the Pequots (*Puritanism in America*, 74).

with any Indian."[42] The third law passed during this Court term gave a committee the power to send out troops against the Pequots, including furnishing the troops with arms, provisions, and vessels.[43] As part of an overall effort to secure the colony, these laws were passed contemporaneously with the exclusionary law aimed at Hutchinson and her sympathizers. Thereafter, the colonists attacked the Pequots.

Through her reading of William Hubbard's *Narrative of the Indian Wars in New England*, John Trumbell's *Complete History of Connecticut*, and John Winthrop's *Journal*, Sedgwick was quite familiar with the Puritan desire to eradicate the indigenous population and the religious rationalizations for their actions.[44] The basic facts of the war, as they are depicted in *Hope Leslie*, are not in dispute with historical accounts. Succinctly stated, by the "war's end, the English executed scores of Pequot warriors, enslaved Pequot women and children, and terminated Pequot sovereignty."[45] A sampling of the original Puritan narratives by colony leaders and the military commanders readily reveals the brutality of the conquest that Sedgwick sought to emphasize:

John Mason: The Captain [Mason] told them that We should never kill them after that manner [with swords]: The captain also said, WE MUST BURN THEM: and immediately stepping into the Wigwam where he had been before, brought out a Fire Brand, and putting it to the Matts with which they were covered, set the Wigwams on Fire.[46]

John Underhill: Many were burnt in the fort, both men, women, and children. Others forced out, and came in troops to the Indians, which our soldiers received and entertained with the point of the sword. Down fell men, women and children; those that scaped us, fell into the hands of the Indians that were in the rear of us. It is reported by themselves, that there were about four hundred souls in this fort, and not above five of them escaped out of our hands.[47]

John Winthrop: Our English from Connecticut, with their Indians, and many of the Naragansetts, marched in the night to a fort of the Pequods at Mistick, and, besetting the same about break of the day, after two hours' fight they took it, (by firing it,) and slew therein two chief sachems, and one hundred and fifty old men, women, and children (*WJ*, 220).*

---

* Although this 25 May 1637 journal entry states that the "story is more fully described in the next leaf," such was never written (see *WJ*, n. 97).

William Bradford: More were burnt to death than was otherwise slain; It burnt their bowstrings and made them unserviceable; those that scaped the fire were slain with the sword, some hewn to pieces, others run through with their rapiers....It was a fearful sight to see them thus frying in the fire and streams of blood quenching the same, and horrible was the stink and scent thereof; but the victory seemed a sweet sacrifice, and they gave the praise thereof to God, who had wrought so wonderfully for them, thus to enclose their enemies in their hands and give them so speedy a victory over so proud and insulting an enemy.[48]

Edward Johnson: The Lord in mercy toward his poore Churches having thus destroyed these bloudy barbarous Indians ...they brought away onely their heads as a token of their victory. By this means the Lord strook a trembling terror into all the Indians about, even to this very day.[49]

There is nothing apologetic about any of these narratives; the Puritans viewed the Pequot War as simply a victory over a pernicious enemy. Indeed, the colony records also note that it was ordered that a day be kept of public thanksgiving to God for his great mercies in subduing the Pequots ans for bringing the soldiers home safely.[50]

SEDGWICK'S BROADER PERSPECTIVE ON THE PEQUOT WAR

In a letter to her father, expressing her awe at his public achievements, Sedgwick said, "You may benefit a nation, my dear papa, and I may improve the condition of a fellow-being."[51] This correspondence reflects the concern about others that Sedgwick expresses in *Hope Leslie*. By challenging "the official history of original settlement by exposing the repositories of the nation's early history, the Puritan narratives, as justifications of genocide,"[52] Sedgwick prompts her contemporaries to think in broad historical terms about roots of American democracy.

What is strikingly different about Sedgwick's depiction of the war in *Hope Leslie* is the human perspective as told by Nelema and Magawisca. Each of these women recounts the personal toll of the massacre of their families. The colonial family of William Fletcher provides the locus for both to relate their stories. The aging Nelema, who lives a short distance from the Fletcher home, Bethel, mourns for her lost offspring; the youthful Magawisca, a prisoner of the Pequot

War who was taken in by the Fletchers, tells of the loss of her brother and many others from her tribe. Magawisca experiences a kind of kinship with Fletcher's son, Everell, and the orphaned Hope Leslie, who has come from England to live with the family. Through Nelema's and Magawisca's narratives, it becomes clear that colonial expansion was at the expense of innocent men, women, and children who were slain and incinerated.

Nelema, who is maimed and essentially a lone survivor, relates a very dramatic and visceral side of the war. Although not from the Pequot tribe herself, Nelema is "one of the few survivors of a tribe who had been faithful allies of the Pequods" (*HL*, 36). Staring at Mrs. Fletcher's infant and Everell, Nelema groans that she "had sons too—and grandsons; but where are they?" With great anguish she laments that her offspring, "have fallen like our forest trees, before the stroke of the English axe" and that of all of her race, "there is not one, now, in whose veins [her] blood runs" (*HL*, 37). Nelema agonizes, "Sometimes, when the spirits of the storm are howling about my wigwam, I hear the voices of my children crying for vengeance, and then I could deal myself the death-blow" (*HL*, 37). Throwing back her cloak to expose her shriveled arm, Nelema concludes her diatribe with "They spared not our homes...there where our old men spoke, where was heard the song of the maiden, and the laugh of our children; there now all is silence, dust, and ashes" (*HL*, 37). The vehemence of her words is at once mediated by the translation in Magawisca's soft voice, yet Nelema's accompanying wild gesturing with her "naked, shriveled, trembling arm" creates a macabre scene.

The cause of Nelema's impaired limb is not revealed, but it may have its source in an event in the life of Sedgwick's beloved "Mumbet." While she was still one of Colonel Ashley's slaves, Mrs. Ashley was attempting to punish Freeman's sister with a shovel. When Freeman attempted to intervene, she suffered a debilitating blow to her arm.[53] This physical similarity between Freeman and Nelema tends to infuse Nelema with the moral voice of Freeman, who prevailed despite the prejudices she experienced in her early life. On a much smaller scale than Freeman's life with the Sedgwick family, Nelema has experienced kindness from the Fletchers. She tells Mrs. Fletcher to "fear me not, I have had kindness from thee, thy blankets have warmed me, I have been fed from thy table, and drank of thy cup" (*HL*, 37), yet there is a hysterical unpredictability in Nelema's grief and her hasty departure which is filled with inarticulate murmuring. Understandably, Mrs.

Fletcher recoils in fear, hugging her infant "closer to her breast." Nelema is nearly mad from the decimation of her people. Even though she is no real threat to the Fletchers, she is depicted as an unsettling character who is feared at an instinctive level.

Unlike Nelema, Magawisca presents herself with great strength and resolve, which makes her narrative about the Pequot War particularly immediate and compelling. She presents herself as a formidable intellectual opponent to the colonists; Magawisca represents the power of the Pequot presence. Before she begins her story, Magawisca pauses for a few moments, sighs deeply, then begins "the recital of the last acts of tragedy of her people" (*HL*, 47). She implicitly lays claim to the land through her panoramic description of the countryside, their hunting-grounds. The sanctity of their homes was undisturbed by predators: "No enemy's foot had ever approached this nest, which the eagles of the tribe had built for their mates and their young" (*HL*, 47). She tells how, on the night of the attack, Magawisca's mother sensed impending danger. Depicted as being in harmony with the natural world, Magawisca relates that all "the servants of the Great Spirit spoke to" her "mother's ear," whispering "that some evil was near" (*HL*, 47). Magawisca suggests that the just nature of the Great Spirit helped to warn her mother against colonial aggression.

Sedgwick's continuation of the war scene adds the human details missing from the accounts by John Mason, John Underhill, John Winthrop, and William Bradford. Through Magawisca's voice, she recreates the story of how Magawisca's mother went out into the darkness, fearing for the safety of her son, Samoset. Shortly thereafter, a "rushing sound was heard" along with a tribesman's cry, "Owanox! Owanox! (the English! the English!)" (*HL*, 48). By this time, the English have surrounded the palisade where the Pequots are sleeping, and they open fire. Led to the tribe by a traitor, who had been a guest in Magawisca's household, the English are "flanked by the cowardly Naragansetts." This story is deliberately calculated to place her oppressors in an extremely unfavorable light.

Magawisca continues her description of the destruction with calm deliberateness, leveling a clear indictment against the English:

> Those fearful guns that we had never heard before—the shouts of your people—our own battle yell—the piteous cries of the little children—the groans of our mothers, and oh! worse—worse than all—the silence of those that could not speak...Some of our people threw themselves into the

midst of the crackling flames, and their courageous souls parted with one shout of triumph; others mounted the palisade, but they were shot and dropped like a flock of birds smitten by a hunter's arrows. Thus did the strangers destroy, in our own homes, hundreds of our tribe. (*HL,* 49)

Seeking refuge in a cavity under a rock, Magawisca, her mother, and several siblings escape the carnage. She then describes how, "when the last sound had died away," they emerged from their shelter to a sight that made them "lament to be among the living." Their homes had vanished and the bodies of their "people were strewn about the smouldering ruin; and all around the palisade lay the strong and valiant warriors—cold—silent—powerless as the unformed clay" (*HL,* 49). Magawisca's sixteen-year-old brother, Samoset, is killed in the mayhem as he defends the family hut. Struck down and disarmed by a saber-blow that severs his bow string, Samoset is taken captive. When he refuses to act as a subversive guide for the English, "with one saber-stroke they severed his head from his body" (*HL,* 51). The colonists were often outraged at the way Indians treated their enemies, yet Sedgwick depicts the kind of brutality that the colonists were also capable of perpetrating.

Refusing to be enslaved by the colonists, at the end of her account, Magawisca pauses, and "she looked at Everell and said with a bitter smile": "You tell us, Everell, that the book of your law is better than that written on our hearts, for ye say it teaches mercy, compassion, forgiveness—if ye had such a law and believed it, would ye thus have treated a captive boy?" (*HL,* 51). This critical statement by Magawisca reveals her allegiance to her own law in blatant defiance of English rule. As Sedgwick acknowledges, this quotation has important historical roots. It is derived from missionary John Heckewelder's reports that the Indians pointed out the hypocrisy of the English who held the Bible, "their big Book in one hand" and "in the other they had murderous weapons, guns and swords" which they used to kill the Indians (*HL,* 352–53).* Magawisca's challenge slashes at the basis of English authority. Touching Everell's imagination with "the wand of feeling," Sedgwick effectively advances a new perspective on the war, "a very different picture of those defenceless families of savages, pent in the recesses of their natural forests, and there exterminated, not by

---

* Jennings acknowledges that whereas Heckewelder's work has been "maligned by historians of the Parkman school," further study has confirmed "substantial issues." Jennings defends Heckewelder as "unimpeachably honest" (325 n. 44).

superior natural force, but by the adventitious circumstances of arms, skill, and knowledge" (*HL*, 54). For extra emphasis, Sedgwick quotes from William Bradford's account in *Of Plymouth Plantation*. His widely accepted Puritan narrative of triumph is reduced to an admission of brutality, and what he negatively deemed the ferocity of the Pequots is transformed into a testimonial of their great courage.

Sedgwick, however, does not end her revision on this high point, which would have skewed history in favor of the Pequots. She complicates the Puritan relations with the Indians through their retaliation on Bethel.† The attack was not without warning. After Nelema's denunciation of the English for killing her friends and family, she drops at Mrs. Fletcher's feet "a little roll...an arrow, and the rattle of a rattle-snake enveloped in a skin of the same reptile" (*HL*, 38). When Mrs. Fletcher implores an explanation of the symbolism from Magawisca, she learns that the token is "the warning voice that speakth of danger near" and that the arrow is "the symbol of death" (*HL*, 39). Nelema actually attempts to warn the Fletchers about the impending danger. Knowing that peril is at hand, Magawisca precedes her account of the Pequot war by telling Everell "when the hour of vengeance comes, if it should come, remember it was provoked" (*HL*, 47). Magawisca presumes that her father, Mononotto, a Pequot leader who survived the massacre, will attempt to liberate his children from captivity. When her father finally arrives, Magawisca makes a dramatic appeal to him crying out: "save them—save them ...take vengeance on your enemies—but spare our friends—our benefactors."

Sedgwick takes the anonymity out of the attack. Magawisca feels a kind of kinship with the Fletchers, claiming that she bleeds "when they are struck"; she shields Mrs. Fletcher, saying, "You shall hew me to pieces ere you touch her" (*HL*, 63). Despite Magawisca's pleas, the ensuing attack results in tragedy for the Fletcher family, leaving a bloody scene of death for Mrs. Fletcher and most of her children. Reclaiming his children to the forest, Mononotto attempts the regeneration of his people through violence against the intruders in his land.

---

† There may have been several sources for Sedgwick's fictional attack on Bethel. It may have been inspired by the account of the Deerfield massacre in *The Redeemed Captive Returning to Zion* by John Williams (1707) (see Michael Bell, 217) or a 1775 attack by Indians on a Stockbridge family that Sedgwick may have known about (Edward Foster, 77).

LEGAL CULPABILITY BASED ON FEAR

For their defiance of colonial authority and their firm adherence to their non-Christian heritage, Nelema and Magawisca are subjected to spurious legal charges.[54] Neither Nelema nor Magawisca has participated in the aggressive acts against the Fletchers—each actually take steps to prevent the slaying—yet they are viewed with great suspicion simply by virtue of their race. The Fletchers' house servants, Jennet and Digby, embody the colonial distrust of these Native American women. After Nelema relates her tale of loss, Jennet's appraisal of the scene is a harsh rebuke: "It's a shame and a sin...a crying shame, for this heathen hag to be pouring forth here as if she were gifted like the prophets of old; she that can only see into the future by reading the devil's book" (*HL*, 37-38). Jennet is equally severe in her suggested disposition: "it were best, forthwith, to deliver her to the judges and cast her into prison" (*HL*, 38). Extending her suspicions, Jennet issues her parting accusation that Magawisca "is ever going to Nelema's hut, and of moonlight nights too, when they say witches work their will—birds of a feather flock together" (*HL*, 39). Likewise, Digby admonishes Everell that the Pequots "are a treacherous race...They are a kind of beast that we don't comprehend—out of the range of God's creatures—neither angel, man, nor yet quite devil" (*HL*, 41-42). This characterization of Nelema and Magawisca as crafty establishes a basis for them to become likely targets for persecution.

This fear is further exacerbated by their resistance to even the semblance of conformity to the prevailing standards for women. In *Hope Leslie*, most of the women are domestic heroines that serve as "a model of genteel behavior."[55] Mrs. Fletcher accepts her husband's decisions with "meek submission," "deeming it the duty of a wife to never disquiet her husband with household cares" (*HL*, 16 and 30). In turn, she is praised by her spouse for her "obedience" and her "careful conformity" to his wishes (*HL*, 20). Mrs. Fletcher epitomizes the expectations of women by expressing her love for her family "by that self-doubting, self-sacrificing conduct to her husband and children, which characterizes, in all ages and circumstances, a faithful and devoted woman" (*HL*, 36). The depiction of John Winthrop's house likewise "exemplifies the well-ordered Puritan household, demonstrating the proper attitude toward political, religious, and personal life."[56] In Winthrop's estimation, "passiveness...next to godliness, is a woman's best virtue" (*HL,* 153). Like Mrs. Fletcher, Madam Winthrop is the example of proper womanhood, and her niece, Esther Downing,* is "always respectful, always patient; always governed by the slightest intimation of her aunt's wishes" (*HL,* 206-7).[57] Esther is described as "a reserved, tender, and timid cast of character, and being bred in the strictest school of the puritans, their doctrines and principles easily commingled with the natural qualities of her mind. She could not have disputed the nice points of faith, sanctification, and justification, with certain contemporary theologians" (*HL,* 135). Mr. Fletcher's swipe at Anne Hutchinson—who is referred to with the derogatory phrase "poor deluded"—underscores Puritan discontent with women who step out of their place (*HL,* 19). Because they have spoken out against the injustice of the Pequot War, the behavior of Nelema and Magawisca is viewed with suspicion.

The mere appearance of Nelema and Magawisca further emphasizes their difference from the models of domestic conformity who fully submit to male authority. Nelema is described as a hag: her "brow was contracted, her lips drawn in, and her little sunken eye gleamed like a diamond from its dark recess" (*HL,* 36). Her appearance conveys a kind of nefarious unpredictability. Equally unpredictable, yet "beautiful even to an European eye," Magawisca is a kind of enchantress, richly garbed with "an air of wild and fantastic grace" (*HL,* 23). The daughter of a chieftain, Mononotto, Magawisca has inherited the noble demeanor of high birth. As her mistress, Mrs. Fletcher observes, "it appears impossible to her to clip the wings of her soaring thoughts, and to keep them down to household matters" (*HL,* 32). Magawisca is a free thinker who cannot be contained by convention or rules.

Nelema: A Criminal Folk Remedy

Nelema's only "crime" is engaging in a folk remedy that is frightening to the colonists. Approximately seven years after the attack on Bethel, Hope Leslie's tutor, Cradock, nearly dies after a rattlesnake sinks its venomous fangs into his hand. Only Hope Leslie is willing to save his life by sucking the poison from his hand, but Cradock refuses to let her

---

* Note that Esther is a fictional character but that the other members of the Winthrop family are based on historical figures.

do so. Recalling that Nelema had once said that she knew an antidote to the poison, Hope Leslie sets out with Jennet and Digby to enlist her help. Not surprisingly, Jennet uses the occasion to vent her rancorous opinions against "the old heathen witch" asserting that "It were better ...to die than to live by the devil's help" (*HL*, 103). After filling a deerskin pouch from a "repository of herbs," Nelema accompanies the trio back to Bethel, where "poor Cradock's death was regarded as inevitable" (*HL*, 102–3). Already established in the text as a kind of witch, Nelema is vulnerable to the deep distrust of the medical abilities that enable her to save Cradock's life.

In her letter to Everell, who was then living in England, Hope Leslie undertakes to describe the life-saving scene, which only she has witnessed: "She first threw aside her blanket, and discovered a kind of wand, which she had concealed beneath it, wreathed with a snake's skin. She then pointed to the figure of a snake delineated on her naked shoulder. 'It is the symbol of our tribe,' she said" (*HL*, 104). Upon seeing Hope Leslie shudder, Nelema had explained the significance of the tattoo as "a sign of honour, won for [her] race by him who first drew from the veins the poison of the king of all creeping things" (*HL*, 104). Keenly aware of the irony of the circumstances, Nelema delivers a reminder that she is the last of her race and has been "bidden to heal a servant in the house" of her tribe's enemies (*HL*, 104). This is particularly significant, because Nelema does what she thinks is right to save another life, without imputing the evil deeds of the white race onto the dying Cradock. In her own way, Nelema expresses graciousness under circumstances in which she could easily have refused to help. Unlike Jennet, Nelema resists blanket racism and offers her aid.

Nelema taps the full extent of her medicinal powers to revive Cradock. The mystical scene that follows drains the colour from Hope's cheeks. Nelema bends over Cradock, muttering

> an incantation in her own tongue. She then, after many efforts succeeded in making him swallow a strong decoction, and bathed the wound and arm with the same liquor. These applications were repeated at short intervals, during which she brandished her wand, making quick and mysterious motions, as if she were writing hieroglyphics on the invisible air. She writhed her body into the most horrible contortions, and tossed her withered arms wildly about her...so violent was her exercise, that sweat poured from her face like rain. (*HL*, 104–5)

After repeating this strange process with great dedication until she is satisfied that Cradock had "turned his back on the grave," Nelema departs.

Nothing more would have likely come from this exercise, save gratitude, if Hope had been the only witness. The entire scene, however, has been observed by Jennet, who was peeping through the keyhole. After accusing Hope of aiding and abetting an "emissary of Satan," Jennet takes it upon herself to instigate trouble for Nelema by reporting the result of her covert surveillance to Mr. Fletcher. Deeply disturbed, he in turn calls upon Hope Leslie to corroborate Jennet's accusations. Like Jennet, Mr. Fletcher's bigotry is unmistakable, as he tells Hope that "it was time to look grave when a pow-wow dared to use her diabolical spirits, mutterings, and exorcisms, beneath a christian roof, and in the presence of a christian maiden, and on a christian man" (*HL,* 107). Mr. Fletcher treats Hope like a misdirected child, sending her to her room with the admonishment to "meddle no farther." Dismissing Hope's opinion that Nelema did not use witchcraft to heal Cradock, the matter is turned over to the magistrates for their consideration. Hope's initial inclination is to be the "good girl"; she admits that whereas her "heart rebelled," that she "dared not disobey" (*HL,* 108). The reality and injustice of Nelema's prosecution, however, causes Hope to muster her strength and to come to Nelema's defense.

Pursuant to local procedures, Nelema is sent the next morning to appear before a triumvirate of magistrates. Messrs. Pynchon, Holioke, and Chapin hear the primary charge against Nelema, namely "the crime of curing Cradock," which was then amplified by "Jennet and some of her gossips," who imputed to Nelema "all the mischances that have happened for the last seven years" (*HL,* 108). Such malfeasance is perhaps best encompassed by the rubric of "witchcraft," which was apparently not yet on the books as a crime in the 1630s. In any event, many of the colonists would have been quite familiar with witchcraft as a crime, since the English Parliament first made it a capital offense in 1542.[58] Most of those accused of and condemned for witchcraft in England were poor women from the lowest ranks of the social order.[59] Furthermore, "women who healed people or relieved symptoms which doctors had unsuccessfully treated could come under suspicion of using magic in their medical practice."[60] As an impoverished, disfigured, Native American woman who practiced herbal medicine, Nelema is particularly vulnerable to charges of sorcery.

The details of the proceeding are, at best, sketchy and devoid of the evidentiary safeguards that were eventually enacted in the American judicial system. The primary evidence comes from Hope, who claims that her testimony was "extorted" from her, because she could not disguise her "reluctance to communicate any thing that could be made unfavorable" to Nelema. Hope continues her letter to Everell, reporting on her exchange with the magistrates:

Holioke:	Take care, Hope Leslie, that thou art not found in the folly of Balaam, who would have blessed, when the Lord commanded him to curse...
Hope:	It was better to make a mistake in blessing than in cursing, and that I was sure Nelema was as innocent as myself...
Pynchon:	Thou art somewhat forward, maiden...in giving thy opinion; but thou must know, that we regard it but as the whistle of a bird; withdraw, and leave judgment to thy elders. (*HL*, 109)

The magistrates' paternalistic posturing is characteristic for the time. Needless to say, Hope stands firm in her attempt to advocate on Nelema's behalf. Unswayed by the sternness of the judiciary or by the murmur of "shame—shame!" on her way out of the room, Hope extends her hand to Nelema "in a token of kindness." With no evidence offered in favor of Nelema, she is "pronounced worthy of death." Because the magistracy lacks the power to levy a sentence that extended to life, limb, or banishment, the matter is then referred to the full court in Boston. Because the colony does not yet have a jail, Nelema is incarcerated in Mr. Pynchon's cellar pending the imposition of a final sentence. Predictably, the Boston court affirms the opinion of the triumvirate, condemning her to death. Thus, popular prejudice is allowed to prevail and become the "law" under which Nelema is prosecuted.

An interesting side note to the trial is added by Digby's apparent change of heart in favor of Nelema. Hope notes in her letter that Digby himself was "summoned before the magistrates, and publickly reproved for expressing himself against their proceedings" (*HL*, 109). Harshly admonished by Mr. Pynchon and directed to "speak no more against godly governors and righteous government," Digby joins the ranks of those high-minded souls who exercised their prerogative to denigrate injustice. Like Anne Hutchinson, Digby's feelings are "suppressed, but not subdued" (*HL*, 109). Relegated to the sidelines of the narrative, Digby becomes part of the covert acts to free Nelema.

Sedgwick undertakes to rework the judicially institutionalized prejudice of the time through Hope Leslie's independent action. Emboldened by her own sense of justice, and by Digby's support, Hope effects Nelema's escape. Unpersuaded by the "wisdom" of the magistrates, Hope "took counsel from her own heart, and that told her that the rights of innocence were paramount to all other rights" (*HL*, 120). Hope rejects the authority of her patriarchal elders, taking action that reconfigures their rule. Never suspecting Hope's involvement in spiriting Nelema away, some in the town persist in their witch fantasy, even claiming that they "could smell sulphur from the outer kitchen door to the door of the cell" (*HL*, 112). Nelema may have been tried and convicted by popular prejudice and religious intolerance, but through the hand of Hope Leslie, Sedgwick ultimately crafts a just result.* Because she has the internal fortitude and confidence to answer to a higher sense of law, Hope prevents this innocent woman—who should be a hero for saving a life—from being executed. The rebellious upshot of this action, however, is noted by Sedgwick's narrator: "she had, before the grave and reverend magistrates, declared her belief in Nelema's innocence, and thereby implied a censure of their wisdom" (*HL*, 119).

MAGAWISCA: IMPUTED PERFIDY

The prosecution of Magawisca is no less egregious than the legal assault on Nelema; the paucity of credible evidence is supplemented with a strategic ploy using overt racism. Sedgwick fictionalizes the degree to which fear and distrust could result in injustice. The events that precede Magawisca's becoming ensnared in the prosecutorial net on vague charges of treachery are particularly telling of her allegiances and sense of equity. Like Nelema and Hope Leslie, Magawisca answers to her internalized law of the Great Spirit about matters of justice. After the attack on Bethel, in which Everell is taken prisoner, Magawisca's father and tribesmen feel fully justified in killing Everell as a *quid pro quo* for Samoset's death. Believing the execution to be "exact and necessary justice," Mononotto exclaims, "I will pour out

---

* Regarding this act of justice, Gregory Garvey argues that Sedgwick "implicitly casts the context in which a woman can enter the public realm as a breakdown in the functioning of a women's moral influence" (293).

this English boy's blood to the last drop, and give his flesh and bones to the dogs and wolves" (*HL,* 91, 92). Defying her father and her tribe, Magawisca saves Everell's life. She interferes with the operation of Indian "justice" when she screams "Forbear!" and interposes her arm just as Everell is about to receive the mortal hatchet blow. Her brave act leaves Everell unharmed, but Magawisca's arm is severed—the "lopped quivering member" drops over the precipice (*HL,* 93).* Like Nelema's arm injury, Magawisca's loss of a limb has resonances in Freeman's history. Accordingly, when Magawisca proclaims the deliberateness of her defense: "I have bought his life with my own" (*HL,* 93), she is imbued with Freeman's great sense of justice and selflessness. The warriors' vitriol evaporates as the "voice of nature rose from every heart...responding to the justice of Magawisca's claim." Everell is allowed to go free, and Magawisca establishes herself as "a superior being, guided and upheld by a supernatural power" (*HL,* 93).

When Magawisca's benevolence also extends to Hope Leslie for her good deed in freeing Nelema, she is betrayed, captured, and subjected to baseless legal charges. After Hope frees Nelema, the old woman vows to use her last bit of strength to reunite Hope with her lost sister, Mary, who had renounced her English heritage and crossed over to the Native American way of life when she married Magawisca's brother, Oneco. In her dying declaration, Nelema asks Magawisca to follow through with the promise to reunite Hope and Mary. It is this very act of loyalty to both Nelema and Hope that results in Magawisca's arrest. Like Nelema administering to Cradock, Magawisca deliberately undertakes the aid of her white friend out of noble principles. In so doing, Magawisca falls victim to one Sir Philip Gardiner† and his subversive attempt to gain Hope's affections.

As the colonial laws that were passed just before the Pequot war reveal, there was rampant distrust of the Indians. Hearing a rumor "of a conspiracy among the natives," Gardiner correctly suspects that he could play on colonial fears about their security. Accordingly, Gardiner secures a meeting with the Magistrates to lay the ground-

---

* There is some speculation that this event may have been "inspired by the story of John Smith and Pocahontas" (Michael Bell, 217).
† As Michael Bell notes, the "seduction plot is based on the career of the historical Sir Christopher Gardiner, who came to New England before Winthrop to validate a prior claim to land." Like the fictional Gardiner, he was accompanied by a mistress (217).

work for his conspiracy theory, proceeding to "state plots and underplots, and artfully exaggerate the number and power of the tribes" (*HL*, 248). His strategy works: The "magistrates lent a believing ear to the whole story." Believing that the Naragansetts "felt a secret dread and jealousy of the power and encroachments of the English" and that they "only waited for an opportunity to manifest their hostility" (*HL*, 248), the magistrates were very receptive to Gardiner's machinations.

Once again, Governor Winthrop plays a key role in the prosecution of a woman who is perceived as a threat to the community. In this fictionalized account, Winthrop is no less concerned about maintaining order than he was in the trial of Anne Hutchinson. The carefully detailed prosecution of Magawisca makes his motivation equally apparent. Before the trial even begins, Everell and his father advocate on Magawisca's behalf, beseeching Winthrop to acknowledge the injustice of Magawisca's confinement. Ignoring the Fletchers' pleas for Magawisca's release, Winthrop relies on hearsay, claiming that: "this young woman is suspected of being an active agent in brewing the conspiracy forming against us among the Indian tribes" and that Everell's "redeemed life is to be put in the balance of the public weal" (*HL*, 234). The threat of subversive activity is a particularly seductive rationale for Winthrop, who knows the usefulness of employing judicial power to ensure his political security.

Even before Magawisca appears before the court, Hope Leslie attempts to plead her case to Governor Winthrop. Petitioning Winthrop to release Magawisca from captivity "on her merits, her rights" (*HL*, 273), Hope endeavors to circumvent the impending legal proceeding. Winthrop takes issue with Hope's deviation from the parameters of appropriate behavior for a woman, stating, "Methinks, my young friend, you have lost right suddenly that humble tone, that but now in the parlor graced you so well" (*HL*, 273). In all likelihood, Winthrop probably has not forgotten about Hope's earlier refusal to be forthcoming with the details of her evening outing and her mighty stance: "I have offended, I know; but I should commit a worse offence—an offence against my own conscience and heart—if I explained the cause of my absence" (*HL*, 175). Hope's plea is wholly unsuccessful and, worse, she is confronted with the racism that becomes the dark undertone of the trial. Winthrop acknowledges his animosity toward the Pequots and cautions Hope and Everell "not to stir in this matter." He maintains that the Pequots are "a hateful race to the English. And, as the old chief and his daughter are accused, and I fear justly, of kindling the enmity of the tribes against us, and attempting to stir up a war that would lay our villages in ruins, it will be difficult to make a private benefit outweigh such a public crime" (*HL,* 274). Hope is unpersuaded by Winthrop's concerns and undoubtedly fully concurs with Everell's sentiment that "the sternest conscience would permit [one] to obey the generous impulses of nature, rather than to render this slavish obedience to the letter of the law" (*HL,* 278). Winthrop's views, however, reflect the animosity that persisted in Massachusetts Bay even after the conquest of the Pequots.

The parallels between Magawisca's trial and Anne Hutchinson's proceeding are striking: Both are called to answer to allegations of subversive activity before community leaders who seek to solidify the power of the government against dissension. Both vociferously refuse to embrace the religious views that are pressed upon them. For her failure to recant her beliefs, Magawisca—like Hutchinson—is condemned. Even the courtroom scene is a familiar one: "At one extremity of the apartment was a platform of two or three feet elevation, on which sat the deputies and magistrates, who constituted the court; and those elders who had, as was customary on similar occasions, been invited to be present as advisory counsel" (*HL,* 281). This is clearly deemed a weighty matter requiring "wisdom" of the court and community leaders.

Uncharacteristically for the early colonial times when there were not yet any official lawyers in New England, Magawisca is accompanied by her "defense" attorney, John Eliot. Known as the "apostle of New England" and "the apostle to the Indians," Eliot is famous for his attempts to convert the Indians to Christianity and for translating the Bible into "their language"(*HL,* 282).[61] Described as having an "ascetic complexion," Eliot is the quintessential portrait of self-denial (*HL,* 282). Called the "originary American reformer," Eliot is known for his work reforming the Indians, leading them from their "spiritual exile."[62] His appearance in *Hope Leslie* is particularly noteworthy because it suggests that if Magawisca can be made to appear as part of the mainstream of the community, then she should be freed. If this respected "man of God" is on her side, then perhaps Magawisca does not pose a threat to the community. Moreover, Eliot's representation illustrates the degree to which the church and religious values were intertwined with the judicial system.

The mere presence of Eliot lends credibility to Magawisca's innocence, yet her own appearance flaunts her Indian culture in the courtroom filled with distrustful onlookers. One such observer brands Magawisca "Jezabel"—creating a clear echo of Hutchinson—as she walks into the court with "neither guilt, nor fearfulness, nor submission" (*HL*, 282). Magawisca's presence radiates great composure and the "power and dignity of her soul" (*HL*, 282). Disdainfully rejecting Winthrop's "offer of an English dress," Magawisca's costume reflects her national pride; she wears a "collar—bracelet—girdle—embroidered moccasins, and purple mantle" with a rich border of bead-work" (*HL*, 282). Steadfastly maintaining her difference, Sedgwick compares Magawisca's attire to Horatio Nelson's "when he emblazoned himself with stars and orders to appear before his enemies, on the last day of his battle" (*HL*, 282). The politics of Magawisca's identity as expressed by her clothing are clear because she does not even attempt to present herself as a member of the community.

The importance of the Bible as a supplement to the few existing laws in the mid-1630s is readily apparent in the trial. Unfettered by what would later become constitutional guarantees separating church and state, Governor Winthrop as chief magistrate requests John Eliot to "supplicate divine assistance in the matter they were about to enter on" (*HL*, 283). Eliot's "prayer" exceeds the apparently customary scope of thankfulness for God's providence by weaving a brief narrative about Magawisca's family. Ostensibly, this is Eliot's strategic posturing to condition the audience to his statement of the case before the prosecution presents its version. The upshot of the benediction is, however, a justification of Christianity. As God's "chosen people," the colonists should seek to "enlarge God's heritage" by converting the heathen savages. The entire trial and Magawisca's only opportunity for acquittal is overshadowed by these righteous and religious overtones. Concluding with a plea for "justice and mercy" to "publicly kiss each other" (*HL*, 284), Eliot seems to have at least momentarily abdicated his role as Magawisca's defender. He seems to assume a posture that concedes guilt, thus necessitating the application of mercy.

Governor Winthrop (yet again, here in fiction) engages in the ethically questionable dual role of judge and prosecutor. Sedgwick aptly recreates the problematic paradigm that Winthrop engaged in during the examination of Hutchinson, where he attempted to be an impartial trier of fact and also an advocate on behalf of the state. After outlining the "charges" against Magawisca—which are never specifically articulated for the reader—Winthrop summarizes the testimony that "would be adduced to support them" (*HL*, 284). The so-called charges are left undefined as some vague sort of perfidy.

The "star witness" for the state, Gardiner, helps the prosecution build its case on mere innuendo. Pretending to have information of a "direful controversy," Gardiner engages in the dramatic gesture of tossing a packet of letters onto the judges' table. The loathsome basis of his allegations is then revealed by his twinge of apprehension; he begins to fear that he may have "counted too far on popular prejudices, which he knew were arrayed against Magawisca, as one of the diabolical race of the Pequods" (*HL*, 284). Alarmed that he might be exposed as a fool, Gardiner quickly decides that the best course to pursue is one that would "inflame the prejudices of Magawisca's judges." Accordingly, he embarks on a racist lie which is contrived to evoke intolerance; he claims to have witnessed "violent contortions," the kind that "characterized the devil-worship of the powwows" (*HL*, 286). Gardiner is persuasive: "The notion that the Indians were the children of the devil, was not confined to the vulgar; and the belief in a familiar intercourse with evil spirits...was then universally received" (*HL*, 286). After Gardiner completes his false testimony, with all "the evidence being now before the court," the prosecution rests its case. Ostensibly, sufficient evidence has been presented upon which Magawisca should be convicted.

Refusing to acknowledge the authority of the tribunal on her, Magawisca abstains from engaging in posturing that might result in her acquittal. When called upon for her defense, Magawisca does not merely plead her innocence or assert that the state has failed in its burden of proof. Even in preconstitutional times, it seems that defendants were deemed innocent until proven guilty. She also ignores the counsel of both Everell and Eliot to show deference to the court and to feign ignorance of the English laws and customs. Raising "her eyes to the judges" she is direct in her defiance of their authority, asserting: "I am your prisoner, and ye may slay me, but I deny your right to judge me. My people have never passed under your yolk—not one of my race has ever acknowledged your authority" (*HL*, 286). Like Hutchinson, who damns herself through her own testimony, Magawisca unequivocally presents herself as outside of the law of the colony. Making it clear that she stands before the enemy that exterminated her people, she is unflinching in her allegiance to her tribe. For a moment there was "silence throughout the assembly," and it seemed for an instant that "no human power could touch the spirit of the captive" (*HL,* 287). Indeed, Magawisca makes a powerful presence in the courtroom, one that commands the attention of her persecutors, and has, initially, the potential to undermine Gardiner's credibility.

Seizing on the opportunity to rehabilitate the beleaguered case against Magawisca but lacking any evidence to do so, Gardiner reintroduces the issue of religion into the proceeding. Whispering to a magistrate, "Is it not awful presumption for this woman thus publicly to glory in her heathen notions?" he rekindles religious intolerance. Magawisca's veracity comes under suspicion when the magistrates realize that she is not Christian. The unspoken question looms in the court: If she does not believe in the Bible, then she must feel no strictures against lying. Instead of attempting a conciliatory response, Magawisca once again directly confronts the magistrate, asserting the primacy of the laws of the "Great Spirit" (*HL,* 287) over any biblical or colonial law dictates. Even though there may not be sufficient testimony from others to convict Magawisca, her own words become the damning evidence. Magawisca's rejection of Christianity, which forms the basis of early law in Massachusetts Bay colony, is not tolerated. One magistrate accuses, "She is of Satan's heritage, and our enemy—a proved conspirator against the peace of God's people" (*HL,* 287). A second of the brethren, who is more concerned about the lack of substantive charges against Magawisca, reminds the court that the testimony presented is insufficient, and suggests that Winthrop "put it to her" for her own admission about the charges presented. Again, the high-principled Magawisca flouts her complete disregard for the court's authority, declaring "I neither confess nor deny aught...I stand here like a deer caught in a thicket, awaiting the arrow of the hunter" (*HL,* 287). Still attempting to prejudice the court against Magawisca, Gardiner yet again spews ethnocentric hatred: "She hath the dogged obstinacy of all the Pequod race...and it hath long been my opinion, that we should never have peace in the land till their last root was torn from the soil" (*HL,* 288).

Unlike his receding role in the Hutchinson hearing, here Winthrop takes the lead at this point in Magawisca's defense by noting inconsistencies in Gardiner's testimony. Apparently, his pretrial, unsworn testimony is embellished upon in the court. Gardiner is then sworn in; the very act seems to embolden Magawisca, who whips out a crucifix that she claims Gardiner had dropped in her prison. The very strict Puritans are aghast at the vision of such a papist, idolatrous symbol, yet are mesmerized by Magawisca's bold insistence and reminder to Gardiner that if the crucifix "is a charmed figure" that "hath power to keep thee in the straight path of truth" that he should press it to his lips and take back his false testimony against her. Magawisca uses great savvy to play the colonists' veneration of the oath to her favor. She turns the tables on her accuser, placing him "on the verge of condemnation." The confrontation results in a dramatic change of events in which Gardiner's mistress, who has been disguised as a page, is exposed.

Attempting at least a semblance of due process, Governor Winthrop decides that the prudent course would be to suspend the proceedings. Clearly, the prosecution's case against Magawisca is materially affected by Gardiner's testimony. Attempting to adjourn the proceedings for a month, Winthrop is abruptly interrupted by Magawisca, who cries out that she would rather be sent to death at that moment than linger "through another moon" in prison. What happens next becomes a critical juncture in the sufficiency of the evidence. Magawisca makes it clear that Gardiner will never testify truthfully under oath; she says that they might as well "expect the green herb to spring up" in the "trodden streets" "as the breath of truth to come from his false lips." Like Anne Hutchinson, Magawisca then proceeds to voluntarily testify against herself: "Take my own word, I am your enemy; the sun-beam and the shadow cannot mingle. The white man cometh—the Indian vanisheth. Can we grasp in friendship the hand raised to strike us? Nay—" (*HL,* 292). After reminding Winthrop that he had promised her dying mother "kindness to her children," Magawisca, herself, issues the ultimatum: "I demand of thee death or liberty." The initial effect is a favorable one for the defendant.

Magawisca's stance, however, places the colonists in a difficult position. Sedgwick presents this as a critical moment in the trial, placing the possibility of Magawisca's liberty in direct conflict with the need for security and order in the community. Onlookers shout for liberty, yet the same "gentleman" who had hissed as Magawisca entered the court reminds the crowd that they must fear this treacherous, heathen woman. The trial has come full circle, and the essence of the case against Magawisca remains an attack on her person for her beliefs and allegiance to her tribe—not for any seditious acts.

This final outburst against Magawisca is punctuated with phrases like "flouts the faith," "quicken the savages to diabolical revenge" and "confederacy with Satan" (*HL*, 293). The actual adjudication is left unresolved, but all implications in the text suggest that Magawisca will be condemned. Even exposing her mutilated body to the court is not likely to save her. Save Hope Leslie and Everell, no one is concerned about the kind acts Magawisca has done. In the public's view, she presents a threat to the cohesiveness of the collective community, a danger to the society, which will not be tolerated.

The conclusion of the trial is marked by a clear tension between Magawisca's individualism and civil law. As Magawisca is led out, "a strange contrariety of opinion and feelings" is experienced by many in the court: "Their reason, guided by the best lights they possessed, deciding against her—the voice of nature crying out for her" (*HL*, 294).

Should the colonists condemn Magawisca based on their desire to ensure an ordered society free from Indian threats, or should they follow their moral instincts and set her free? Throughout *Hope Leslie*, Sedgwick presents her Nelema and Magawisca with a sense of humanity and the ability to interact with individual English characters as fellow human beings. Both act out of their own sense of what is right under the circumstances, with a sense of the Great Spirit as their guide. To this end, Magawisca is freed; thus, *Hope Leslie*, gives primacy to individual liberty when it is not clearly at odds with the need of the colony for security.

CONCLUSION

Through *Hope Leslie*, Sedgwick shows the human side of the conflict between the colonists and the Pequot Indians. In her portrait, neither group is vilified—in their own way, both are virtuous, yet that does not mean that their existence is harmonious. Magawisca and Nelema remain true to their Native American values and customs, which sets them at odds with colonial pressure to assimilate. Based on the hostility shown to her by Puritan leaders, Magawisca's parting thoughts make it clear that there will never be any true kinship between the Indians and the colonists: "the Indian and the white man can no more mingle, and become one, than day and night" (*HL*, 330).

The law of the Great Spirit is inherently incompatible with English law. Nelema and Magawisca are condemned in an atmosphere of fear and distrust that is brought about, at least in part, by the retaliation on

Bethel. Through this cause-and-effect scenario, Sedgwick's text reveals the generalizations and fear that prevents "justice" from being achieved for these two defendants in the colonial legal system.

Hope Leslie, however, is more than just a historical critique. Sedgwick also uses the individual relationships in the text to present an alternative vision of the never achieved possibility of peaceful racial coexistence. Through Hope and Magawisca she suggests that there is the possibility of an enduring interracial bond, albeit from a distance.* As for what that has to say to a nineteenth-century audience, Sedgwick leaves it to her readers to consider the implications of how black Americans are treated under the law.

---

* Zagarell suggests that *Hope Leslie* presents "the possibility of a sisterhood that crosses racial boundaries" (237).

Part II

OVERCOMING SLAVE LAW

Part II

Overcoming Slave Law

> In this 'land of the free' we are burned, tortured, and denied a fair trial, murdered for any imaginary wrong conceived in the brain of the negro-hating white man. There is no redress for us...We cannot sing, 'My country, 'tis of thee, Sweet land of Liberty'! It is hollow mockery. The Southland laws are all on the side of the white, and they do just as they like to the negro, whether in the right or not.
> —Susie King Taylor, *Reminiscences of My Life in Camp*

African American slave women were afforded no right to liberty under laws that provided institutionalized legitimization of slavery, supported the right of slave owners to treat their slaves as "property," and deemed their racial status inferior. The law offered female slaves no real protection against rape, sexual abuse, or violence. There was little or no sanction of slave marriage and no rights of slave mothers to custody of their children. If they fled, harsh fugitive slave laws provided for their return. As A. Leon Higginbotham, Jr., carefully details in *In the Matter of Color: Race and the American Legal Process*, "In treating the first 200 years of black presence in America...the entire legal apparatus was used by those with the power to do so to establish a solid legal tradition for the absolute enslavement of blacks."[1] There can be no doubt about the power of the law "as an instrument of domination"* or about its ability to circumscribe the freedom of slave women.[2] As such, any action to seek the same rights as those enjoyed by white Americans was in direct defiance of the law.

---

* Genovese observes that, in the context of slavery, "the law cannot be viewed as something passive and reflective, but must be viewed as an active, partially autonomous force, which mediated among the several classes" (26).

Created by social custom and reinforced by law, the nineteenth-century cult of true womanhood was reserved for white women.[3] Black women, who were subjected to slavery, occupied a very separate place. Far removed from the antebellum "privileged"* position of domesticity, they were unprotected by law as women and as individuals. Slave Bethany Veney captured the essence of this plight:

> ...you can never understand the slave mother's emotions as she clasps her new-born child, and knows that a master's word can at any moment take it from her embrace; and when, as was mine, that child is a girl, and from her own experience she sees its almost certain doom is to minister to the unbridled lust of the slave-owner, and feels that the law holds over her no protecting arm, it is not strange that, rude and uncultured as I was, I felt all this, and would have been glad if we could have died together there and then.[4]

The law, in fact, "encouraged the exploitation of black women by white men, and discouraged the legitimization of their sexual relationships by marriage."[5] As Harriet Jacobs laments, the institution of slavery was "far more terrible for women. Superadded to the burden common to all, *they* have wrongs, and sufferings, and mortifications peculiarly their own" (*I*, 77). Stereotypes about black women's sexuality—especially the depiction as being a "bad," licentious Jezebel—had the effect of legitimating white men's sexual abuse of Black women and defining Black women as the opposite of the "ideal mother."[6] By characterizing black women as "lusty wenches in whom sexual impulse overwhelmed all restraint," legislators in many slave-holding states were able to rationalize why it was not a crime to rape a black woman.[7] Sojourner Truth embraced the essence of this injustice when she asked, "Ar'n't I a woman?"†

For many slave women, mere survival was a form of resistance[8]; others, however, took action against their oppressors, violating the law to obtain their freedom. Many literary works illustrate the tribulations of slave women living without those legal and social protections afforded to white women; a few are especially representative. Two

---

* It should be noted, however, that even though white women occupied a "privileged" social position, they had limited legal rights in marriage and child custody matters. This fact is discussed by Wolff in "'Margaret Garner,'" 107.

† This phrase is frequently misquoted as, "Ain't I a woman?" (*Narrative of Sojourner Truth*, 133–34).

nineteenth-century texts, Harriet Beecher Stowe's *Uncle Tom's Cabin; Or Life Among the Lowly* and Harriet Jacobs's *Incidents in the Life of a Slave Girl* were very public statements designed to raise awareness about the evils of slavery. Both present caring mothers who fall short of nineteenth-century standards of maternal perfection. Because of the devastating effects of slavery on their family, these mothers nonviolently defied the laws that reinforced the institution of slavery. Stowe highlights the devastating effects of slavery on African-American family life. Her idealized Eliza is unable to have a meaningful marriage with her husband or control over the custody of her child. Rather than see her young son sold away from her, Eliza becomes a fugitive. She breaks the law to keep her family intact.

Harriet Jacobs also became a fugitive in a brave attempt to escape the sexual advances of her master and save her children from slavery. Writing under the pseudonym Linda Brent, Jacobs describes a plight similar to Eliza's but nonfictional: She hid in the garret of her grandmother's house for seven years before escaping to the North. Like *Uncle Tom's Cabin*, her story also points out many unjust features of slave law. Both Stowe and Jacobs sought to fuel the abolitionist political agenda and, as such, are quite blunt in their commentary about the injustice perpetuated by slave laws, especially the fugitive slave acts. The jurisprudential stories they present are relatively straightforward. In short, they break the law to stress the urgency of the need for legal change.

A creative shift, however, is evident in the focus of two twentieth-century texts, Sherley Anne Williams's *Dessa Rose* and Toni Morrison's *Beloved*, which use the distance of over a century to comment on the harsh laws of the past while attempting to address concerns of the present. Written well after slavery was abolished, these works are free from the overt preaching tone that characterizes Stowe's and Jacobs's work. In these much more oblique texts, historical inspiration is evident, but the depictions yield a more psychological and overall sense of oppression than their nineteenth-century predecessors. Much like what Trudier Harris observed in the context of lynching, "Black writers begin with the realistic depictions of violence in their history, then move to a political level where such depictions become statements of the oppression of a people."[9] Unlike Eliza and Linda, who are presented as idealized mothers, Dessa Rose and Sethe fight against oppression in a much more aggressive manner. Dessa Rose assaults her master and mistress after her lover is brutally murdered. Thereafter, she is influential in leading an uprising in a slave coffle. Pregnant, she murders coffle guards who are leading her to an unknown ultimate destination via the slave market. Dessa Rose physically attacks those who attempt to control her as property pursuant to slave law. Similarly, Sethe's story in *Beloved* involves brutality in the name of resistance—as a fugitive, she murders her child to spare her from the return into slavery. Sethe commits this controversial act in the name of what she believes to be warranted, but it subjects her to legal, social, and psychological censure.

In these morally complicated novels, Dessa Rose and Sethe both are depicted as driven by the injustice of slavery to act out their frustrations and as refusing to be victimized. They act on their own terms, employing means that have troubling jurisprudential implications. Williams and Morrison seem to suggest that under extenuating circumstances murder and other unlawful acts may be justified, that violence is an acceptable form of resistance to unjust laws. By the end of each novel, however, this controversial assertion is deemphasized. The relationships that *Dessa Rose* and *Beloved* ultimately present offer a concluding portrait of justice for the twentieth century based on the hope of interracial cooperation and individual fortitude. Both qualities are essential to ease the pain left from the injustice perpetrated under slave law.

Despite the difference in the political focus of these four books, the primary female characters in each of these texts share common ground with many other slave women who "asserted their equality aggressively in challenging the inhuman institution of slavery."[10] Engaging in acts that they believe will save themselves and their families from the evils of slavery, Eliza, Linda Brent, Dessa Rose, and Sethe boldly defy oppressive slave laws. With an instinctive sense of their own moral code and slavery's violation of its principles, each of these women acts on her own individual sense of what is right, which necessarily violates existing laws of the state and federal government.

Chapter 3

Preemancipation Activism

Harriet Beecher Stowe's *Uncle Tom's Cabin* and Harriet Jacobs's *Incidents in the Life of a Slave Girl*

> Yet all through the darkest period of the colored women's oppression in this country her yet unwritten history is full of heroic struggle, a struggle against fearful and overwhelming odds, that often ended in a horrible death, to maintain and protect that which woman holds dearer than life. The painful, patient, and silent toil of mothers to gain a fee simple title to the bodies of their daughters, the despairing fight, as of an entrapped tigress, to keep hallowed their own persons, would furnish material for epics.
> —Anna Julia Cooper, *Black Women in Nineteenth Century American Life*

Former slave Anna Julia Cooper's statement to the Congress of Representative Women encapsulates the nineteenth-century struggle and triumph of African American women who were unprotected by law as women and mothers.[1] For white women, as Angela Davis observes, by mid-century "the cult of motherhood was in full swing. As portrayed in the press, in the new popular literature and even in courts of law, the perfect woman was the perfect mother."[2] Defined by four cardinal virtues—piety, purity, submissiveness, and domesticity—this vision of "true womanhood" was designed to form the basis of a stable American society.[3] As mothers, women were "attributed social influence as the chief transmitters of religious and moral values."[4] For black women who were slaves, this so-called privileged bastion was unavailable; instead of being regarded as mothers, slave women were producers of human chattel.[5] The emphasis on the black woman's struggle to be a conventionally good mother and virtuous woman in the face of nearly insurmountable forces was thus viewed as particularly persuasive for effecting social change. Many abolitionists knew quite well that with separate spheres developing for women and men, all that is good and domestic was to be guarded by women. Accordingly, they played on this fact in their efforts to abolish slave law.

With an audience of primarily white women in mind, motherhood thus became an essential political component in Harriet Beecher Stowe's *Uncle Tom's Cabin* and Harriet Jacobs's *Incidents in the Life of a Slave Girl.* Designed to fuel the nineteenth-century abolitionist movement, these texts present Eliza and Linda as nearly perfect mothers who were unable to be literally "perfect" and law-abiding under the umbrella of slavery. Instead of nurturing their children to their full ability, Eliza and Linda are forced to live on the fringe of a society that does not sympathize with their needs. Clearly, the pernicious institution of slavery created lawbreakers out of selfless mothers and treated their children as another person's property. The critical leap to law is a short one. Inasmuch as law formally maintained slavery, such laws are, in turn, "bad" and should be abolished. Through their characters' fierce loyalty to their children, these narratives use nonviolent resistance to challenge the established legal order. Eliza and Linda refuse to resign themselves and their children to slavery, the institution that could destroy their familial bonds.* They act according to their code, which is at odds with a legal code widely deemed unjust.

THE FEDERAL LAW CONTEXT: "A WEASEL IN THE CONSTITUTION"

The American slave system may have "originated in international custom and colonial practice" reinforced by the English government; however, as time passed, it "acquired a legal structure consisting essentially of local common and statute law in the thirteen colonies."[6]

---

* Winifred Morgan argues that whereas "male fugitives stressed their individuality, their ability to stand alone and assume responsibility for themselves, women fugitives generally saw themselves as part of communities." As such they were interested in preserving relationships (73–94).

During the eighteenth century, the fear of slave revolt prompted many colonies to enact increasingly repressive slave codes.[7] Furthermore, the laws that sanctioned slavery received a great boost by the formation of a federal government.

Lawyers played a key role in the birth of the United States, comprising twenty-five of the fifty-six signers of the Declaration of Independence and thirty-one of the fifty-five members of the Constitutional Convention.[8] Given the ubiquitous presence of Sir William Blackstone's *Commentaries on the Laws of England* (1765-1769) in legal education, most lawyers were probably well versed in his ideas.[9] Moreover, to the extent that many other "gentlemen" began their "study of legal and political institutions with the *Commentaries*,"[10] most of the founding fathers were likely familiar with Blackstone's belief that the role of government was to protect one's personal liberty and property. He claimed that men have an "absolute right" to property "which consists of the free use, enjoyment, and disposal of all his acquisitions, without any control or diminution, save only by the laws of the land."[11] Later in the *Commentaries,* Blackstone defined "the right of property" as "that sole and despotic dominion which one man claims and exercises over the external things in the world, in total exclusion of the right of every other individual in the universe."[12] Despite Blackstone's belief that slavery could not be justified in natural law, it is from this concept of property that the founding fathers made their pernicious analytical leap. By considering other human beings "property," they had a legal rationale for slavery.* Thus, as property, slaveholders could treat their slaves with an unequivocal right of control like any other thing they owned. The rationale behind the law was quite fundamental: rules of law, such as inheritance, applied uniformly to a master's entire estate, which by definition included slaves as "capital assets."[13]

By the time the Declaration of Independence was signed in 1776, the practice of slavery was well established. On the surface, the

---

* Ironically, Blackstone did not believe that slavery was justified in natural law and maintained that England was therefore opposed to slavery. This idea carried over into the nineteenth century, where one of the central abolitionist arguments was the simple fact that human beings cannot be justly owned. "Now this claim of property in human being is altogether false, groundless. No such right of man in man can exist. A human being cannot be justly owned" (Channing, 14). For a discussion about the impact of the ideology of commodificationism on nineteenth-century proslavery legal writing, see Alexander, 211-40.

signature phrase, "We hold these Truths to be self-evident, that all Men are created equal," seems to be a mere mockery of the possibility of justice in American law. Even so, not all of the founding fathers unequivocally embraced slavery; some, such as Thomas Jefferson felt that the justification for slavery "could never rest upon the higher morality of natural law."[14] A slaveholder himself, Jefferson was filled with inherent contradiction when he expressed reservations in his original draft of the Declaration of Independence. Critical of King George, Jefferson stated that the ruler "has waged cruel war against human nature itself, violating its most sacred rights of life and liberty in the persons of a distant people who never offended him... Determined to keep open a market where MEN should be bought & sold, he has prostituted his negative for suppressing every legislative attempt to prohibit or restrain this execrable commerce."[15] The language may have been stricken from the final document; however, its import continued to hover uneasily over the nation. No lawmaker was willing to jeopardize the formation of the union by opposing slavery.

Thus, the grandiose language in the preamble to the U.S. Constitution belies the status of both free and enslaved black Americans: "We the People...in Order to form a more perfect Union, establish Justice, insure domestic Tranquility,...promote the general Welfare, and secure the Blessings of Liberty to ourselves and our Posterity, do ordain and establish this Constitution for the United States of America." The references to "justice, welfare, and liberty," however, "were mocked by the treatment meted out daily to blacks from the seventeenth to the nineteenth centuries through the courts, in legislative statutes, and in those provisions of the Constitution that sanctioned slavery for the majority of black Americans."[16] The concept of liberty was clearly at odds with slavery.* Attempting to dodge responsibility by treating slavery as an "economic and political rather than a moral matter,"[17] the framers' refusal to use the word "slavery" in the Constitution reveals that they "did not want to acknowledge to the world their legitimization of the precept of black inferiority."[18] Nonetheless, the following constitutional provisions inherently "maximized the political power of southern slaveholders":[19]

---

* The fact that liberty was at odds with slavery was clearly recognized by John Locke in the seventeenth century ("Of Slavery," 1690). Kammen notes that in Lockean terms, slavery was, quite simply, the "denial of *full* freedom" (xvi–xviii).

- Article I, section 2, clause 3: "Three-fifths of all other Persons," that is, slaves, were to be included in the calculation for congressional representatives and taxation purposes;
- Article I, section 9, clause 1: The slave trade, euphemistically referred to as the "Migration or Importation of such Persons," was to be preserved against any Congressional action until at least 1808 and, furthermore, that "a Tax or duty may be imposed on such Importation, not exceeding ten dollars for each Person";
- Article IV, section 2, sanctions the return of fugitive slaves;
- Article V prohibits any amendment that might alter the clauses regarding the unfettered importation of slaves until 1808.

Even though these provisions were "flagrantly at odds with the principles of the American Revolution," the Northern delegates "recognized that without southern support a strong federal government would be impossible."[20]

This blatant lack of equality was not lost on many African Americans, like Sojourner Truth. At an anti-slavery meeting, and following a speaker who praised the Constitution, she responded:

> Children, I talks to God and God talks to me...Dis morning I was walking out and I got over de fence. I saw de wheat a holding up its head, looking very big. I goes up and takes holt of it. You b'lieve it, dere was no wheat dere. I says, 'God, what is de matter wid dis wheat?' and he says to me, 'Sojourner, dere is a little weasel in it.' Now I hears talkin' bout de Constitution and de rights of man. I come up and talks holt of dis Constitution. It looks mighty big, and I feels for my rights, but dere ain't any dere. Den I say, 'God, what ails dis Constitution?' He says to me, 'Sojourner, dere is a little weasel in it.'[21]

Sojourner Truth's "weasel" is a colloquial way of saying what many of the constitutional framers knew, but failed to address—because slavery is against natural law, it could not be justified as manmade positive law.[22] Nor could it be reconciled with the language of freedom and liberty inherent in the Constitution.

Following the ratification of the Constitution, federal statutory and case law continued to perpetuate the grip of slavery and reinforce state slave laws. The passage of fugitive slave laws that provided for the return of runaway slaves is particularly significant. The Fugitive Slave Law of 1793 was adopted following an extradition disagreement between Pennsylvania and Virginia.[23] "For the better security of the peace and friendship now entered into by the contracting parties," the law provided that the parties agreed not to "entertain, or give countenance to, the enemies of the other, or protect, in their respective states, criminal fugitives, servants, or slaves, but the same to apprehend and secure, and deliver to the state or states, to which such enemies, criminals, servants, or slaves, respectively belong."[24] Designed to provide for the swift return of a slave owner's "property," the law provided that when an owner or his agent could provide some proof of identity, the slave would be promptly turned over. Alleged fugitives were not afforded the due process of a trial and were not even permitted to give testimony in their defense.[25] In fact, there was no constitutional or other legal protection for blacks who were falsely arrested or unjustly accused. This was further exacerbated by the passage of laws in some southern states, such as Virginia, offering lucrative rewards for the return of fugitive slaves. Naturally, these measures only increased the number of wrongful arrests.[26]

Because even free blacks could be wrongly accused of being fugitive slaves and were in jeopardy of being enslaved under the Fugitive Slave Law, a number of northern states enacted "personal liberty laws." These laws were designed to "strike a balance between the rights of slaveholders and the rights of free" blacks threatened by the federal law.[27] One such law in Pennsylvania resulted in the conviction of Edward Prigg on kidnaping charges for taking a captured fugitive back to Maryland without obtaining the required documentation. The Supreme Court heard Prigg's appeal and, in its landmark decision, *Prigg v. Pennsylvania* (1842), struck down the Pennsylvania statute as inconsistent with the Constitution and the Fugitive Slave Law of 1793.[28]

The opinion underscores the legality and presence of slavery in the Constitution. In reaching his decision, Justice Story found that the fugitive slave clause (Article IV, Section 2) "constituted a fundamental article, without the adoption of which the Union could not have been formed."[29] One of the most disturbing aspects of this opinion is the holding that the Fugitive Slave Law of 1793 was constitutional. Justice Story took the path of least resistance by demonstrating that Congress had the power to enact such legislation under the fugitive slave clause. As Don Fehrenbacher notes, what Justice "Story cooly ignored was the argument by counsel for Pennsylvania that the law of 1793, in certain of its provisions, violated personal rights guaranteed by the privileges-

and-immunities clause, by the Fourth Amendment, and by the due-process clause of the Fifth Amendment."[30] In short, free blacks were denied the fundamental constitutional protections afforded to white Americans.

The chilling effect of the *Prigg* decision may have essentially halted further passage of personal liberty laws, yet slaves continued to flee to the north. Inasmuch as the *Prigg* decision concentrated responsibility for enforcement of the fugitive law in the federal government, abolitionists hailed this aspect of the opinion as freeing states from that obligation. As a practical matter, this impeded a slave holder's ability to recover slaves and resulted in vocal complaints that the Fugitive Slave Law of 1793 was inadequate. From this history, the Fugitive Slave Act of 1850 became a key feature in the Missouri Compromise. In response to the southern constituents, Senator James Mason of Virginia introduced a bill to reassert the constitutional right of slave holders to apprehend fugitive slaves.[31] A great deal of contention ensued—some southerners felt that the bill fell short of fully protecting their property interest in slaves and a northern contingent was concerned about the lack of protection for free blacks. Massachusetts Senator Daniel Webster became the pivotal voice in the final agreement, casting his persuasive oratorical powers on the side of slavery. Webster was publicly rebuked by Ralph Waldo Emerson who denounced the law: "There was an old fugitive law, but it had become, or was fast becoming, a dead letter...The new Bill made it operative, required me to hunt slaves, and it found citizens in Massachusetts willing to act as judges and captors. Moreover, it discloses the secret of the new times, that Slavery was no longer a mendicant, but was become aggressive and dangerous."[32]

Walt Whitman likewise joined in opposition to the law, incorporating a stanza about aiding a fugitive in his poem "Song of Myself." Describing how the "runaway slave came to my house and stopt outside...limpsy and weak" the slave was brought water for a bath, clean clothes and bandages. In a great egalitarian gesture, both slave and host defy the law: "He staid with me a week before he was recuperated and pass'd north, / I had him sit next me at the table."[33] Later in the poem, Whitman graphically empathizes with the horror of being a hunted human being: "I am the hounded slave...I wince at the bite of the dogs, / Hell and despair are upon me...They beat me violently over the head with their whip-stocks."[34] The Fugitive Slave Act may have marked a horrifying low point in American statutory law; however, as Emerson and Whitman illustrate, the law coalesced anti-slavery forces with renewed vigor.

Passed on 18 September 1850, the new law rigorously set forth the duties and powers attendant to apprehending and returning fugitive slaves. Specifically, the law provided that commissioners appointed by the United States Circuit Courts were to execute "duties and powers conferred" by the act, and their jurisdiction was concurrent "with the judges of the Circuit and District Courts of the United States" and the "judges of the Superior Courts of the Territories."[35] The commissioners had authority to grant certificates to claimants (upon satisfactory proof) for the return of the fugitives. The "aiding and abetting" provision outraged many abolitionists:

> any person who shall knowingly and willingly obstruct, hinder, or prevent such claimant, his agent [etc.]...from arresting such fugitive...or shall aid, abet, or assist such person...or shall harbor or conceal such fugitive, so as to prevent the discovery and arrest of such person ...shall...be subject to a fine not exceeding one thousand dollars, and imprisonment not exceeding six months.[36]

The law even went so far as to provide that such activity shall subject violators to "civil damages to the party injured by such illegal conduct, the sum of one thousand dollars, for each fugitive so lost" by the act of aiding and abetting.[37]

An especially disturbing aspect of the Fugitive Slave Act of 1850 was the express provision that "in no trial or hearing under this act shall the testimony of such alleged fugitive be admitted in evidence."[38] This clause made it impossible for the person in custody to refute the allegation that he or she was, indeed, a fugitive slave. The result was that the "434,000 blacks who were free should have been convinced that they had no reasonable protection under the Constitution and the laws of the United States."[39] Condemned as more evil flowing from the fugitive clause in the Constitution, the law resulted in the flight of many free blacks to Canada.[40]

If there was any hope that America would legally recognize the rights of blacks as citizens, it was extinguished by *Dred Scott v. Sandford* (1857). Because he was a temporary resident in Illinois, a free territory, Dred Scott sought to be adjudicated a free man under the doctrine of *Somerset v. Stewart*, a famous English case. In *Somerset*, a slave who accompanied his master to England, escaped, and was thereafter captured. He was subsequently freed by the court because England had no statutes authorizing slavery, an institution "so odious, that nothing can be suffered to support it, but positive law."[41] Dred Scott's challenge was unsuccessful. Deemed "nothing more than a southern manifesto on the institution of slavery" the Supreme Court decision in *Dred Scott* represents nothing "more than two hundred years of racial oppression and slavery."[42] Chief Justice Roger B. Taney framed the issue before the Supreme Court in cold historical terms: "The question is simply this: Can a negro whose ancestors were imported into this country, and sold as slaves, become a member of the political community formed and brought into existence by the Constitution of the United States, and as such become entitled to all the rights, and privileges, and immunities, guaranteed by that instrument to the citizen?"[43]

To reach his conclusion, Justice Taney went "back in time in an attempt to determine what the founding fathers had intended" and "argued from the untenable position that the Constitution might never be any larger than the restrictive version of eighteenth-century America."[44] Based on the Court's finding that Dred Scott was not a citizen of Missouri, the case could have been resolved on procedural grounds; that is, he could not invoke federal court diversity jurisdiction to resolve his dispute. Justice Taney, however, went much further, holding that African Americans were not citizens under the Constitution and invalidated the Missouri Compromise of 1820, thereby denying Congress the power to prohibit slavery in the territories.

Whereas there is some debate about the weight of Justice Taney's opinion on behalf of the majority,[45] his feelings about the inferiority of African Americans were made quite clear:

> They had for more than a century before been regarded as beings of an inferior order, and altogether unfit to associate with the white race, either in social or political relations; and so far inferior, that they had no rights which the white man was bound to respect; that the negro might justly and lawfully be reduced to slavery for his benefit. He was bought and sold, and treated as an ordinary article of merchandise and traffic, wherever a profit could be made by it. This opinion was at the time fixed and universal in the civilized portion of the white race. It was regarded as an axiom in morals as well in politics, which no one thought of disputing, or supposed to be open to dispute; and men in every grade and position in society daily and habitually acted upon it in their private pursuits, as well as in matters of public concern, without doubting for a moment the correctness of this opinion.[46]

Justice Taney's ensuing justification for denying African Americans rights as citizens under the Constitution is equally laden with racism:

> For if they were...entitled to the privileges and immunities of citizens...it would give persons of the negro race...the right to enter every other State whenever they pleased...to go where they pleased at every hour of the day or night without molestation...and it would give them the full liberty of speech in public and in private upon all subjects upon which its own citizens might speak; to hold public meetings upon political affairs, and to keep and carry arms wherever they went. And all of this would be done in the face of the subject race of the same color, both free and slaves, and inevitably producing discontent and insubordination among them, and endangering the peace and safety of the State.[47]

Chief Justice Taney made it clear that the Constitution did not grant blacks citizenship; to the contrary, it "treated blacks as property, and granted them no rights."[48] For those who believed in the inferiority of blacks, *Dred Scott* was hailed as the long-awaited "culminating point of the wildest, the most senseless, the most disgusting, and withal the most dangerous delusion that ever afflicted an intelligent people, or threatened to destroy the peace, order, and safety of human society."[49] There can be no doubt that the *Dred Scott* decision "codified into law, at the highest level of the American legal process, the precept of black inferiority."[50] This sobering history of laws designed first to enslave, then to ensure the social inequality of African Americans forms the backdrop for the legal issues in *Uncle Tom's Cabin* and *Incidents of a Slave Girl*.[51]

UNCLE TOM'S CABIN:
THE ILLEGAL FLIGHT OF A CHRISTIAN ANGEL

Harriet Beecher Stowe wrote *Uncle Tom's Cabin* to initiate legal change. Realizing that "injustice is an *inherent* one in the slave system,—it cannot exist without it" (Concluding Remarks, *UTC,* 619), she urged her readers to oppose slavery. Stowe's opposition to slavery was galvanized by a number of factors,* including the impact of the institution upon the family and the passage of the Compromise of 1850,

---

* Wolff (595–618) argues that *Uncle Tom's Cabin* was written as a direct consequence of the Fugitive Slave Act, and Thomas (161) points out that Stowe was also affected by *State v. Mann,* the case that she used to structure *Dred: A Tale of the Great Dismal Swamp* and one that she noted in her *Key.* Inasmuch as Stowe's focus was primarily

which included the Fugitive Slave Act.[52] After Stowe lost a beloved son to cholera, she felt the kind of anguish that she imagined a slave mother must experience when her child is "torn away from her."[53] She was heartbroken about this aspect of slavery. Later, when the Fugitive Slave Act was passed, requiring Northerners to seize and return runaway slaves, she began to see slavery as much more than merely a Southern institution. Deeply disturbed about how slavery affected both individual families and the entire country, Stowe vowed to her children to "write something" so that the nation would "feel what an accursed thing slavery is."[54] "I beseech you," she wrote in the novel, "pity the mother who has all your affections, *not one legal right* to protect, guide, or educate, the child of her bosom!"

As Elizabeth Ammons effectively argues, Stowe "heartily embraced the Victorian idealization of motherhood and channeled it into an argument for widespread social change."[55] Stowe critiques slave law through the character of Eliza, a mother who must violate the law to save her young son.[56] Notwithstanding the fact that she is a lawbreaker, Eliza is deliberately crafted to evoke sympathy. As Amy Lang observes, "Stowe rewrites Anne Hutchinson's defiance as not lawlessness but piety."[57] Relatively recent commentary has heaped harsh criticism on Stowe, accusing her of presenting an "utter distortion of slave life" that "miserably fails to capture the reality and truth of Black women's resistance to slavery"[58] and of presenting every African American character who is not "truly human" as fitting "neatly into a particular stereotype."[59] Moreover, James Baldwin dismissed *Uncle Tom's Cabin* as a "very bad novel" that forms "the cornerstone of American protest fiction" and deemed Stowe an "impassioned pamphleteer" who wrote the book to "prove that slavery was wrong."[60] While that kind of critique is certainly understandable, and while Stowe's message may very well have been "effective because it did not challenge the beliefs of her audience,"[61] *Uncle Tom's Cabin* presents a very pointed and successful assault on an egregious system of laws that denied African Americans the slightest acknowledgment of their humanity.

In boldly attacking well established slave law, Stowe was met with vigorous resistence. When *Uncle Tom's Cabin* was published, she was bitterly criticized for her alleged legal mischaracterizations. In her *Key*

---

on a national level, the discussion of Kentucky law appears later in this book in connection with Toni Morrison's *Beloved.*

to *Uncle Tom's Cabin*, Stowe recaps two of the rebukes: "The New York *Courier and Enquirer* proffers law from Virginia and Louisiana to dispute Stowe's dramatization stating: 'had its inventor [Stowe] looked in the statute-book of Louisiana, she would have found' that the law prohibited selling mothers separately from their children '*who shall not have attained the full age of ten years*.'" One of Stowe's "much-valued" correspondents from Richmond, Virginia claimed "The laws of the Southern States...have not been so loosely framed as to fail of their object where person and property are one" (*Key*, 147, 149).

Stowe's response is clear enough: "The author still holds to the opinion that slavery in itself, as legally defined in law-books and expressed in the records of Courts, *is* the SUM AND ESSENCE OF ALL ABUSE" (*Key*, 154). Lest there be any doubt about her legal research skills, Stowe then asserts that, with regard to some of the passages she quotes, the "language of certain enactments was so incredible that she would not take it on the authorship of any compilation whatever, but copied it with her own hand from the latest edition of the statute-book, where it stood and still stands" (*Key*, 154). Stowe thoroughly researched her book, incorporating the most egregious legal aspects of slavery in her story.

In subsequent chapters of her *Key*, Stowe elaborates on her knowledge of statutory and case law.[62] Her analysis of the Louisiana so-called "protective" statute (quoted above) is particularly telling. After first acknowledging that her critic correctly noted the existence of the statute that restricts the separation of mothers and children, Stowe points out the practical shortcomings. If a master decided to separate a slave mother from her children under ten, she would have no recourse; as a slave, she could not bring suit to restrain and enjoin the sale; as a black woman, she could not testify against her white master; and, as property, if she lodged her objection with the master, he could "whip the child within an inch of its life... lock her up in a dungeon, sell her on to a distant plantation, or do any other despotic thing he chooses, and there is nobody to say–Nay" (*Key*, 205–6). Stowe confidently concludes her point by saying that "by this time, the reader will agree...that the less the defenders of slavery say about protective statutes the better" *(Key,* 206). Resolute in her opposition to slave law and its pernicious application, Stowe held her ground.

The Effect of Slave Law on Families

Proclaiming that the "worst abuse of the system of slavery is its outrage upon the family," Stowe expressed her horror at the particularly evil side of slavery that prevented slaves from becoming legally married and that wrenched children from their mothers (*Key*, 299). By treating slaves "only as so many *things* belonging to a master," the "portentous shadow—the shadow of *law*" gave legitimacy to this social system (*UTC*, 51). Stowe addressed this situation through Eliza, a character who has been subjected to much criticism. Eliza may be "white motherhood incarnate...in just-a-little-less-than-white-face," but it is an overstatement to accuse her of being "practically oblivious to the injustices of slavery."[63] Nearly the entire characterization of Eliza's plight epitomizes the effects of slavery on women—albeit in a way that would appeal to Stowe's audience.

Indeed, by Stowe's own words, she implored "mothers of America" to "pity those mothers that are constantly made childless by the American slave-trade" by asking "is this a thing to be defended, sympathized with, passed over in silence?" (*UTC*, 623–24). Thus, Eliza is set up as an idealized mother to facilitate the answer to this question. Using nonviolent resistence,* Eliza becomes a lawbreaker and fugitive from justice to escape the atrocities that are legally sanctioned by slavery.[64] She is presented as an idealized "young quadroon woman apparently about twenty-five," her dress neatly fitted to set off her "finely moulded shape" (*UTC*, 45), the physically flawless mother of young Harry. Her son has already been introduced in the story as "between four or five years of age...remarkably beautiful and engaging...black hair, fine as floss silk, hung in glossy curls about his round dimpled face, while a pair of large dark eyes, full of fire and softness, looked out from beneath the rich, long lashes" (*UTC*, 43). Eliza shares his "same rich, full, dark eye, with its long lashes" (*UTC*,

---

* Romero argues that "Stowe identifies the situation of slaves with that of middle-class white women, and in so doing she obliterates the power differentials making their experiences incommensurable" (70). At the time Stowe was writing *Uncle Tom's Cabin*, it is unclear whether she had read Henry David Thoreau's 1949 essay "Civil Disobedience" (Reed, 37–38). Indeed, recent biographical studies (Hedrick, Boydston et al., Rugoff, Gerson) do not explore Stowe's relationship with Thoreau and, thus, fail to shed any light on this issue. In any event, as Charles Foster observes, "'Civil Disobedience' and *Uncle Tom's Cabin* imprudently spoke the truth when duty and justice demanded it" (224).

45). This emphasis on eyes is evocative of the humanity of this mother and child, urging readers immediately to see the injustice in their legal classification as property.

In terms of her experience, Eliza does have an idealized existence for a slave, yet this does not undercut Stowe's anti-slavery message. Eliza herself is sold away from her mother, Cassy, who is held for the sexual gratification of her master, Simone Legree. Moreover, in *Uncle Tom's Cabin* there are a number of other slave mothers who are driven to extreme measures because of intolerable incidents: One woman for sale in the slave market "jest went ravin' mad, and died in a week" after watching her baby be carried off (*UTC*, 47); a woman in her sixties pleads not to be separated at auction from her last son, and her fingers have to be pried from her son when no one will buy them together (*UTC*, 194–98); and another woman whose child is stolen from her on a boat commits suicide by diving into the water with a "wild look of anguish and utter despair" (*UTC*, 207–11). The story of Old Prue, the servant in the St. Clare household, who was used to breed children for market, is equally disturbing. All of her children are sold off except the last one, who starves to death after Prue's milk dries up and she is unable to nurse. Unable to cope with such overwhelming loss, she seeks refuge in alcohol (*UTC*, 323–25). The experiences of these women, which are based on historical fact, form an important background for Eliza's acts (Concluding Remarks to *UTC*, 618–19; *Key* 99–106).

Eliza's life highlights the fact that even a female slave living under the best possible conditions is still subjected to plenty of the horrors of slavery. Consistent with Eliza's Madonna-like quality, she is spared from sexual abuse by her master. Stowe does, however, gently remind her readers that "Eliza had reached maturity without those temptations which make beauty so fatal an inheritance to a slave" (*UTC*, 54). Unlike many slave women who were at odds with their mistresses over sexual advances by their masters, Eliza actually is kept safe from rape by the "protecting care of her mistress" (*UTC*, 54), and she is courted by George Harris, a slave on a neighboring plantation who lives much like a free man. Furthermore, Eliza and George are "married" by a minister in the Shelby home and actually see each other frequently during the first year or so of their marriage. With the exception of the loss of two infants (to death, not the slave trade), Eliza and Harry are a "happy" slave couple with a new infant son.

Eliza's indoctrination into the harsh reality of her slave status comes late in life, but the lessons about her lack of legal protection are no less difficult to bear. After several years of marriage, George is rudely "brought under the iron sway of his legal owner" who suggests that George "take a wife"—mate with someone other than Eliza (*UTC*, 57, 63). George then educates Eliza about the law, stating "Don't you know that a slave can't be married? There is no law in the country for that" (*UTC*, 63). A matrimonial bond was not legally superior to a master's ownership rights. Lacking any legal protection, Stowe's ideal slave family is on the brink of decimation; George laments: "I can't hold you for my wife, if he [master] chooses to part us. That's why I wish I'd never seen you,—why I wish I'd never been born; it would have been better for us both,—it would have been better for this poor child if he had never been born. All this may happen to him yet!" (*UTC*, 63). George becomes a fugitive, and naive Eliza must consider the nearly inconceivable idea that her "kind master" would sell her son, Harry. The couple parts with Eliza haunted by the memory of the swaggering, slave-trading Haley. He has already admired Harry as a good candidate to be raised for the market as a handsome waiter and has actively sought to have Harry added to the slave deal.

Mr. Shelby may have been a well-meaning master; however, economics and his legal right to dispose of his property come before promises to slaves. Mrs. Shelby's Christian plea is carefully crafted to pit religious values against the pernicious power of the slave holder to divide families. She implores

> I have taught them the duties of the family, of parent and child, and husband and wife; and how can I bear to have this open acknowledgment that we care for no tie, no duty, no relation, however sacred, compared with money? I have talked with Eliza about her duty to him as a Christian mother, to watch over him, pray for him, and bring him up in a Christian way; and now what can I say, if you tear him away, and sell him, soul and body, to a profane, unprincipled man, just to save a little money? (*UTC*, 83–84)

Mrs. Shelby continues, "I have told her that one soul is worth more than all the money in the world; and how will she believe me when she sees us turn around and sell her child?"

Her incredulousness is firmly grounded in a religious indictment of slave law: "This is God's curse on slavery!...It is a sin to hold a slave under laws like ours" (*UTC*, 84). Stowe depicts religious devotion as squarely at odds with slave law. Eliza's Christian indoctrination, thus, becomes the justification for her resistance to the law. As a good

Christian mother, she must take whatever steps necessary to save the soul of her child, even if it means violating man-made law.

Stowe then effectively puts a human face on the Fugitive Slave Act. Eliza's flight and her desperate barefoot traverse across an icy river ultimately lead her to the home of Senator Bird, who has voted in favor of the Act. Mrs. Bird, a mother whose pain over the recent loss of a child causes her to identify with Eliza, becomes an immediate ally. The two women are united in their sorrow, forming a maternal moral front against slave law. Much more reserved with his feeling, Senator Bird finds himself caught in a moral pocket—his patriotic allegiance to the law versus the reality of Eliza and young Harry on his doorstep. Just a week earlier, he had been "spurring up the legislature of his native state to pass more stringent resolutions against escaping fugitives, their harborers and abettors" (*UTC*, 155). The smug complacency he had exhibited in Washington with "his hands in his pockets" while looking down on "all sentimental weakness of those who would put the welfare of a few miserable fugitives before great state interests" is called into question (*UTC*, 155). With his previous vision of runaway slaves replaced by "a hapless mother, a defenceless child,—like that one which was now wearing his lost boy's little well-known cap," Senator Bird violates his own law and risks being fined and imprisoned by aiding and abetting Eliza's escape from the slave catchers (*UTC*, 156).

Likewise, as a fugitive from "justice," Eliza is vulnerable to capture and return to her master. For her bold defiance of the law, however, the story ends with Eliza reunited with her husband. Both are free and their son is a "fine bright boy" doing well in school. Perhaps because of the unrealistic "story-book" ending, Stowe's point about the Fugitive Slave Act is abundantly clear; readers with the slightest sense of humanity should be persuaded to join her opposition to the legislation. With its focus on happy endings, Eliza's story makes a powerful statement for civil disobedience. In this, Stowe urged others to follow her example and challenge slave law. In her *Key to Uncle Tom's Cabin*, Stowe states,

> A generous man, instead of regarding the poor slave as a piece of property, dead, and void of rights, is tempted to regard him rather as a helpless younger brother, or as a defenceless child, and extend to him, by his own good right arm, that protection and those rights which the law denies him...if left to itself, individual humanity would, in many cases, practically abrogate the slave code (249).

Thus, using Eliza and the other mothers in *Uncle Tom's Cabin* as powerful examples of the need for legal change, Stowe made a persuasive appeal to her nineteenth-century audience.

INCIDENTS IN THE LIFE OF A SLAVE GIRL:
WRITTEN BY HERSELF

Unlike Harriet Beecher Stowe, who gives credit to God for writing *Uncle Tom's Cabin*, Harriet Jacobs asserts the authority of her authorship. The authenticity of the narrative was originally questioned;* however, many critics now accept Jacobs's story about her experiences as largely true.[65] Certifying "this narrative is no fiction," (Preface to *I*, 1) Jacobs "went public in the most national medium available to her," albeit using the pseudonym Linda Brent.[66] Similar to Stowe, however, Jacobs wrote with an earnest "desire to arouse the women of the North to a realizing sense of the condition of two million women at the South, still in bondage" (Preface to *I*, 1). Even Jacobs's epigraph, taken from Isaiah, is a call to action: "Rise up, ye women that are at ease! Hear my voice, ye careless daughters! Give ear unto my speech." Through literature, she sought to add her "testimony to that of abler pens to convince the people of the Free States what Slavery really is" (Preface to *I*, 2). In this endeavor, Jacobs appreciated the power of the narrative to effect legal change, because only "by experience can any one realize how deep, and dark, and foul is that pit of abominations" (Preface to *I*, 2). Jacobs's story and her life deliver a "sustained and rather rigorous critique of slaveholding and patriarchal power vis-a-vis the ideologies and constructed ideologies of antebellum culture."[67]

Like Stowe, Jacobs understood the appeal of her position as an "outraged mother"[68] and sought to elevate black motherhood to the same plane of protection that was afforded to white mothers.† She

---

* One of Jacobs's harshest critics is Blassingame, who has rejected the work as "too orderly" and "too melodramatic," and questioned the authenticity of the "miscegenation and cruelty, outraged virtue, unrequited love, and planter licentiousness appear[ing] on practically every page" (373).

† Barbeito argues that "while Jacobs certainly uses the conventions of sentimental fiction to identify slavery as the denial of natural human bonds, she seems to be doing much more than prudishly positing redemptive domestic female virtue as an antidote to the perversions of slavery" (368).

presented herself as a "new kind of hero."[69] As "a poor Slave Mother" she spoke on behalf of "Slave Mothers" that were still in bondage with the hope that "their hapless Children" might enjoy the same liberties as Jacobs's children enjoyed after her escape to freedom.[70] Jacobs knew from her own grandmother's experience that white motherhood was privileged over the slave's. When Jacobs's mother was only three months old, she was weaned so that "the babe of the mistress might obtain sufficient food" (*I*, 7). Jacobs writes that a "slave mother...may be an ignorant creature, degraded by the system that brutalized her from childhood; but she has a mother's instincts, and is capable of feeling a mother's agonies" (*I*, 16). On behalf of herself and other slave mothers Jacobs argued that laws which failed to protect mothers and children and which permitted slavery to tear families apart must be eradicated. To this end, she presented her own story of civil disobedience.[71]

Making Her Story Public

Just about the time *Uncle Tom's Cabin* was published, Harriet Jacobs was considering how to make her story public. Jacobs was concerned about how her out-of-wedlock (since slaves could not legally marry) pregnancies might be perceived by Northern, white, middle-class readers.[72] An obvious solution was to enlist the help of Stowe, who was quite well known and generally respected. Jacobs originally planned to dictate her narrative to Stowe, who would have endorsed Jacobs's credibility.† Working as a nursemaid for the wife of New York publisher Nathaniel P. Willis, Jacobs had access to many public figures. However, believing that Willis was "too proslavery," Jacobs declined to enlist Willis's help.[73] Jacobs feared that Willis might tell her that it was "very wrong...that [she] was trying to do harm or perhaps he was sorry" for Jacobs to undertake the writing while she was still in his family.[74] After reading in the newspaper that Stowe planned to travel to England, Jacobs, in an attempt to attract Stowe's interest in her story, persuaded Mrs. Willis to write to Stowe suggesting that she allow Jacobs's daughter Louisa to accompany her on that trip.[75]

---

† The summary of Jacobs's plans for how to present her story is taken from Yellin's ground-breaking scholarship, which used a cache of Jacobs's letters to authenticate *Incidents* ("*Written By Herself*"; "Texts and Contexts"; Introduction to *I*, xiii–xxxiv).

Stowe's response, however, was not favorable. In correspondence with Quaker abolitionist Amy Post, Jacobs reports that Stowe declined to take Louisa with her, claiming that if Louisa's "situation as a Slave should be known it would subject her to much petting and patronizing which would be more pleasing to a young Girl than useful."[76] An outraged Jacobs sarcastically wrote: "Mrs. Stowe thinks petting is more than my race can bear? Well, what a pity we poor blacks can't have the firmness and stability of character that you white people have!"[77] Even more disturbing to Jacobs was the fact that Stowe apparently forwarded a copy of Amy Post's sketch of Jacobs's life to Mrs. Willis, seeking to incorporate the story in her *Key to Uncle Tom's Cabin*. Jacobs had not disclosed details regarding her children to her employer who, through "the Charitableness of her own heart...sympathized with [Jacobs] and never asked their origin."[78] Mrs. Willis and Jacobs thereafter wrote several letters urging Stowe not to include Jacobs's story in her *Key*; there was no response.[79] After this disconcerting epistolary encounter with Stowe, Jacobs decided to write her own story.

Jacobs ultimately found an ally in abolitionist L. Maria Child, who shared her desire to see slave laws changed.[80] Like many other abolitionist women, Child's anti-slavery work had a strong religious component.[81] At the 1837 Anti-Slavery Convention of American Women, Child referred to her abolitionist work as "the cause of God, who created mankind free."[82] Child was also well known for her commitment to being publically outspoken about the sexual violation of female slaves,[83] and acknowledged that some may accuse her of "indecorum" for presenting Jacobs's story to the public, stating that this "peculiar phase of Slavery has generally been kept veiled" (Introduction, *I*, 3–4). She stated plainly that she would "take the responsibility of presenting" the "monstrous features" "with the veil withdrawn" for the sake of her "sisters in bondage, who are suffering wrongs so foul, that our ears are too delicate to listen to them" (Introduction, *I*, 4). Her motive in this was clearly designed to rally the abolitionist spirit:

> I do it with the hope of arousing conscientious and reflecting women at the North to a sense of their duty in the exertion of moral influence on the question of Slavery, on all possible occasions. I do it with the hope that every man who reads this narrative will swear solemnly before God that, so far as he has the power to prevent it, no fugitive from Slavery shall ever be sent back to suffer in that loathsome den of corruption and cruelty. (Introduction to *I*, 4)

This sentiment is likewise echoed by Amy Post in her statement at the end of the book: "It is a sad illustration of the condition of this country, which boasts of its civilization, while it sanctions laws and customs which make the experiences of the present more strange than any fictions of the past" (Appendix to *I,* 204). Child's and Post's statements in support of Jacobs reinforced the activist anti-slavery message of *Incidents in the Life of a Slave Girl.*

A Brief History of Slave Laws in North Carolina

Jacobs's narrative has been viewed on a number of levels, but criticism of the effect of slave law is generally limited to a very general acknowledgment of the law's "indifference" to her plight with only passing reference to the Fugitive Slave Law. The legal context for *Incidents in the Life of a Slave Girl,* however, is essential to an understanding of the depth of Jacobs's fear of the law and its lack of protection for African Americans. At the time Jacobs was born in 1813, the slave code in North Carolina was a deeply entrenched part of American life. In addition to well established federal law, a number of laws pertaining to slaves had been enacted and were being enforced in North Carolina. These laws were designed to keep control over slaves and curtail the activity of free blacks. The earliest of those laws was passed in 1715 and, among other things, created special courts to hear cases brought against slaves for serious crimes; provided for a pass system restricting slave travel; allowed those who killed runaway slaves to escape punishment if they merely swore that they acted in self-defense; and required emancipated blacks to leave the colony within six months.[84] Such restrictions on free blacks were seen as an important aspect of keeping slaves isolated from those free persons who might prompt dissatisfaction.

To make sure that freed slaves who left North Carolina did not return, in 1723, a law was passed providing that free blacks reentering North Carolina would be sold into servitude for seven years.[85] Moreover, legislation enacted in 1729

> for the better suppressing of Negroes travelling and associating themselves together in great Numbers, to the Terror and Damage of the white People [provided that]...if any Negro or Negroes shall presume to travel in the night, or be found in the Quarters or Kitchens among other Persons Negroes, such Negroes so found shall receive Correction, not exceeding

forty Lashes...and such Negroes in whose Company they shall be found, shall receive Correction, not exceeding twenty Lashes.[86]

More restrictions were enacted in 1741, further defining the limitations on slaves and the rights of masters, including rewards for persons taking up runaways, punishments for slaves who "shall go armed with a Gun, Sword, Club, or any other Weapon," and a provision that no slaves shall be set free "except for meritorious services, to be adjudged and allowed by the County Court."[87]

A key aspect of the 1741 legislation refined the jurisdiction of the special slave courts and severely restricted the fair operation of the judicial system. Narrowly defining the scope of minority testimony sufficient to prosecute a case, the law provided that evidence necessary for conviction should be the "Confession of the Offender, the Oath of one or more credible Witnesses, or such testimony of Negroes, Mulattos, or *Indians*, bond or free, with pregnant Circumstances, as to them shall seem convincing."*[88]

Of course, "credible witnesses" meant white witnesses. Nonwhite testimony was implicitly deemed inherently inferior and, therefore, was required to be corroborated by "pregnant circumstances." The law further provided that if such "Negro, Mulatto, or *Indian*...be found to have given a false testimony, every such Offender shall, without further Trial, be ordered, by said Court, to have one Ear nailed to the Pillory, and there stand for the space of one Hour, and the said Ear to be cut off, and thereafter the other ear to be nailed in like Manner, and cut off, at the Expiration of one other Hour; and moreover, to order every such Offender thirty-nine Lashes, well laid on, his or her bare Back, at the common Whipping-post."[89] In a further attempt to control slaves and prevent rebellion, in 1753 a new law permitted patrols to search slave quarters on a regular basis, seizing any weapons that might be found.[90] In light of the inadmissibility of black testimony against white defendants, little comfort was felt following the enactment of a 1774 law that declared the malicious killing of a slave to be murder.[91]

---

* Later, in 1816, a law was enacted giving superior courts exclusive jurisdiction and requiring that "the trial shall be conducted in the same manner, and under the same rules, regulations and restrictions, as trials of freemen for a like offence" with the exception that the defendant slave was "entitled to the right of challenge for cause only" (Act of 1816, ch. XIV, *Laws of the State of North Carolina*, 10).

In addition to such statutory laws, two notorious North Carolina cases effectively illustrate the power of the law over slaves. In Judge Thomas Ruffin's infamous decision in *State v. Mann* (1829), for example, the emphasis on the unmitigated authority of the master over the slave is especially apparent. In this case, the court acknowledged that a slave is "doomed in his own person, and his posterity, to live without knowledge, and without the capacity to make anything his own."[92] Notwithstanding the severe struggle he claimed to feel in his "own breast between the feelings of the man, and the duty of the magistrate," Judge Ruffin held that such "services can only be expected from one who has no will of his own; who surrenders his will in implicit obedience to that of another. Such obedience is the consequence only of uncontrolled authority over the body...The power of the master must be absolute, to render the submission of the slave perfect."[93] He went on to state that it "will be the imperative duty of the Judges to recognize the full dominion of the owner over the slave, except where the exercise is forbidden by statute."[94] In general, many states had statutes requiring masters to treat slaves with "a certain minimal fairness, to feed them and clothe them, and to punish no more severely than the situation demanded."[95] Such statutes were, of course, open to a wide range of subjective and discretionary abuse by masters, just short of murder.

Similarly, in *State v. Will* (1834), the North Carolina Supreme Court addressed a situation in which Will, a slave, was charged with murder for defending himself against an attack by his overseer. Under circumstances described as "strongly calculated to excite his [Will's] passions of terror and resentment," the court took the opportunity to refine the master-slave relationship.[96] Recognizing that "[u]nconditional submission is the *general* duty of the slave" and "unlimited power, is in general, the *legal*, right of the master," Judge Gaston found that there are exceptions to this rule: "It is certain that the master has not the right to slay his slave, and I hold it to be equally certain that the slave has a right to defend himself against the unlawful attempt of his master to deprive him of life."[97] The court then went on to hold that an "attempt to take a slave's life is then an attempt to commit a grievous crime, and may rightfully be resisted."[98] Accordingly, Will was convicted of manslaughter instead of the more serious charge of murder.

This sampling of North Carolina statutory law leaves little doubt about the degree to which the legislature desired to control both free and enslaved blacks. The North Carolina law supplements the federal legal reinforcement of slavery and establishes the restrictive context in which Jacobs and her family lived.

"RISE UP, YE WOMEN": THE EFFECTS OF SLAVE LAW IN *INCIDENTS*

Through her narrator, Linda Brent, Harriet Jacobs lays bare her defiance of slave law by declaring, "My master had power and law on his side; I had a determined will" (*I*, 85). Acknowledging that there is "might in each," Linda summons her strength from a "woman's pride" and a "mother's love" for her children, resolving that "out of the darkness...a brighter dawn should rise" for her daughter and son (*I*, 85). Significantly, Jacobs reminds her readers that not only did the laws not protect black slave women, the laws allowed cruelties to be inflicted upon them (*I*, 121). Lest there be any doubt about the disparity of treatment she received—twice—Jacobs directly addresses her readers, pointing out the protections afforded to white women and their children that were not enjoyed by slaves:

> But, O, ye happy women, whose purity has been sheltered from childhood, who have been free to choose the objects of your affection, whose homes are protected by law....Pity me, and pardon me, O virtuous reader! You never knew what it is to be a slave; to be entirely unprotected by law or custom; to have laws reduce you to the condition of a chattel, entirely subject to the will of another. (*I*, 54, 55)

In so doing, Jacobs calls upon the humanity of her white readers in order to recognize the injustice perpetuated by slave laws and to rally to her cause.

Undoubtedly unfamiliar with Blackstone's theories about property, Jacobs nevertheless knew, as an oppressed human being, that the concept of property was at the heart of a slave's status under the law. Through Linda, Jacobs begins her narrative with childhood, noting "I was so fondly shielded that I never dreamed I was a piece of merchandise" trusted to her parents for "safe keeping, liable to be demanded of them at any moment" (*I*, 5). When her mother dies, Linda is sent to live with her maternal grandmother in the household of Margaret Horniblow,[99] where she is claimed as property and becomes part of Mrs. Horniblow's estate. When Linda is twelve years old her mistress dies, bequeathing Linda to her five-year-old niece, Emily (the fictionalized Matilda Norcom). This transfer places Linda under the control of the young girl's father, Dr. Flint (the fictionalized James Norcom), a prominent physician in Edenton, North Carolina. From this point, Linda finds herself caught in legal technicalities about her ownership and control; Dr. Flint is quite fond of making the point that she "is my daughter's property and I have no legal right to sell her" (*I*, 35). Flint, however, is quick to invoke the law when it serves his interests. Later, as a fugitive, Linda considers using the money she had earned to purchase herself, but decides this would be "unjust"—she could not possibly regard herself as "a piece of property" (*I*, 187).

This issue of legal ownership of human beings haunts Jacobs throughout her narrative. The sale and separation of slave families was done without compunction. Driven "like cattle, ...[h]usbands were torn from wives, parents from children, never to look upon each other again this side of the grave" (*I*, 106). On New Year's Day, slaves were routinely sold and expected to go with their new masters the following day. Linda describes one particularly devastating scene in which she sees a mother "lead seven children to the auction-block" (*I*, 16). The mother "knew that *some* of them would be taken from her; but they took *all*," selling the children to a slave trader who would, in turn, sell them one by one to the highest bidder (*I*, 16). The mother "wrung her hands in anguish" in the street, exclaiming "Gone! All gone! Why *don't* God kill me?" (*I*, 16). Jacobs also illustrates that elderly slaves were treated with an equal lack of compassion, describing through her narrator how one woman who had worked for a family for seventy years is left to be sold for twenty dollars after her owners had moved to Alabama (*I*, 16). Masters were free under the law to dispose of their property in virtually any way they saw fit.

Linda Brent's family was no exception to a master's mercenary legal right to separate and sell his slaves. The fact that her grandmother, aunts, and uncles are ultimately regarded as merely other pieces of property is abhorrent to Linda, who comments: "Notwithstanding my grandmother's long and faithful service to her owners, not one of her children escaped the auction block. These God-breathing machines are no more, in the sight of their masters, than the cotton they plant, or the horses they tend" (*I*, 8). Linda's grandmother tries to save money to buy back her children, especially following the sale of her youngest son, Benjamin, when he is only ten years old. She manages to save three hundred dollars, but loans the money to her mistress, who is in great financial need and "promises" to repay the loan soon. Jacobs dryly notes the naive trust that the grandmother exhibited: "The reader probably knows that no promise or writing given to a slave is legally binding; for, according to Southern slave laws, a slave, *being* property, can *hold* no property" (*I*, 6). Thus, the mistress's promise that her will contained a provision to free Linda's grandmother is equally unenforceable. After years of service, Flint tells Linda's grandmother that "under existing circumstances, it was necessary that she be sold" (*I*, 11). Rejecting Flint's hypocritic offer to have a private sale, "Aunt Marthy" (as she was known by many in the community) "took her place among the chattels, and at the first call she sprang upon the auction block" (*I*, 11). Having laid bare the shame of the sale, the grandmother is finally granted her freedom by the elderly sister of her deceased mistress.

With great anguish, Linda also has to come to terms with the legal reality that her children are also deemed the property of her master. Even before she has children, she knows that they "must 'follow the condition of the mother'" (*I*, 42). After the birth of her first child, Benjamin, Flint threatens to sell the child if she continues to refuse "to accept what he called his kind offers"—that is, his sexual advances. (*I*, 76). Linda is well aware that this is not an empty threat, and that "the law gave him power to fulfill it; for slaveholders have been cunning enough to enact that 'the child shall follow the condition of the *mother*'" (*I*, 76). Her bitterness is seething in her observation that slave owners have taken "care that licentiousness shall not interfere with avarice" (*I*, 76). The arrival of her second child, Ellen, only further exacerbates Flint's anger and threats.

Much of Linda's life is driven by trying to free her children from their legal classification as slaves. The purchase of her children by their father, Mr. Sands (the fictionalized Samuel Tredwell Sawyer*), a respected white man, gives Linda only short-term solace. Her initial relief that her "little ones were saved" (*I*, 109) and that slavery could not shackle her children quickly gives way to legal questions over ownership. Mr. Sands now ostensibly owns the children as slaves, but Linda fears that Sands might die, leaving their children "at the mercy of his heirs" (*I*, 125). Coming out of hiding, Linda pleads with Sands to emancipate the children and allay her fears. Instead, she receives a

---

* Samuel Tredwell Sawyer was a United States Congressman (Yellin, Introduction to *I*, xv). Vermillion makes an interesting argument that Linda Brent's "decision to have sexual relations with Sands" begins the "rewriting of her body into her life story" and challenges the "hegemonic culture's perception of her as a mere body" (246–47).

report that Sands's wife "wanted to take Benjamin" and that Mrs. Sands's sister is "so much pleased with Ellen, that she offered to adopt her, and bring her up as she would a daughter" (*I*, 138). Linda responds, "Never should I know peace till my children were emancipated with all due formalities of law" (*I*, 138). In the midst of this distress, Linda then learns that Flint is claiming that the children are his daughter's property and, "as she was not of age when they were sold, the contract" selling Benjamin and Ellen to Sands is "not legally binding" (*I*, 138).

Linda knows that she is powerless to resolve this legal entanglement because there "was no protecting arm of the law" for her to invoke (*I*, 138). Years later, when Jacobs considered the legal status of her children and herself, she acknowledged that she "knew the law would decide that" she was James Norcom's property and "would probably still give his daughter a claim" to her children (*I*, 187). Linda, however, refuses to succumb to the authority of man-made law, defiantly declaring "I regarded such laws as the regulations of robbers, who had no rights that I was bound to respect" (*I*, 187). Linda may acknowledge the legal reality of a slave's status as property, but she refuses to subvert her will to unjust law.

The other consequence of being deemed property was a master's nearly unmitigated right to treat slaves as he pleased. In the chapter titled "Sketches of Neighboring Slaveholders," Jacobs details the mistreatment of a number of slaves.* One such neighbor, "Mr. Litch," an "ill-bred, uneducated...but very wealthy" man operated his own judicial system for his six hundred slaves (*I*, 46). Complete with a jail and a whipping post, Litch inflicted whatever cruelties he deemed appropriate and was never held accountable for his hideous "punishments." Jacobs also details the mistreatment of a slave named James who attempted to escape his bondage. Upon recapture, James was whipped to the overseer's satisfaction, washed in strong brine, then "put into the cotton gin, which was screwed down, only allowing him room to turn on his side" (*I*, 49). After four days, James's dead body was found partly eaten by rats and vermin. No inquiry followed and no questions were asked; because James was a slave, "the feeling was that the master had a right to do what he pleased with his own property" (*I*, 49).

---

* The one major change Maria Child made to Jacobs's narrative was to put all of the "savage cruelties" into this chapter (Karcher, 436).

In addition to physical abuses that were sanctioned by law, female slaves were wholly unprotected from sexual abuse by their masters. By legal definition, "rape" meant the rape of a white woman.[100] Under North Carolina law, "Any slave, or free negro, or free person of color, convicted by due course of law, of an assault with intent to commit a rape, upon the body of a white female, shall suffer death."[101] In contrast, the systematic rape of black women went wholly unprosecuted, as an "uncamouflaged expression of a slaveholder's economic mastery and the overseer's control over Black women as workers."[102] As an institutionalized part of slavery, rape "was a weapon of domination, a weapon of repression, whose covert goal was to extinguish slave women's will to resist, and in the process, to demoralize their men."[103]

Linda feels this lack of legal protection at the most fundamental level. When she is told that her second child is a girl, her "heart was heavier than it had ever been before" (*I*, 77). She knows that as a slave her daughter will be subjected to the sexual whim of her master: "Slavery is terrible for men; but it is far more terrible for women. Superadded to the burden common to all, *they* have wrongs, and sufferings, and mortifications peculiarly their own" (*I*, 77). Jacobs is very careful to provide her readers with a sense of this aspect of the "all-pervading corruption produced by slavery" (*I*, 51). Slave girls must live in an "atmosphere of licentiousness and fear," because as soon as she is fourteen or fifteen the unwelcome attention of her master, his sons, and the overseer will begin. If their initial bribes with presents are unsuccessful, she may be "whipped or starved into submission of their will" (*I*, 51). The pervasiveness of this sexual corruption undermined slave owners' marriages and created hostile mistresses.

Linda herself is not spared from sexual abuse. Flint is the father of at least eleven slaves and fully intends to add Brent to his list of exploited women.[104] When she is just fifteen, Flint begins to "whisper foul words" in her ear. Flint, nearly forty years older than Linda, repeatedly tells her that she is his property and that she must "be subject to his will in all things" (*I*, 27). Flint "boasted much of his forbearance," reminding Linda that "there was a limit to his patience" (*I*, 32). By keeping within the sight of others during the day and sleeping with her great aunt during the night, Linda succeeds in eluding Flint, who would often hold a razor to her throat to force her to change her "line of policy" (*I*, 32). Flint's pursuit of Linda does not go unnoticed by his wife; by the time Linda is sixteen, marital altercations are frequent.[105] Later, Mrs. Flint allows Linda to sleep adjoining her room, promising to protect her—but in an attempt to stem the desecration of her marriage, rather than out of sympathy for the girl. Undaunted by his wife's protests and Linda's resistance, Flint threatens, "Do you know that I have a right to do as I like with you,— that I can kill you if I please?" (*I*, 39). The nearly absolute legal right of a master to control his slaves sanctioned such persistent abuse.

Consistent with the legality of using slave women as "breeders" to generate more slave capital and permitting them to be raped on a regular basis, laws prevented slaves from enjoying any sanctity of marriage. By law, only with their master's permission were slaves allowed to marry freemen.[106] Even then, this "marriage" would have no protection against a slave holder separating and selling off the partners. Jacobs knew from the experiences of her Great Aunt Nancy what can happen to slaves that marry. Nancy had permission to marry, yet in reality it was "a mere form, without any legal value," because her "master or mistress could annul it any day they pleased" (*I*, 143). Indeed, as a married woman, Nancy was still required to sleep near her mistress's chamber and was so overworked night and day that several of her infant children died.

Marriage would give Linda no legal protection from the whim of her master. When she falls in love with a freeborn carpenter in the neighborhood, Flint is enraged. Inflicting a blow, he asks whether Linda wants his permission to marry. There is little question about his lack of acquiescence to such a union. Linda realizes that even if her lover could have obtained permission to marry her, "the marriage would give him no power to protect" her from her master, and any children would merely be additions to Flint's chattel (*I*, 42). If they were to marry without permission, the law provided that her lover "shall be liable and held to pay to the Master or Mistress…the Sum of ten Pounds; and on failing to pay such Sum, shall be held to service to the Master or Mistress of such Slave for and during the Term of one Year."[107] Linda knows that the relationship is doomed, lamenting, "when I reflected that I was a slave, and that the laws gave no sanction to the marriage of such, my heart sank within me" (*I*, 42). She knows that her only hope is for her lover to buy her, but knows also that the jealous Flint will never consent to such a sale.

The laws providing for the return of runaways were also the source of great anguish for Jacobs. Her own story and the vignette about her uncle Benjamin illustrate a slave's desperate desire to flee and the great force of the law to ensure his or her return. When Jacobs was about fourteen, Benjamin briefly escaped from his master. Benjamin's flight took place after he resisted his master's whipping, throwing his master to the ground. It was a serious crime for a slave to assault a white man, especially when his master was one of the richest men in the town. Benjamin believed that his only way out was to flee to the North. Unfortunately, he was soon recaptured and placed in jail. Remembering the Christian leanings of her readers, Jacobs is careful to include Benjamin's despair and loss of faith. From his jail cell he told his mother that he did not think of God when he was on the run, that "when a man is hunted like a wild beast he forgets there is a God, a heaven. He forgets everything in his struggle to get beyond the reach of the bloodhounds" (*I*, 22). Lest any other slaves think about fleeing, Benjamin was kept in the jail in heavy chains and covered with "vermin" as a reminder to others of their fate upon recapture. Ultimately, however, Benjamin did successfully flee to New York, giving Jacobs hope for her own freedom in the North.

Jacobs is understandably outspoken in her anger about the fugitive slave laws. She is critical of the northern states for enforcing the Fugitive Slave Act and sustaining a "law which hurls fugitives back into slavery" (*I*, 43). She levies a good share of the blame on the free states because "[*t*]*hey* do the work" consenting "to act the part of bloodhounds, and hunt the poor fugitive back into his den" (*I*, 44, 36). Seeing no other way out of her own enslavement, Jacobs became a fugitive when she was in her early twenties. Soon after she fled, a notice for her return was posted "at every corner, and in every public place for miles around":

> $300 Reward! Ran away from the subscriber, an intelligent, bright, mulatto girl...21 years of age. Five feet four inches high. Dark eyes, and black hair inclined to curl; but it can be made straight. Has a decayed spot on a front tooth. She can read and write, and in all probability will try to get to the Free States. All persons are forbidden, under penalty of law, to harbor or employ said slave. $150 will be given to whoever takes her in the state, and $300 if taken out of the state and delivered to me, or lodged in jail. (*I*, 97)

In an attempt to reclaim his chattel, Flint invokes the power of the law to have Linda's uncle Phillip arrested. Charged with aiding and abetting her flight, Phillip is held without any evidence, save the accusation of Flint. Linda fears that her uncle will lash out in frustration, giving the authorities legal cause to prosecute him. Any act he might commit would place him in peril, because under the evidentiary rules, as a black man, Phillip's word could not be used to controvert the testimony of any white man (*I,* 110). Fortunately, Phillip is soon released without further incident.

Until her freedom was bought in 1852, Jacobs was a fugitive from "justice" in violation of federal and state runaway laws. Her initial "flight" actually entailed hiding for seven years in the garret of her grandmother's house. At the behest of Flint, Linda is hunted by slave catchers, even overhearing a conversation in which one slave hunter said that he would "catch *any* nigger for the reward" because a "man ought to have what belongs to him, if he *is* a damned brute" (*I,* 117). Under North Carolina law, slave catchers received a reward based on the distance of the slave from the master: "For the taking up servants or slaves, if ten miles or under, from the house or quarter where such servant or slave was kept...as reward to the taker up, seven shillings and six pence, proclamation money, and for every mile above ten, three pence, over and above said sum."*

Jacobs was continually in jeopardy, fearing for her safety at the hands of these legal mercenaries. Finally, in 1842, she escaped to Massachusetts, a place that she had heard "that slaveholders did not consider...a comfortable place to go to in search of a runaway... before the Fugitive Slave Law was passed" (*I,* 131). Jacobs resisted the efforts of her mistress to lure her back to the South with promises of freedom. When Jacobs's location was revealed by one Mr. Thorne, she fled Boston upon the advice of a judge and attorney. Thorne's rationale for exposing her whereabouts is revealed in his letter to Norcom, where he writes, "I am a patriot, a lover of my country, and I do this as an act of justice to the laws" (*I,* 179).

This kind of false patriotism is remarkably similar to justifications given by politicians such as Senator Albert Gallatin Brown of Mississippi, who is quoted as declaring "that slavery was 'a great moral, social, and political blessing; a blessing to the master, and a blessing to the slave!'" (*I,* 122)†

---

* Acts of 1741, ch. XXVII, *Laws of the State of North Carolina,* 90. This statute was still in full force in the 1814 Code, chapter 107, section 8. Later, in the 1855 *Revised Code of North Carolina,* chapter 107, section 8, the reward for capturing a runaway slave is noted as "five dollars, when the owner resides in the county in which the slave may be apprehended, and ten dollars, if he reside beyond the limits of such county," with extra money rewarded if the slave was apprehended in certain swamps.

† Jacobs's recollection captures the gist of this statement by Senator Brown, which was made during an 1854 congressional debate. The full quotation reads, "I believe that

The passage of the Fugitive Slave Act in 1850 renewed Jacobs's anxiety about being captured and returned to her master, who had never given up on the hunt. She devotes an entire chapter to delineating the injustices generated by the law. Jacobs is quick to point out that the status of runaway slaves in Massachusetts changed dramatically with this Act. For its part in the passage of this law, Jacobs denounced Massachusetts as consenting "to become a 'nigger hunter' for the South" (*I,* 131). Jacobs is equally harsh in her characterization of the judges who enforced the law, declaring that they "stooped under chains to enter courts of justice, so called" (*I,* 187). By this time Jacobs was living in New York City, which she described as being "a city of kidnappers" (*I,* 193). Like many other fugitive slaves living in New York, Jacobs was filled with anxiety about her safety. She relates the example of Hamlin, the first slave who was apprehended under the new law, "given up by the bloodhounds of the north to the bloodhounds of the south," which prompted an exodus of families from the city (*I,* 190–91). The Fugitive Slave Act renewed the effect of slave law by threatening established families; wives discovered that their husbands were fugitives and husbands discovered that their wives were fugitives. Inasmuch as children of fugitive slave women were deemed by law to "follow the condition of their mother," such children were "liable to be seized and carried into slavery" (*I,* 191). In short, "hundreds of intelligent and industrious people" now risked being returned to slavery (*I,* 191).

Jacobs's own experience and defiance of the law placed her in great jeopardy. When she informed her employer, "Mrs. Bruce," about the danger that the law posed, prompt measures were taken to ensure Jacobs's safety. Amazingly enough, Mrs. Bruce offered her baby as a traveling companion for Jacobs, stating "It is better for you to have baby with you...for if they get on your track, they will be obliged to bring the child back to me; and then, if there is a possibility of saving you, you will be saved" (*I,* 194). Jacobs was fortunate to work for a woman whose idea of justice was more expansive than the law. When her aristocratic and pro-slavery husband "remonstrated her for harboring a fugitive slave" asking "if she was aware of the penalty," Mrs. Bruce responded, "I am very well aware of it. It is imprisonment and one thousand dollars fine. Shame on my country that it *is* so! I am

---

slavery is of divine origin, and that it is a great moral, social, and political blessing—a blessing to the slave, and a blessing to the master" (Cluskey, *Speeches,* 335).

ready to incur the penalty. I will go to the state's prison, rather than have any poor victim torn from *my* house, to be carried back to slavery" (*I*, 194). Thereafter, Jacobs fled to New England, to the home of a senator who opposed the Fugitive Slave Act. However, the Act struck fear in even those who condemned the law. Because the senator was concerned about having Jacobs in his house, arrangements were made for her to stay in the country with the baby. Ultimately, she safely returned to New York.*

As one critic notes, throughout her narrative, Jacobs continally insists "that domestic values prevail by nature and *should* prevail politically over the marketplace values."[108] Through Linda, Jacobs's own defiance of the law was a call to action. As a "rebel with a moral cause," Jacobs distinguished herself by "breaking out of the boundaries others set for black females in white America."[109]

CONCLUSION

By depicting the devastating power of slave law on women and children, Stowe and Jacobs added narrative power to the abolitionist movement. They both created brave characters who were able to overcome their plight by nonviolent defiance to the law. Their civil disobedience inspired other women to join in their cause and abolish the pernicious laws that permitted the ownership of other human beings. *Uncle Tom's Cabin* and *Incidents in the Life of a Slave Girl* were designed to present a relatively straightforward jurisprudential story revealing the dark side of slave law. Crafted as caring women and selfless mothers, Eliza and Linda were persuasive messengers for the abolitionist call to action. Even though they break the law by acting on their internal sense of what was right, their goal of freedom is a laudable one. Eliza and Linda act as moral agents consistent with constitutional principles of liberty and justice for all.

---

* Yellin notes that "Messmore apparently assumed—correctly—that Jacobs did not know that Norcom, acting as his daughter's natural guardian, had in 1837 legalized his sale of the children with a bill of substitution that assigned two other slave children of equal value to his daughter's estate" (Notes to *I*, 291 n.10).

Chapter 4

Perspectives after Civil Rights

Sherley Anne Williams's *Dessa Rose* and Toni Morrison's *Beloved*

> The Elizas, if they indeed existed, were certain oddities among the great majority of Black women. They did not, in any event, represent the accumulated experience of all those women who toiled under the lash for their masters, worked for and protected their families, fought against slavery, and who were beaten and raped, but never subdued.
> —Angela Y. Davis, *Women, Race & Class*

Unlike the preemancipation literary activism of Harriet Beecher Stowe and Harriet Jacobs, contemporary twentieth-century authors dealing with slavery write from a markedly different political perspective. By their own admission, Stowe and Jacobs wrote as spokeswomen, speaking for enslaved women, men, and children. Calculated to rouse their abolitionist audience to action, their sentimentalism and often stereotypical characters served a practical agenda: They wanted the law changed. With slavery abolished for over a hundred years and modern civil rights laws enacted, the need for such overt posturing has arguably been obviated. Authors like Sherley Anne Williams and Toni Morrison are free to create more artistic narratives which, in James Baldwin's words, "bear witness to the truth"[1] as they comment about nineteenth-century justice. Anchoring *Dessa Rose* and *Beloved* in historical incidents, Williams and Morrison draw from the past and then add the interior lives to their characters.[2] In so doing, they withdraw the "veil" of slavery to which L. Maria Child refers in her introduction to *Incidents in the Life of a Slave Girl* (*I*, 4).* Accordingly, Dessa Rose in Williams's novel of the same name and Sethe in Morrison's *Beloved* are imbued with a range of human emotions—both positive and troubling—in response to the "monstrous" laws that maintained slavery.

The effects of slavery are depicted in all facets of these characters' existence, without romantic posturing of Dessa Rose and Sethe as "perfect mothers." Unlike Eliza and Linda, their strength is not tied to "some mystical power attached to motherhood, but rather to concrete experiences as slaves."[3] Motherhood is "both annihilation and empowerment" for these women, who, like many other slave women, are "driven to defend their children by their passionate abhorrence of slavery."[4] In the spirit of what Herbert Aptheker concluded after he compiled *American Negro Slave Revolts*, Dessa Rose and Sethe are crafted to be heroes who refuse to be victimized by their oppression: "They were fireballs in the night; cries from the heart; expressions of human need and aspiration in the face of the deepest testing. They manifest that victimization does not simply make victims; it also produces heroes."[5]

Dessa Rose and Sethe, however, are not heroes in any conventional sense. "Heroism for Black Americans," Williams observes in *Give Birth to Brightness*, "has always meant some measure of revolt against social structures, for these structures were the instruments of their oppression rather than their protection."[6] No social structure in the history of the country has been more oppressive than slavery. Dessa Rose and Sethe are, thus, characterized as rebelling against what historian Kenneth Stampp deemed the "peculiar institution"[7] by killing out of an overriding sense of loyalty to those they love.

These literary depictions of the human toll taken by the perniciousness of slavery weave a complicated indictment of the laws which sustained this institution. Most, if not all, of the reasons raised by Stowe and Jacobs for the abolishment of slavery are reinforced and delineated in great psychological detail. Williams's *Dessa Rose* and Morrison's *Beloved* do more, however, than merely witness the legally

---

* Moody considers the treatment of "literacy, community, and romantic love in relation to the self-esteem of the central characters of *Incidents, Beloved,* and *Dessa Rose*," concluding that for Morrison and Williams "community precedes autonomy, and only collective authority permits personal ability" (633–34, 646).

sanctioned horrors of slavery to a new audience. They appropriate historical stories to suggest that the harsh laws of slavery drive Dessa Rose and Sethe to murder and, moreover, that these violent acts are reasonable under the circumstances of each character's life. By reworking history to spare their characters from capital punishment and the return to slavery, respectively, Williams and Morrison offer readers a radical vision of justice: Under the extenuating circumstances, murder may be justified. By depicting the violent acts of Dessa Rose and Sethe as the outgrowth of social forces, Williams and Morrison tap into the ideas expressed by Richard Wright in *Native Son*. During the legal proceedings against Bigger Thomas, his attorney, Boris Max, argues that "warping influences" "played down hard" on his client.[8] In an attempt to convince the court to spare Bigger from the death penalty, Max continues,

> We are dealing here not with how man acts toward man, but with how a man acts when he feels that he must defend himself against, or adapt himself to, the total natural world in which he lives. The central fact to be understood here is not who wronged this boy, but what kind of vision of the world did he have before his eyes, and where did he get such a vision as to make him, without premeditation, snatch the life of another person so quickly and instinctively that even though there was an element of accident in it, he was willing after the crime to say: "Yes; I did that. I had to."[9]

Similar to Bigger Thomas, Dessa Rose and Sethe are depicted as acting violently because they see no other alternative. By the end of both texts, however, this controversial assertion is deemphasized and largely subsumed into an expanded vision of humanity and justice. Williams and Morrison do not fall prey to the protest novel genre. Unlike Bigger Thomas, Dessa Rose and Sethe do not "accept a theology" that denies them life[10]; the power of each work lies in its embrace of life.

Thus, Williams and Morrison remind readers that health and wholeness requires remembering not only the parts of the past that are pleasant, but also those which are painful.* Ann Trapasso's perceptive observation about *Dessa Rose* is equally applicable to *Beloved*. She says,

---

* Smith-Wright takes this assertion a step further and argues "that not only do historical novels by African-American women writers chart the journey toward wholeness, but by correcting misrepresentative accounts of their history and writing history where there was none, these writers also critique hegemonic historical boundaries of those discourses to include race and gender experience in the writing of the lions' history" (263).

"We must never forget how horrible it was and we must also free ourselves from the horror so that we can move on."[11] By retrieving traumatic memories, the "history" in the texts "acquires the function of communal 'talking cure': its characters, author, and readers delve into the past, repeating painful stories to work toward the health of fuller awareness."[12] *Dessa Rose* and *Beloved* "begin to perform a textual healing for all readers."[13] In terms of the law, this act of healing through writing is particularly noteworthy because African Americans were "once legally proscribed from attaining literacy or having access to education."[14] In *Dessa Rose* and *Beloved*, Williams and Morrison "reclaim" and reshape a part of history.[15] Their narratives are, however, more than historical novels; they "illustrate how the memory process of creative reconstruction can re-remember the fragments so as to transform the past and its implications, and give it new life in the present."[16] By taking little-known slave women and making them "live for a twentieth-century readership,"[17] Williams and Morrison make a concluding gesture for a more positive future: *Dessa Rose* underscores the importance of interracial cooperation, and *Beloved* celebrates the power of the individual to overcome adversity. Both of these factors are crucial in the twenty-first century for the just execution of civil rights laws.

THE FEDERAL LEGAL CONTEXT: BEYOND *DRED SCOTT*

When *Uncle Tom's Cabin* and *Incidents in the Life of a Slave Girl* were published, Supreme Court Justice Taney's opinion in *Dred Scott* encapsulated the status of African Americans in the United States as a legally inferior race. Moreover, the Fugitive Slave Act of 1850 sanctioned ruthless interstate manhunts for runaway slaves, and slave states all had their own oppressive statutory codes. Stowe and Jacobs very publically fought against these laws. In fact, Abraham Lincoln is often quoted for his remark that Harriet Beecher Stowe started the Civil War. It is fanciful to think of literature as that powerful, but suffice it to say that Stowe certainly rallied abolitionists and other writers, like Jacobs, who did have an impact on the ensuing legal changes.

Williams's and Morrison's work in the 1980s is, of course, informed by a much different legal consciousness than that of Stowe and Jacobs. They are writing in a post-Martin Luther King world in which comprehensive civil rights legislation has been passed. Moreover, through affirmative action and effective litigation, the legal status of African Americans has dramatically improved over their nineteenth-century counterparts. Nonetheless, race relations in the United States are far from resolved. As Mae Henderson points out, "the politics of civil rights generated a counter-response from an empowered religious right, a reconstituted conservative Supreme Court, and a polarizing presidential politics of Reaganomics in the 1980s."[18] With the primary focus now shifted away from changing the law to enforcing existing laws, *Dessa Rose* and *Beloved* can be seen as creating empathy for the human effects of slavery with the larger goal of increasing understanding about the treatment of black Americans. In turn, such heightened awareness can contribute to the fair execution of the law. This more expansive goal intended to lead to justice, however, is built upon historical understanding and casting a critical eye on the law. As such, Williams and Morrison are no less effective than Stowe and Jacobs in their depictions of the injustices perpetrated under slave law.*

A survey of federal civil rights laws after *Dred Scott* to contemporary times serves to round out the legal history that precedes *Dessa Rose* and *Beloved.* In the midst of the Civil War, the next major legal development regarding the status of African Americans was the Emancipation Proclamation. Effective 1 January 1863, "all persons held as slaves within any state or designated part of a state, the people whereof shall then be in rebellion against the United States, shall be then, thenceforward, and forever, free."[19] As Leon Higginbotham is quick to point out, despite revisionist history, Lincoln did not free slaves *carte blanche.* The *"in rebellion"* clause makes the Emancipation Proclamation a restrictive document; *all* slaves were not freed.[20] The fate of many slaves was left unresolved.

On 28 June1864, the Fugitive Slave Acts of 1793 and 1850 were repealed, yet another incremental gain toward abolishing slavery.[21] Runaway slaves could no longer be captured and returned to their masters under federal law. Thereafter, in December 1865, the

---

* At least one critic has extended this kind of analysis into the present. In her discussion of four recent legal cases involving mothers, Elizabeth Tobin uses *Beloved* to critique the way the contemporary legal system deals with issues involving mothers (140–74).

constitutional protection of slavery ended with the ratification of the Thirteenth Amendment: "Neither slavery nor involuntary servitude, except as a punishment for crime whereof the party shall have been duly convicted, shall exist within the United States, or any place subject to their jurisdiction."[22] Slavery and involuntary servitude were plainly outlawed, yet the issue of black citizenship was left unresolved. The Thirteenth Amendment also gave Congress the "power to enforce this article by appropriate legislation," but it was unclear whether this included the authority to grant African Americans all of the rights and privileges of full citizenship.[23]

Just over a year after the ratification of the Thirteenth Amendment, in an attempt to further the goals of the reconstruction, the Civil Rights Act of 1866 was passed. This legislation was sponsored, in part, to eradicate the severe restrictions enacted by several states—known as "black codes"—that were tantamount to slavery. The language in Section 1 of the Civil Rights Act is unequivocal: "*all persons* born in the United States" were declared "citizens of the United States" (emphasis added).[24] Furthermore, the Act mandated that

> citizens, of every race and color, without regard to any previous condition of slavery...shall have the same right, in every State and Territory in the United States, to make and enforce contracts, to sue, be parties, and give evidence, to inherit, purchase, lease, sell, hold, and convey real and personal property, and to full and equal benefit of all laws and proceedings for the security of person and property, as is enjoyed by white citizens.[25]

Even though the Thirteenth Amendment gave Congress enforcement power by "appropriate legislation," doubts existed about the constitutionality of the Amendment to support the Civil Rights Law. Accordingly, the Fourteenth Amendment was ratified on 9 July 1868. Under this key Amendment,

> *All persons* born or naturalized in the United States and subject to the jurisdiction thereof, are citizens of the United States and of the State wherein they reside. No State shall make or enforce any law which shall abridge the privileges or immunities of the citizens of the United States; nor shall any State deprive any person of life, liberty, or property, without due process of law; nor deny to any person within its jurisdiction the *equal protection of the laws* (emphasis added).[26]

The 1866 Act was thus validated.

During the 1870s, as the country struggled with Reconstruction, several laws were passed. In 1870, the Fifteenth Amendment was ratified giving black men the vote. The Amendment prohibits the denial of franchise, providing that "the right of citizens of the United States to vote shall not be denied or abridged by the United States or by any State on account of race, color, or previous condition of servitude."[27] The 1870 Enforcement Act dealt primarily with the denial of voting rights, yet the entire system was not without flaws: The Amendment was not effectively enforced until nearly a century after its passage and women continued to be disenfranchised until 1920.[28]

Likewise, the other civil rights laws passed during this decade were fraught with practical problems. Congress amended the 1870 Act through the Civil Rights Act of 1871.* Known as the "Ku Klux Klan Act," this law established civil and criminal liability for depriving a person of his or her civil rights.[29] Thereafter, the Civil Rights Act of 1875 was designed to make "public accommodations" for the enforcement of the Constitutional Amendments. Specifically, Section 1 provided that

> all persons within the jurisdiction of the United States shall be entitled to the full and equal enjoyment of the accommodations, advantages, facilities, and privileges of inns, public conveyances on land or water, theatres, and other places of public amusement; subject only to the conditions and limitations established by law, and applicable alike to citizens of every race and color, regardless of the previous condition of servitude.[30]

The law, however, was ineffective; U.S. marshals were not even provided with a copy of the law so they could effectively enforce the terms of the Act.[31] Thereafter, in 1883, the Supreme Court declared the law unconstitutional in the *Civil Rights Cases*. This decision involved five cases growing out of exclusions of blacks from hotels, theaters, and railroads in Kansas, California, Missouri, New York, and Tennessee. Justifying its decision, the court found that there "were thousands of free colored people in this country before the abolition of slavery...yet no one, at that time, thought it an invasion of his personal status as a freeman because he was not admitted to all the privileges enjoyed by white citizens...Mere discriminations on account of race or color were not regarded as badges of slavery."[32] Criticizing the majority opinion

---

* The codification of this Act, 42 U.S.C. §1983, provides for civil action for deprivation of rights by state actors.

as "too narrow and artificial," Justice Harlan dissented, holding that since slavery was the "moving or principal cause of the adoption of" the 13th Amendment,

> and since that institution rested wholly upon the inferiority, as a race, of those held in bondage, their freedom necessarily involved immunity from, and protection against, all discrimination against them, because of their race...Congress, therefore, under its express power to enforce that amendment, by appropriate legislation, may erect laws to protect that people against deprivations *because of their race* (emphasis added).[33]

As such, Justice Harlan argued that Congress was within its rights to enact the Civil Rights Act of 1875.

The final blow to civil rights in the nineteenth century came with another Supreme Court decision, *Plessy v. Ferguson*, which established in 1896 the doctrine of "separate but equal."[34] Rejecting the appeal of a man of mixed descent ("seven eighths Caucasian and one eighth African"), the Court asserted that, "If the two races are to meet upon terms of social equality, it must be the result of natural affinities, a mutual appreciation of each other's merits and a voluntary consent of individuals...Legislation is powerless to eradicate racial instincts or to abolish distinctions based on physical differences, and the attempt to do so can only result in accentuating the difficulties of the present situation."[35] The Court then held that a Louisiana law that provided for "equal but separate accommodations for the white, and colored races" was constitutional.[36] Once again, Justice Harlan spoke out against the majority. In a powerful dissent, Justice Harlan argued that in view of the Constitution and

> in the eye of the law, there is in this country no superior, dominant, ruling class of citizens. There is no caste there. Our Constitution is color-blind, and neither knows nor tolerates classes among citizens...The destinies of the two races [are] indissolubly linked together, and the interests of both require that the common government of all shall not permit the seeds of race hate to be planted under the sanction of law...The thin disguise of "equal" accommodations for passengers in railroad coaches will not mislead anyone, nor atone for the wrong this day done.[37]

The rule of law articulated in *Plessy* was undisturbed for over fifty years before Justice Harlan's words were finally vindicated.

The era of *Plessy* was brought to an abrupt halt by *Brown v. Board of Education* in 1954. In this case, plaintiffs from Kansas, South Carolina, Virginia, and Delaware contended that segregated public schools were not "equal" and could not be made "equal."[38] Delivering the majority opinion, Chief Justice Warren concluded that "in the field of public education the doctrine of 'separate but equal' has no place," that separate educational facilities are "inherently unequal."[39] The Court restricted its landmark decision to education, but was unequivocal in its announcement that such "segregation is a denial of the equal protection of the laws."[40]

Congress finally revived civil rights legislative activity in the late 1950s. First, there was the Civil Rights Act of 1957[41] and the Civil Rights Act of 1960,[42] which expanded remedies for racial discrimination in the context of voting. The first modern comprehensive civil rights law since the Reconstruction, however, was the Civil Rights Act of 1964.[43] With provisions similar to the Civil Rights Act of 1875, there was one significant difference. Unlike the nineteenth-century legislation that was enacted using legislative power obtained through the Fourteenth Amendment, the 1964 Act was tied to the regulatory power granted by virtue of the interstate commerce clause of the Constitution.[44] Key aspects of this law included Titles I and VIII regarding voting rights, Titles III and IV dealing with desegregation in schools and other public facilities, and Title VII prohibiting employment discrimination.

In the period between 1964 and the late 1980s when *Dessa Rose* and *Beloved* were first published, there were several significant events relating to the continuing campaign to enforce laws ensuring civil rights for all citizens. Some of the more momentous events included Martin Luther King's voting rights campaign in Alabama and his march to Montgomery, the assassination of Malcolm X, and rioting in the Watts section of Los Angeles all in 1965, the formation of the Black Panther Party in 1966, and the assassination of Martin Luther King in Memphis, Tennessee, in 1968.[45] Notwithstanding these advances, however, as prodemocratic litigation flourished, a backlash began with some arguing that affirmative action had gone too far, thereby creating reverse discrimination. In 1978, in *Regents of the University of California v. Bakke*, an unsuccessful white applicant to the Medical School of the University of California at Davis challenged the school's policy of reserving a specific number of places for minority students. The court held that this policy was unlawful, but that the state had a substantial interest that legitimately may be served by an admissions program that considered race and ethnic origin.[46] The kinds of issues raised in *Bakke* are the source of ongoing litigation, as educators attempt to decide if race should be a factor in the admissions process. *Bakke* continues to be the source of bitterness and was even cited by James Baldwin as a gloomy sign of the state of race relations.*

Nevertheless, the law has come a long way since the founding fathers wrote slavery into the Constitution. Even though modern civil rights laws have not yielded and are not likely to yield racial equality in the United States, narratives like *Dessa Rose* and *Beloved* help to highlight the effects of racist laws and raise questions about the nature of justice.

DESSA ROSE: THE NECESSITY OF SISTERHOOD

In *Dessa Rose*, Sherley Anne Williams has created a "place in the American past" where she can "go and be free" (Author's Note, *DR*, x). She breathes "wonderful life into the bare bones of the past"[47] as she demonstrates that "slavery eliminated neither heroism nor love" (Author's Note, *DR* x). Part of the motivation for this endeavor was her outrage about William Styron's critically acclaimed 1966 novel, *The Confessions of Nat Turner*. Williams denounced the white Southern novelist's work, saying that it "travestied the as-told-to memoir of slave revolt leader Nat Turner" (Author's Note, *DR*, ix). Williams's retort to Styron began with her short story "Meditations on History" which she later elaborated into *Dessa Rose*.[48] Her novel is a counternarrative that taps the "moral energy generated by revisiting the slave past."[49] By building on a slave narrative, Williams also seeks to create certain cultural meanings and displace others. Unlike Styron, who has been accused of taking "away Turner's dignity and his love for his fellow slaves," Williams leaves those qualities in "her characters intact and even creates the potential" for interracial friendship.[50]

In the process of celebrating her characters' ultimate triumph over slavery, Williams's text denigrates the oppressive slave laws. Through Dessa Rose, a pregnant fugitive slave, and Ruth Elizabeth ("Rufel"), a plantation mistress, Williams lays bare the laws intended to keep slaves under strict control, details the reasons for Dessa Rose's violent

---

* *Conversations with James Baldwin*, 172. In his epilogue to his discussion about civil rights in the twentieth century, Lawrence Friedman also notes that the "white backlash...is not to be underestimated" and that even though progress is real, "so is rage and reaction" (*History of American Law*, 666–73).

rebellion, and offers hope for justice through interracial cooperation and friendship.

Inspired to write stories about "black women's struggles and their real triumphs" Williams was moved by Angela Davis's 1971 essay, "Reflections on the Black Woman's Role in the Community of Slaves" in *The Black Scholar*.[51] In her Author's Note to *Dessa Rose*, Williams informs her readers that her story is based on two historical incidents, which she learned about from reading Davis's essay and tracking the sources of Herbert Aptheker's *American Negro Slave Revolts* (1947) (ix).[52] With this legacy, Williams melds the two stories to create a powerful narrative about interracial friendship and rebellion against oppressive laws.

The first incident occurs in 1829 in Kentucky and involves a pregnant black woman who helped to lead an uprising on a coffle (a group of slaves chained together, generally destined for the slave market). She was apprehended, convicted, and sentenced to death. However, for "reasons of economy," capital punishment[53] was "mercifully" delayed until after the birth of her baby—rightful property of her owner. Aptheker elaborates a bit on the details of the August morning in which "two male slaves in a coffle of ninety men, women, and children recently bought in Maryland and being led to the South for sale, suddenly dropped their shackles...and began to deal blows to each other."[54] When William B. Petit, one of the three men "leading and guarding this valuable group of humans" "rushed in with his whip to compel them to desist," he realized that the men's shackles had been filed through.[55] According to a newspaper account, at "this moment, every negro was found to be perfectly at liberty."[56] Along with the guard who came to his aid, Petit was killed and Henry Gordon, a well-known slave trader, was attacked.[57] Gordon escaped, a posse was formed, and all of the slaves were recaptured. The six rebel leaders, including the pregnant woman, were sentenced to hang. On 25 May 1830, the woman was publically hanged after the birth of her child.[58] Consistent with Williams's theme of triumphant rebellion, the convicted "all maintained to the last, the utmost firmness and resignation to their fate. They severally addressed the assembled multitude, in which they attempted to justify the deed they had committed."[59]

Williams describes the second incident as involving "a white woman living on an isolated farm" who "was reported to have given sanctuary to runaway slaves" (Author's Note, *DR*, ix). Williams also located the historical basis for this in Aptheker's *Slave Revolts*. After an "outlaw" fugitive slave named Moses was captured in 1830, he divulged information to authorities that an "uprising was imminent" and that the "conspirators 'had arms & ammunition secreted.'"[60] Thereafter, arms were located in North Carolina in a place named by Moses "in possession of a white woman living in a very retired situation—also some meat, hid away & could not be accounted for— a child whom the party [of citizens] found a little way from the house, said that his mamy dressed victuals every day for 4 or 5 runaways, shewed the spot...where the meat was hid & where it was found."[61] Out of these two women Williams creates Dessa and Rufel, building on historical fact and inventing the rich, internal stories history does not record. The relationship that evolves between Dessa Rose and Rufel "allows them both to escape the roles and concepts of race and gender that antebellum society forced on them."[62] In so doing, Williams challenges nineteenth-century slave laws and offers hope for the future of improved race relations in the United States.

"You just asking for trouble":
The Effect of the Law in *Dessa Rose*

Even though the actual historical events upon which *Dessa Rose* is based happened in Kentucky and North Carolina in 1829–1830, Williams selected 1847 and Alabama as the setting for her novel.* Of course, it comes as no revelation that Alabama's slave law was, in terms of oppression, equal to that of North Carolina and Kentucky.

Like most states, the Alabama code contained a general perfunctory provision making cruel and unusual punishment of slaves an "offence against the public morals." Without further definition or elaboration, the law stated that "No cruel or unusual punishment shall be inflicted on any slave, and any master, or other person having charge of a slave," and provided that upon conviction, punishment would be "by a fine not less than fifty and not exceeding one thousand dollars" with the added proviso that such a defendant shall be "required

---

* Williams has not indicated why she selected this year or place for her novel. Henderson (288–89) and Walker (26–28) both compare the historical contexts of the production of "Meditations" (1970s) and *Dessa Rose* (1980s), as well as the fictional time setting of each (1829 and 1847, respectively). Note that inasmuch as the laws of Kentucky and North Carolina are discussed in detail in connection with *Incidents in the Life of a Slave Girl* and *Beloved*, Alabama law is the focus of this section.

to give security for his good behavior, for the space of twelve months."* Inasmuch as slaves were prohibited from presenting evidence against their masters, this provision was little more than something the state could point to while attempting to argue that slaves were treated humanely.[63]

Moreover, the law sanctioned and promoted the use of "patrols" to police African Americans living in Alabama. The law gave each patrol detachment wide latitude to "visit all negro quarters, all places suspected of entertaining unlawful assemblies of slaves or other disorderly persons unlawfully assembled" and to remove any such persons to the nearest justice of the peace to be "dealt with according to law."[64] Slaves found without a pass could be whipped, and runaways could be returned for rewards.[65] The law essentially gave roving groups of white men the right to "regulate"—terrorize—slaves and free blacks.

In the epilogue of *Dessa Rose* Williams makes this point clear: "*Negro can't live in peace under protection of law, got to have some white person to stand protection for us*" (259). *Dessa Rose* is replete with examples of the legal disparity between whites and blacks. Adam Nehemiah, the white historian who attempts to capitalize on his interviews with Dessa Rose, embodies the detachment of the law. As the author of *The Masters' Complete Guide to Dealing with Slaves and Other Dependents*, he is clearly a proponent of slavery on a philosophical and practical level. At work on a second book, *The Roots of Rebellion in the Slave Population and Some Means of Eradicating Them*, Nehemiah seeks to make mercenary use of his interviews with Dessa Rose. He attempts "to master Dessa in his reading of her character and his writing of her history," and that reading is an act of control that "has to do solely with assuming mastery over others."[66] Through Nehemiah, however, Williams continues her own mastery and revision of history. Williams

---

† Laws of the State of Alabama, Penal Code, Ch. VI, §1. It is interesting to note that in 1848, the year after the events in *Dessa Rose*, the Alabama legislature enacted a provision supplementing the "offences against the public morals." The law stated that it shall be the duty of every master or person having charge of slaves "to treat them with humanity, and provide for them necessary food and clothing; and if any master...shall fail to provide and furnish him, her or them with a sufficiency of healthy and substantial food and necessary clothing, he shall be subject to indictment therefor, and on conviction thereof, be punished by a fine, not less than twenty-five and not exceeding one thousand dollars" (Acts Passed at the First Biennial Session of the General Assembly of the State of Alabama, 103–4).

plays on the historical figure of Boston clergyman Nehemiah Adams (1806–1878) who, after visiting the South in 1854, reported that it was "deeply affecting to hear the slaves give thanks in their prayers that they have not been left like the heathen who know not God, but are raised, as it were, to heaven in their Christian privileges."[67]

Like his historical counterpart, Nehemiah's posture with Dessa Rose is akin to that of a judge writing an opinion: He is concerned merely with ascertaining a set of facts that can be interpreted in terms of a larger framework. It is important that in the course of his questioning, Nehemiah fails to see the connection between Dessa Rose's violent acts and her lapses into monologues about Kaine. A clear connection, however, is to be made between the injustice that Dessa Rose perceives and her resulting unlawful acts. After she describes seeing Kaine bleeding and near death, Nehemiah sharply rebukes Dessa Rose for her involvement with the murderous uprising against the trader. Like a dogged prosecutor, he merely wants to get to the bottom of who had the file that allegedly allowed members of the coffle to go free. When Dessa Rose defends Kaine, Nehemiah scowls, stops writing, and becomes frustrated at what he views as another irrelevant digression about "the young buck" (*DR*, 32). Ironically, he is blind to the roots that led to the deadly attack and, in turn, to Dessa Rose's retaliatory assault.

Again, Nehemiah's position is much like nineteenth-century law, which viewed slaves as property. Understanding the chain of events would have required Nehemiah's seeing Dessa Rose and Kaine as human beings, not assets. This was an inconceivable vision for one whose consciousness is steeped in the tradition that supported nineteenth-century slave laws designed to control human chattel. There was no leeway to indulge in human emotion under such laws, no legal defense for Dessa Rose's attack.

Likewise, when the plantation master murders Kaine, he presumably acts out of his "right" to handle his property as he sees fit. The attack is unprovoked by any act of violence by Kaine, who is summoned to the House. Presumably, Kaine's master is angry about the plantation mistress's enthusiasm for Kaine's banjo playing. The very act of playing the banjo is a gesture of independence and freedom for Kaine, who has learned to play from an African man (*DR*, 33). Kaine is taken with the idea that in Africa nobody "belongs to white folks" and makes the banjo himself (*DR*, 33–34). The master's smashing of the banjo is a symbolic attempt to break Kaine.

Frustrated, Kaine says, "Nigga can't do shit. Masa can step on a nigga hand, nigga heart, nigga life, and what can a nigga do? Nigga can't do shit" (*DR*, 34). The clever song Kaine makes out of this sentiment, along with his singing and laughing in defiance, is not appreciated by his master. Dessa Rose is later summoned to the nightmare of Kaine's cold, clammy body and crushed skull, while her master laughs at her.

Alabama law provided such wide latitude for masters to deal with their slaves that even the murder of a slave could be "justified" by a master so as to avoid any criminal liability. The penal code drew a distinction between homicides against whites and slaves. If an owner

> of any slave or slaves, shall cause the death of the slave, by cruel, barbarous, or inhuman whipping, beating, or by any other cruel, inhuman treatment, although with the intention to kill, or shall cause the death of any such slave by the use of an instrument in its nature calculated to produce death, though without intention to kill, *unless in self defence, or in the use of so much force as is necessary to procure obedience* on the part of the slave, such killing shall be deemed murder in the second degree. (emphasis added)*

Under all but the most extreme and wanton circumstances, a master could get away with murdering his slaves pursuant to the statutory defenses of self-defense and necessary force. In any event, a successful prosecution would be highly unlikely for lack of witnesses. Few, if any, white people would speak out against a plantation master, and the law prevented any slave from testifying "against any person, in any matter, cause, except in criminal cases, in which the evidence of one slave shall be admitted for or against another slave."[68] Simply stated, there could be no legal redress for Kaine's murder.

Dessa Rose may have "had no idea what 'court' was," but she certainly knows injustice at the most visceral level (*DR*, 53). Refusing to idly stand by and accept her lot, Dessa Rose undertakes her own form of justice by attacking her master and mistress. Williams's description and Dessa Rose's intense glee expose the deliberateness of the attack, even though she knows that if she had killed the white woman, the death sentence would have awaited her—albeit without the "due process" that was provided for by law. Under the separate

---

* Laws of the State of Alabama, Penal Code, Ch. III, §7. Note that such treatment by an overseer or manager was not afforded the "procure obedience" defense and that the act of a killing of a slave by anyone one else under similar circumstances was deemed first-degree murder. Laws of the State of Alabama, Penal Code, §§5–6.

penal code for crimes committed by blacks, the punishment for killing or assaulting a white person was capital punishment: "Every slave, who shall be guilty of murder, or commit an assault with an intent to kill any white person, or shall be guilty of the voluntary manslaughter of a white person, or of the involuntary manslaughter of a white person, in the prosecution of an unlawful act, and be convicted thereof, shall suffer death."[69]

Of course, there was no point for Dessa Rose's master in having her punished by death under the criminal justice system when he could as easily sell her away from his plantation for a profit. As such, the law actually prompts the master to undertake his own vigilante form of justice, "lashing her about the hips and legs" and branding Dessa Rose with an R along the insides of her thighs (*DR*, 143, 245). Her master is careful to focus his abuse on body parts that would not necessarily be seen by a slave trader, so as not to "impair her value." As if his point might not be sufficiently made, Dessa Rose is then placed in a sweatbox—a closed box in the sun used "for wilful darkies" and which contained a few breathing holes so that she might not suffocate (*DR*, 142). When she is finally let out, Dessa Rose's face is swollen, she is bloody and dirty, but she stands up. Momentarily quieted, but never crushed, Dessa Rose has withstood the beating with her resolve intact; her mere survival is a form of resistance. Even at a "bargain price…*because* she'd attacked her master," Dessa Rose is still a source of four hundred dollars in revenue (*DR*, 13, 143).

Dessa Rose's second, and most significant, act of rebellion as part of a coffle is based on the historical incident in Kentucky. While being transported to her new owner, Dessa Rose leads an uprising against a slave trader named Wilson. Again, an egregious yet lawful event precedes Dessa Rose's rebellion. After most in the camp are asleep, one of the drunken guards seeks out a mulatto girl named Linda and leads her into the bushes. Every night since Linda was purchased in Montgomery one of the white men has taken her into the bushes, prompting "pleas and pitiful whimperings" for help that go unanswered. In Alabama, as in other slave states, it was not a crime to rape a black woman. Nevertheless, it is easier for the guard to conjure up a story about a file used by one of the slaves to facilitate the uprising than to acknowledge that in his "lust and alcoholic daze" he had neglected to resecure the chains in Linda's group. Dessa Rose seizes on the opportunity to "kill as many of them as she could" (*DR*, 60). The result is horrifying: "Five white men had been killed. Wilson himself lost an arm. Thirty-one slaves had been killed or executed; nineteen branded or flogged; some thirty-eight thousand dollars in property destroyed or damaged" (*DR*, 14; also 10 and 23). When questioned about the mayhem and what the story of Kaine had to do with "trying to kill white men," Dessa Rose's response is most illustrative: "I kill white mens...I kill white mens cause the same reason Masa kill Kaine. Cause I can" (*DR*, 12, 13). At this point, Dessa Rose has nothing to lose; the law offered no real protection against the murder and rape of slaves. What the law did offer was protection for whites against blacks. The penalty for consulting or conspiring "to rebel or be in any wise concerned in an insurrection or rebellion of the slaves against the white inhabitants" of Alabama was death.[70] Like the circumstances surrounding her attack on her master and mistress, Dessa Rose is depicted as lashing out at the coffle guards because of the oppressive conditions of her life and those around her.

Without any sense of the proceedings in the novel, Dessa Rose is duly convicted, but due to the "extenuating circumstances" of her pregnancy, hanging is delayed (*DR*, 19, 24). Unlike her historical counterpart, however, Dessa Rose becomes a fugitive, eluding the death penalty and her "rightful owner." Just as her evening meal is delivered, three of Dessa Rose's friends free her from the makeshift jail cell. Sheriff Hughes gives up the search in the rain, but Nehemiah resolves, "the slut will not escape me. Sly bitch, smile at me, pretend—. She won't escape me" (*DR*, 72). Although the more stringent federal Fugitive Slave Act of 1850 had not yet gone into effect, Alabama had its own very liberal provisions for capturing suspected runaways: "All runaway slaves may be lawfully apprehended by any person, and carried before the next justice of the peace, who shall either commit them to the county jail, or send them to the owner, if known, who shall pay for every slave so taken up, the sum of six dollars to the persons apprehending him or her, and all reasonable costs and charges."[71] The patrols were likewise authorized to round up anyone suspected of being a runaway slave for a ten-dollar reward.[72] Lacking any semblance of due process, these laws sanctioned the wholesale rounding up of any black person suspected of being a runaway.

Like so many others, Dessa Rose runs because she does not want her baby to be enslaved (*DR*, 149). She is pregnant with Kaine's baby and knows from her lover's own words that "niggas just only belongs to white folks and that be's all. They don't belong to their mammas and daddies; not they sister, not they brother" (*DR*, 33). She knows that her master would freely sell any offspring, confident that more human property could easily be created. Dessa Rose even considers ways of killing her baby rather than allow it to be wrenched from her home (*DR*, 62). There may have been a law in the Alabama statute books that provided at least a five-year prison sentence for taking "any child under the age of twelve years" from its parent, but slaves knew the reality of their children being sold on economic whim or necessity.[73] This illusory law was merely a formality that proponents of slavery could cite in an attempt to codify the treatment of children under slavery.

At this point in Dessa Rose's narrative, it is important to point out that her acts are depicted as understandable under the circumstances. Her life as a slave has driven her to attack her owners and to join the coffle uprising. Dessa Rose is a product of her environment, reacting to a legal system that offers her no real protection. The fact that Dessa Rose kills because she can is tantamount to saying that this is an understandable outlet for the aggression that slavery has created. It is not difficult to see the dangerous societal implications of such ideas about "justice." The intersection between the lives of Dessa Rose and Rufel, however, takes this novel beyond the mere critique of slave law or the suggestion that violence might be an acceptable form of resistance. Their relationship paves the way for a discussion about the necessity of sisterhood and cooperation, "locating the power of female bonding at the heart of" the vision of a "transformed human community."[74]

The civil disobedience of Dessa Rose and Rufel imbue the novel with its concluding portrait of justice. Dessa Rose is a hunted fugitive in great jeopardy of recapture when her friends take her to the sanctuary of Rufel's plantation, Sutton's Glen. In what begins as an awkward allegiance, Dessa is joined by a white plantation mistress in her defiance of slavery. Out of her own need for self-preservation, Rufel violates the laws prohibiting any aid to runaway slaves. Abandoned by her gambling husband, Rufel and her slave, Mammy, run the plantation with the help of runaway slaves. Rufel's initial fears that she will be "denounced or arrested for harboring runaways" fades with time (*DR*, 116). Considered an offense against "property," the Alabama penal code provided a harsh penalty for harboring and concealing runaway slaves; upon conviction the offender shall "be fined not less than one hundred, and not more than one thousand dollars; or be imprisoned in the penitentiary not more than two years."[75] Rufel, however, is largely undaunted by the law. As their relationship develops, and Rufel learns more about Dessa Rose's escape, even though she "couldn't, of course, approve any slave's running away or an attack upon a master...something in her wanted to applaud the girl's will, the spunk that had made the action possible" (*DR*, 158). They are kindred spirits in their defiance of slave law.

Rufel not only breaks the law by harboring slaves; she also transgresses sexual boundaries by having an affair with Nathan, another runaway slave. Although there was no law against raping a black woman, Alabama law was unequivocal about a black man having sex with a white woman, stipulating that "Every slave, free negro or mulatto, who shall commit, or attempt to commit, the crime of rape on any white female, and be convicted thereof, shall suffer death."* Under the law, it was inconceivable that there could be consensual sex between a white woman and a black man. Rufel's acts, in contravention of this law, become an important statement about the righteousness of defying laws that are merely rooted in racial prejudice and stereotypes.

Dessa Rose and Rufel are both law breakers, gauging their actions by their internal sense of what is right, not by civil law. By the end of *Dessa Rose*, they are engaged in an ingenious money-making scheme that defrauds slave traders. They are collaborative outlaws who subvert the laws of slavery for their own purpose. At this point, what is important, however, is not so much their lawlessness but their commentary about slavery, race relations, and justice. When they are on the road, Dessa Rose thinks that there may come a time when she can "for*give*" but she doesn't think she is "set up to for*get*—the beatings, the selling, the killings" and the state of ignorance in which slaves were kept (*DR*, 227). Rufel believes that "if white folks knew slaves as she knew" Dessa Rose and Nathan, that there "wouldn't be no slavery" (*DR*, 231). That is, if people knew slaves as individuals, instead of as just "a pair of hands, stock, sometimes not even a name" they would know slavery was wrong (*DR*, 232). By the end of the novel, Rufel even acknowledges that she does not want to live around slavery any more, because she does not think she can "without speaking up" (*DR*, 239).

---

* Laws of the State of Alabama, Penal Code, Ch. XV, §3. It is worth noting the disparity between the penal code for whites and blacks: If a white man was convicted of raping a white woman, the punishment was life imprisonment (Laws of the State of Alabama, Penal Code, Ch. III, §14).

When Dessa Rose is confronted by the law in the final episode, Rufel's fidelity to her sentiments is tested. Nehemiah resurfaces, attempting to re-capture Dessa Rose, who is legally still a fugitive from "justice." When she resists, claiming to belong to Rufel, and then flees, Nehemiah invokes the law, yelling, "Stop her, someone...dangerous criminal, reward" (*DR*, 242). After she is taken to the jail, it becomes clear that Nehemiah has been hunting Dessa Rose since her escape. Periodically he has plucked black women off of the street in hopes of apprehending the source material for his book.* When Rufel arrives, she is greeted by the sheriff, who tells her, "This the law job. Ma'am, this darky cused of being a scaped criminal with a price on her head" (*DR*, 248). Nathan had told Rufel about "the scars, about the coffle, something about what the white folks" had done, and in the critical moment, Rufel defends Dessa Rose, protecting her from the power of the law.

As they leave the jail, Dessa Rose is presumably about to thank Rufel for saving her—a foreshadowing of the epilogue "...*got to have some white person to stand protection for us*" (*DR*, 259). She begins, "Mis'ess...Miz—" only to be met with a curt "My name Ruth...Ruth. I ain't your mistress" (*DR*, 255). But Rufel has been mispronouncing Dessa's name all along, calling her Odessa. Thus, Dessa Rose's response is almost comical, sassing back, "Well, if it come to that...my name Dessa, Dessa Rose. Ain't no *O* to it" (*DR*, 256). Through their resistance to slavery, to the law, they have become "testy" friends; Dessa Rose acknowledges, "I didn't hold nothing against her, not 'mistress,'" not Nathan, not ski" (*DR*, 256). Dessa Rose and Rufel part as close to equals as they can be in nineteenth-century southern America. They may not have been able to "hug each other, not on the streets, not in Acropolis, not even after dark" (*DR* 256), but "their relationship shows fiction correcting the failures of history."[76]

Dessa Rose's epilogue reinforces her respect for Rufel and the intended power of her story, which seeks a more just future. She says, "*Well*, this *the childrens have heard from our own lips. I hope they never have to pay what it cost us to own ourselfs. Mother, brother, sister, husband, friends...Oh, we have paid for our children's place in the world again and again...*" (*DR*, 260). These final words "invite readers of the novel to meditate on history, to

---

* Kekeh writes that the novel has successfully restored "the missing voice of the black woman slave and simultaneously disrupt[ed] the writing of the white male historian," (219).

consider the price that has repeatedly been paid to insure what freedoms her children enjoy."[77] Williams also seems to be saying that we should not only remember the past but also embrace the possibility of the future.* For *Dessa Rose*, as a twentieth-century text, that future is to recognize the value of interracial collaboration right now. Williams not only engraves the past "on the memory of the present" but also "on future generations that might otherwise succumb to the cultural amnesia that has begun to re-enslave us all in social and literary texts that impoverish our imagination."[78] The process of remembering is important to acknowledge the legal injustice of the past, and to use that knowledge to ensure that contemporary laws are administered fairly.

BELOVED: THE POWER OF THE INDIVIDUAL

Toni Morrison has been quite outspoken about the focus of her work: "I am not interested in indulging myself in some private, closed exercise of my imagination that fulfills only the obligation of my personal dreams—which is to say yes, the work must be political."[79] In *Beloved*, she attempts to shape and define a political consciousness about slavery for a twentieth-century audience. Dedicating her book to "Sixty Million and more," Morrison invokes the memory of the Middle Passage, "the four-hundred-year holocaust that wrenched tens of millions of Africans from" their homeland "in a disorganized and unimaginably monstrous fashion."[80] She "situates herself at the boundary of fantasy and realism," remembering the "collective tragedy that, as history, must be remembered and redeemed."[81] Through Sethe, Morrison critiques the horror of slave law and asserts that the ultimate power to overcome injustice lies within each individual.

Over a century removed from her subject matter, Morrison has historical distance from various nineteenth-century slave narratives, including Harriet Jacobs's *Incidents in the Life of a Slave Girl*. She has commented that such works were written for two reasons: "One: 'This is my historical life—my singular, special example that is

---

* This vision, however, is not always viewed as utopian. Porter acknowledges that where as "black and white people in *Dessa Rose* confront and transcend racial and class perceptions to become real to one another, the ending of the novel is not utopian" (264). Patricia Ferreira likewise views *Dessa Rose* as problematizing the "dynamic of power" as it relates to "privilege and authority among women"(15-20).

personal, but also represents the race.' Two: "I write this text to persuade other people—you, the reader, who is probably not black—that we are human beings worthy of God's grace and the immediate abandonment of slavery.'"[82] Using the story of Margaret Garner, Morrison builds on this tradition in *Beloved* and moves beyond the limitations of nineteenth-century works. Morrison has been viewed as writing in response to a variety of authors and, most notably, for endeavoring to "remodel" *Uncle Tom's Cabin*.[83] Both Stowe and Morrison wrote for political reasons, yet their "rhetorical modes" differ dramatically.[84] As Eileen Bender points out, Stowe used "the languages of empowerment, political oratory, and that of the 'bully pulpit,' the white Christian Church" to argue for the abolition of slavery.[85] By contrast, Morrison uses a "circuitous, multivocal, choral, and oral form" to set up a "rhetorical challenge to rules of order"—to the laws which supported slavery.[86] Morrison's purpose is "never simply to recapture the texture of a world gone by"; rather, she seeks to "explore and dramatize the complex interaction between the present in search of itself" and the past.[87] Because her imagination "transcends ideology and polemics,"[88] Morrison presents a much more complicated portrait of race and the effects of slavery than her historical counterpart.

Drawing on history, the effect of slave law in *Beloved* is depicted as producing tragic circumstances for the main character, Sethe. By using the technique of "rememory," Morrison creates an interior life for her character to "yield up a kind of truth" about slavery.[89] She demonstrates how Sethe's life as a slave drives her to kill her child. Pregnant, Sethe is subjected to sexual violations by those charged with the responsibility of overseeing the slaves; she then becomes a fugitive rather than subject her children to the horror of enslavement. Sethe, however, goes a step further than Stowe's Eliza and Harriet Jacobs's Linda. When Sethe believes that capture is imminent and that she will be returned to slavery with her children, she engages in the almost unthinkable act of killing her young daughter. Sethe's deliberate and desperate act is the direct result of her experience as a slave; she kills so her daughter will be spared abuse as a slave. Morrison raises questions about the degree to which murder might be justified. She tests the limits of her reader's willingness to stand by the laws that were used to maintain slavery and social order, even when they have driven a woman to commit infanticide. Sethe's response to slavery, however, is not uniformly met with approval. Morrison, herself, has commented on the complexity and paradoxical nature of the act, saying that it "was the right thing to do, but she had no right to do it... It was the *only* thing to do, but it was the wrong thing to do."⁹⁰ Moreover, in the text, both Sethe's mother-in-law, Baby Suggs, and another former slave, Ella, express their reservations about the act, undercutting the suggestion that the abuse Sethe suffered is sufficient to mitigate any criminal wrongdoing. By the end of *Beloved*, Sethe is transformed from a victim who commits criminal acts without regard to the law to a survivor and testament to the power of the individual to overcome the forces of oppression through internal fortitude.

THE STORY OF MARGARET GARNER

Margaret Garner's story provides a compelling basis for *Beloved*. When Morrison was an editor at Random House, she learned about Garner in connection with working on *The Black Book* (1974), a scrapbook of "the folk journey of Black America."⁹¹ Morrison was "obsessed by two or three little fragments of stories," including an 1851 newspaper clipping.⁹² In Morrison's own recollection, the newspaper article "said that the Abolitionists made a great deal out of her case because she had escaped from Kentucky, I think, with her four children. She succeeded in killing one; she tried to kill two others. She hit them in the head with a shovel and they were wounded but they didn't die."⁹³ The other details Morrison recounts are, perhaps, most telling of why this story caught her attention:

> In the inked pictures of her she seemed a very quiet, very serene-looking woman and everyone who interviewed her remarked about her serenity and tranquility. She said, "I will not let those children live how I have lived." She had run off into a little woodshed right outside her house to kill them because she had been caught as a fugitive. And she had made up her mind that they would not suffer the way that she had and it was better for them to die. And her mother-in-law was in the house at the same time and she said, "I watched her and I neither encouraged her nor discouraged her."⁹⁴

Morrison was inspired by Garner, who "loved something other than herself so much" that "she would not see them sullied" by slavery.⁹⁵

There is a quiet majesty in this recollection, yet Morrison resists presenting Garner (through the fictionalized Sethe) as an idealized mother. The life Morrison creates for Sethe provides a much more complicated portrait of a woman who would break the law to save her children. Other accounts of Margaret Garner's ordeal are equally compelling. In *Reminiscences*, the president of the Underground Railroad, Levi Coffin, used Garner's story to illustrate the harshness of the Fugitive Slave Law.[96] According to Coffin, along with several other slaves, Garner escaped with her four children from her master's Kentucky plantation in the snow in January 1856. In Ohio, the fugitives fought against slave catchers, but when Garner saw "that their hopes of freedom were vain, seized a butcher knife that lay on the table, and with one stroke cut the throat of her little daughter, whom she probably loved the best. She then attempted to take the life of the other children and to kill herself, but she was overpowered and hampered before she could complete her desperate work."[97] Garner and her cohorts were arrested as runaways under federal law, the Fugitive Slave Act of 1850.

By nineteenth-century standards, this high-profile case attracted media coverage in the *Cincinnati Daily Enquirer,* and the courtroom was crowded. As Coffin notes, the "case seemed to stir every heart that was alive with the emotions of humanity." He remarks, "interest manifested by all classes was not so much for the legal principles involved as for the mute instincts that mold every human heart—the undying love of freedom that is planted in every breast—the resolve to die rather than submit to a life of degradation and bondage."[98] The matter was heard by a commissioner appointed under the provisions of the 1850 Act to hear such matters.[99] During the two-week trial in Ohio, Garner's defense attorney, Mr. Jolliffe, argued, in part, that she had been brought to Ohio by her owners a number of years earlier to act as a nurse. Because the law provided that "liberated slaves who were brought into free States by the consent of their masters" were free, Garner should have been free as a result of the Ohio trip.[100] Accordingly, all of Garner's children—who were born after the trip to Ohio—would follow the condition of their mother and, likewise, be free.

During the trial, the legal issues became much more complicated. Warrants were issued by Ohio authorities charging Garner with murder and the others of complicity in murder. The commissioner sought to defer these charges until the fugitive matter was disposed of, which would take the defendants out of his jurisdiction. Jolliffe, however, sought to turn the additional charges to his client's advantage. He argued that "the fugitives" had assured him that they would rather "*go singing to the gallows* rather than be returned to slavery." In so doing, Jolliffe sought to take advantage of a somewhat obscure provision of the Fugitive Slave Act which provided that if the defendants were returned to Kentucky no warrant could be served upon them.[101] In a novel use of the First Amendment, Jolliffe then asserted that the Fugitive Slave Act of 1850 was unconstitutional. In an impassioned argument, he asserted that the Constitution "'expressly declared that Congress should pass no law prescribing any form of religion or preventing the free exercise thereof. If Congress could not pass any law requiring you to worship God, still less could they pass one requiring you to carry fuel to hell.'"[102] Unfortunately, the defendants were not permitted to testify in their defense and could not recount their personal experiences in this hell; in accordance with the 1850 Act no testimony of the fugitives could be admitted into evidence.[103] Garner, however, was permitted to speak briefly on behalf of her children. She confirmed that she had been in Ohio previously with her owners and that her three children were born after that Ohio visit.[104]

The argument was unsuccessful; the commissioner decided that "a voluntary return to slavery, after a visit to a free State, re-attached the conditions of slavery, and that the fugitives were legally slaves at the time of their escape."[105] Remanding the defendants back to slavery, he rejected the "touching appeals...of eloquent pleadings." Like so many judges he rejected the appeal to his humanity and opted to hide behind the law which "made it a question of property."[106]

Enlisted by Jolliffe to speak out and act as a guardian for Garner's children, abolitionist Lucy Stone also attempted to advocate on Garner's behalf. She had earlier visited Garner in prison and allegedly "beseeched the jailor to give the slave mother a knife to kill herself, as the women preferred death to a life of slavery."[107] An eloquent orator, Stone made a speech in Garner's behalf at trial:

> The faded faces of the negro children tell too plainly to what degradation female slaves submit. Rather than give her little daughter back to that life, she killed it. If in her deep maternal love she felt the impulse to send her child back to God to save it from coming woe, who shall say she had no right to do so?...With my own teeth I would tear open my veins and let the earth drink my blood rather than wear the chains of slavery. How then could I blame her for wishing her child to find freedom with God and the angels, where no chains are?[108]

Stone also appealed to Garner's owner to release her, telling him "that these were *heroic* times, and that this *heroic* action of his slave might send his name to posterity as her oppressor—or if he chose—as the generous giver of her freedom" (emphasis added).[109] All of these efforts were unsuccessful.[110]

Ultimately, the fugitives were delivered to their owners and nothing came of the murder charges. It was reported that, on the way down the river, Garner "sprang from the boat into the water with her babe in her arms," that she was seized, but the child drowned. Margaret Garner was, as her attorney characterized it, lost in the "'seething hell of slavery.'"[111]

It was this story about Margaret Garner that inspired Morrison. It is important to remember, however, that even though Morrison "did research about a lot of things in this book [*Beloved*] in order to narrow it, to make it narrow and deep" she "did not do much research on Margaret Garner other than the obvious stuff" because she "wanted to invent her life."[112] Morrison explains this as freeing her to "be accessible to anything the characters had to say about it" and that recording Garner's "life as lived" might restrict the creative process from pertinent development of the story.[113]

A BRIEF HISTORY OF SLAVE LAWS IN KENTUCKY

As with *Incidents in the Life of a Slave Girl* and *Dessa Rose*, state law forms an important backdrop in understanding the oppression expressed in *Beloved*. A brief excursion into Kentucky law sketches the historical legal context for Sethe's acts. Kentucky's system of laws grew out of those of its "mother state," Virginia. In fact, Kentucky's first constitution in 1792 provided that, with certain restrictions, "all laws then in force, in the State of Virginia, not inconsistent with the Constitution...should be in force here, until altered or repealed by the Legislature."[114] Article IX specifically addressed the issue of slavery. First, and foremost, it protected the rights of slaveholders, providing that the "legislature shall have no power to pass laws for the emancipation of slaves without the consent of their owners, or without paying their owners."[115] In a surprisingly benevolent gesture, the constitution gave the legislature "full power to pass such laws as may be necessary, to oblige the owners of slaves to treat them with humanity, to provide for them necessary clothing and provisions, to abstain from all injuries to them extending to life or limb, and in case of their neglect, or refusal to comply with the directions of such laws, to have such slave or slaves sold for the benefit of their owner or owners."[116]

Two years later, the Kentucky assembly drafted a law concerning the "importation and emancipation of slaves," but this law merely modified Virginia law.[117] The 1798 slave code, however, was much more comprehensive in scope. Chapter II provided for apprehending and securing runaways.[118] The power conferred was broad: "Any person may apprehend a servant or slave, suspected to be a runaway"; similar to federal fugitive acts, the statute exposed free African Americans to wrongful detention. Key provisions of chapter LXIII likewise circumscribed the actions of "Slaves, Free Negroes, Mulattoes and Indians." All nonwhite persons living in Kentucky were restricted by this statute. Section 2 provided that "No negro or mulatto shall be a witness, except in pleas of the commonwealth against negroes or mullatoes, or in civil pleas where negroes or mullatoes alone shall be parties."[119] This precluded slaves from testifying against their owners or any other white person, leaving slaves without any criminal or civil legal recourse for wrongful acts by their masters. Sections 3 and 4 prevented slaves from leaving their masters' property "without a pass, so some letter or token whereby it may appear that he is proceeding by authority from his master, employer or overseer."[120] Furthermore, the law provided that "it shall be lawful" to punish slaves traveling without such a writing with "ten lashes on his or her bare back, for every such offence." Section 5 prohibited such individuals from keeping or carrying "any gun, powder, shot, club, or other weapon whatsoever, offensive or defensive."[121] Lest there be any doubt about a slave's status, Kentucky law in 1798 deemed slaves "real estate" that "shall pass by the last will and testament of persons possessed thereof in the same manner...as landed property."[122] Each of these laws was designed to subdue and prevent slaves from gaining any power against their masters.

Slaveholders, however, feared that the 1798 Act did not offer them enough protection against possible aggressive acts by their slaves. Accordingly, on 25 January 1811, the legislature approved chapter CCXXXV, an Act "for the more effectual preventing of Crimes, Conspiracies and Insurrections of Slaves, free Negroes and Mullatoes, and for better government." The language of each section is reflective of the kinds of acts feared and provides for capital punishment:

> §1...if any negroes or other slaves shall at any time hereafter conspire to rebel or make insurrection, every such conspiring shall be adjudged and deemed felony, and the slave or slaves duly convicted shall suffer death.

§2...any slave or slaves shall hereafter be convicted of administering to any person or persons any poison or medicine, with the evil intent that death may thereupon ensue, such slave or slaves shall suffer death.

§3... any slave or slaves, free negro or mulatto, hereafter duly convicted of voluntary manslaughter, shall suffer death.

§4...any slave or slaves hereafter duly convicted of an attempt to commit a rape on the body of any *white* woman, such slave or slaves so convicted shall suffer death. (emphasis added)[123]

Moreover, the statute also provided that "any negro or other slaves" consulting or advising "the murder of any person or persons...shall be punished by any number of stripes not exceeding one hundred."[124] With the exception of willful murder, each of the penalties for the crimes was far in excess of that set forth for white individuals.

When the key events in *Beloved* occurred, the slave laws in Kentucky were essentially the same as these early legislative acts. An overview of these laws is illustrative and sets up the historical legal context for *Beloved.* For example, chapter XCIII of the Kentucky statutes sets forth a comprehensive compilation of the laws pertaining to "Slaves, Runaways, Free Negroes, and Emancipation." The law applied to all "negroes," including mulattoes, defined as persons having "one-fourth, or larger part of negro blood."[125] By this time, slaves were deemed "personal estate"; children of female slaves continued to "follow the condition of the mother" and be personal property of their mother's master.[126] Restrictions still existed with regard to slaves going at large and a separate penal code existed for crimes committed by "slaves and free negroes."[127] Even the constitutional provision requiring the "humane" treatment of slaves was codified in negative terms: "If the owner of any slave shall treat him cruelly and inhumanely, so as, in the opinion of a jury, to endanger the life or limb of such slave, or materially to affect his health, or shall not supply his slave with sufficient wholesome food and raiment, such slave shall be taken and sold for the benefit of the owner."[128] Under the law, "the petition of any person, verified by oath...setting forth, substantially, the ill treatment of a slave" would cause the owner to be summoned to appear.[129] As a practical matter, given the limitations against African Americans testifying in a court of law and the composition of juries as all white men, it is difficult to imagine a slave prevailing in such an action. Thus, the early preemancipation events in *Beloved* took place during one of the darkest times in Kentucky slave history.

"This *Is* a Story to Pass on": The Effect of Slave Law in Beloved

As a novelist with a political bent, Morrison uses Sethe to explore the concept of justice and the validity of law. In the coldest legal terms, Sethe is a fugitive slave who murders her daughter—property that belongs to the Garner estate—when she is confronted with being lawfully returned to her owner. Morrison asks her readers to scorn the law and to consider whether Sethe's acts are justified. Through her narrator, Morrison implicitly captures much of the basis of federal and Kentucky slave law: "White people believed that whatever the manners, under every dark skin was a jungle. Swift unnavigable waters, swinging screaming baboons, sleeping snakes, red gums ready for sweet white blood" (*B*, 198). Many of the restrictive codes were born out of fear. Designed to control slaves and prevent—or severely punish—any form of rebellion, these laws institutionalized racism. Through a series of flashback memories, the effect of these laws on Sethe and the other characters is readily apparent. Sethe relives the abuse she suffered on the Sweet Home plantation, her flight, the desperate murder of her daughter and, finally, life during Reconstruction. The law is inseparable from her experience and, likewise, makes an indelible impression on those around her.*

Sethe is thirteen years old when she becomes part of the "personal estate" of Mr. and Mrs. Garner, the owners of the Sweet Home plantation (*B*, 10). With "iron eyes and backbone to match"—not exactly the makings of submissiveness—Sethe is purchased as a gift for Mrs. Garner (*B*, 9). She joins five male slaves who vie for her attention but are never sexually aggressive. Mr. Garner prides himself on the way he treats his slaves, calling them the "Sweet Home men," the kind of men who could be trusted around women. Unlike the other slaveholders who claimed that "Ain't no nigger men," Garner boasts, "Now at Sweet Home, my niggers is men every one of them, Bought em thataway, raised them thataway. Men every one" (*B*, 11). This is Garner's way of saying that he treats his slaves with respect. He even trusts his men enough to allow them to hire themselves out. Such a practice was prohibited by Kentucky law, which provided that if the owner of a slave "shall permit him to go at large and hire himself out

---

* In the context of slave legal cases, Rockwood considers the narrative power of *Beloved* to advance "an understanding of the human and emotional toll slavery demanded" ("Retakings," 221).

for his own benefit...he shall be fined forty dollars for each offense."[130] Undaunted by the penalty associated with his acts, Garner even goes a step further. After his slave Halle Suggs earns enough money by "renting himself out all over the county" for "five years of Sundays," Garner allows Halle to purchase his mother, Baby Suggs, who is Mrs. Garner's slave (*B*, 23, 11).

Unaware that there was no legal sanction for slaves to be married, at fourteen, Sethe "selects" Halle to be her husband. Unlike many plantation owners, Garner resists the temptation of pairing Sethe with the best breeding choice and allows her to choose her mate. Sethe naively expects there to be a "preacher, some dancing, a party, a something" and wants "[t]wo pounds of currants in the cake...four whole sheep," the kind of reception where people are "still eating the next day" (*B*, 26, 59). When Sethe asks Mrs. Garner about "the next step" after she has accepted Halle's proposal, she is met with a disappointing response: Her mistress laughed a little and "touched Sethe on the head, saying, 'You are one sweet child'" (*B*, 26). Sethe soon realizes that "it wasn't going to be nothing," that the Garners "said it was all right for us to be husband and wife and that was it. All of it" (*B*, 59). The provisions at law regarding marriage did not apply to slaves. In spite of this lack of sanction, Sethe does piece together a makeshift wedding gown and Mrs. Garner gives her a pair of earrings as a wedding gift. Later, Sethe realizes that she had the "amazing luck of six whole years of marriage" to the man who "fathered every one of her children" (*B*, 23). She is also fortunate enough to have custody of all of her children; none have yet been sold off. As the narrator comments, "Everything rested on Garner being alive. Without his life, each of theirs fell into pieces" (*B*, 220).

After Garner's suicide, his benevolence is replaced by harsh legal reality: Sethe and the other slaves are merely chattel under the law; economic necessity changes the way of life at Sweet Home. First, Mrs. Garner immediately sells off one of the men to "the debts that surfaced the minute she was widowed" (*B*, 9). Second, the "schoolteacher arrived to put things in order" (*B*, 9). The schoolteacher takes liberties to the full extent of the law in dealing with Sethe and the remaining Sweet Home men. He beats Sixo "to show him that definitions belonged to the definers—not the defined" (*B*, 190). He also takes away the guns from the men; by law, if "any negro shall keep or carry a gun, or other deadly weapon, powder, or shot" the same could be "seized by any white person."[131] Later, the schoolteacher "broke three more

Sweet Home men and punched the glittering iron out of Sethe's eyes, leaving two open wells that did not reflect firelight" (B, 9). The other slaves are reminded that they each have a cash value. Paul D. hears "the men talking and for the first time [learned] his worth," not of his value as a laborer, but the "dollar value of his weight, his strength, his heart, his brain, his penis, and his future" (B, 226). The same slave traders remind the schoolteacher that Garner spoiled his slaves and that he even broke the law by letting the men hire themselves out. The schoolteacher easily succumbs to the prevailing treatment of slaves that Garner had steadfastly resisted. In short, "the schoolteacher broke into children what Garner had raised into men," (B, 220). It was not merely legal; it was promoted by the law.

The schoolteacher's liberal use of his legal power to control the Sweet Home slaves creates a defining moment in the text. Details, however, are especially important to fathom the difference between the largely benevolent treatment the slaves received from Garner and the latitude the law allowed a despotic overseer to exercise. Well into her third trimester of pregnancy, Sethe was assaulted by the schoolteacher and two nephews. Because she was still nursing her small daughter, Sethe's breasts were full of milk (B, 16). One nephew held Sethe down while his brother "nursed" on Sethe (B, 150). Over and over in the text, Sethe repeats the fact that they took her milk, recalling her disgust about the white boy with the "mossy teeth, an appetite" (B, 32). She never uses the word rape to describe what happened, but there is little doubt about the overall nature of the assault.[132] Taking her milk was merely an egregious insult to the injury already committed. Under Garner's successor, Sethe is subjected to the abominable behavior sanctioned by slavery.

In connection with this assault, it is telling of the law to remember that the standards of conduct were strikingly different for black and white Americans. If Sethe had been a white woman raped by a black man, her assailant would have faced the death penalty. Kentucky law provided that if any "free negro or slave be guilty of...rape committed upon a white woman, or the attempt to commit such rape...upon conviction shall suffer death."* By the very wording of the statute, it

---

* KY Rev. Stat., Ch. XCIII, Art. VII, §4. Cf. KY Rev. Stat., Ch.XXVIII, Art. IV, §4, which provided that a white man who "shall unlawfully and carnally know any white woman, against her will or consent, or by force, or whilst she is insensible, shall be guilty of rape, and shall be confined in the penitentiary from ten to twenty years."

was subject to broad application. There was, however, no legal prohibition against raping or attempting to rape a black woman.

Moreover, Sethe is not free from the schoolteacher's ability to retaliate against her for telling Lillian Garner what happened. Unable to speak because of a tumor in her neck, tears just roll down Mrs. Garner's face, but she continues to abdicate power over her slaves to the schoolmaster (*B*, 16-17). After learning that Sethe has told her mistress what had happened, the schoolteacher digs a hole for Sethe's pregnant belly "so as not to hurt the baby" and begins whipping Sethe with cowhide (*B*, 202 and 17). She feels like she had been "split in two" and accidentally bites off a piece of her tongue when they open up her back (*B*, 202). The beating leaves a wound shaped like a choke cherry tree on Sethe's back, one complete with a trunk split open. The tree becomes a scarred, ugly reminder of the question posed in the text— "How much is a nigger supposed to take? Tell me. How much?"—and the answer—"All he can...All he can" (*B*, 235).

The letter of Kentucky law may have prohibited cruel and inhumane treatment of a slave, but in practice, the highly subjective statute was merely ink on paper.* For all practical purposes, legal protection is unavailable to Sethe: Unable probably to read or write, she cannot not file a "petition"—as a black person, her word cannot be used as evidence against a white man, and, inasmuch as the only witnesses to the crime were also perpetrators, there was no one who would act on her behalf. Moreover, the "remedy" available under the statute would merely mean that Sethe would be sold, which opened up a whole array of negative possibilities at the hands of a slave trader.

The only "choices" available to Sethe are either to submit to the schoolteacher or to break the law. She chooses the latter, and in 1855, with her back slashed and her belly swollen, Sethe flees Sweet Home for Ohio, where her three other children are with their grandmother, Baby Suggs, and becomes a fugitive under Kentucky law and the Fugitive Slave Act of 1850. The schoolteacher "must have believed, what with her belly and her back, that she wasn't going anywhere" (*B*,

---

* KY Rev. Stat., Ch. XCIII, Art. VII, §2. KY Rev. Stat., CH. CVII, §1 provided "A slave, negro or Indian could be a witness in a case of the commonwealth for or against a slave, negro or Indian or in a civil case to which only negros or Indians are parties, but in no other case." This was a long-standing rule in Kentucky. See also Act of February 8, 1798, *Littell's Laws*, II:113, which provided that "No negro or mulatto shall be a witness, except in pleas of the commonwealth against negroes or mulattoes, or in civil pleas where negroes or mulattoes alone shall be parties."

228), but he is wrong. Nevertheless, both Federal and state law give the schoolteacher the power to pursue, apprehend, and return Sethe to Kentucky.[133] Sethe is valuable, "property that reproduced itself without cost" (B, 228), property that is carrying in her belly another part of the Garner estate. As part of his effort to "put the place aright" (B, 226) the schoolteacher seeks to capture Sethe and her four children and recoup some of the plantation losses.

Lest there be any doubt about the source of his authority to capture and return Sethe to slavery, the schoolteacher is described as "busting in...*with the law* and a shotgun (B, 43, emphasis added). When Sethe sees the four horsemen—the schoolteacher, one nephew, one slave catcher, and a sheriff—arrive at 124 Bluestone Road, she is squatting in the garden (B, 148, 163). Recognizing the schoolteacher's hat, she thinks, "No. No. Nono. Nonono. Simple. She just flew" (B, 163). Her instinct is unequivocal and law-breaking. She "collected every bit of life she had made, all the parts of her that were precious and fine and beautiful, and carried, pushed, dragged them through the veil, out, away, over there where no one could hurt them. Over there. Outside this place, where they could be safe" (B, 163). She "split to the woodshed" to take her children to a place where she believes they would be out of the reach of human horror (B, 158). The slave catchers survey the house, focusing finally on the shed, where the schoolteacher's worst fear comes true: "there was nothing to claim" (B, 149). It is a scene of human decimation: "two boys bled in the sawdust and dirt at the feet of a nigger woman holding a blood-soaked child to her chest with one hand and an infant by the heels in the other...she simply swung the baby toward the wall planks...the woman schoolteacher bragged about...gone wild, due to the mishandling of the nephew who'd overbeat her and made her cut and run" (B 149). Sethe has summoned all her strength to pick up a handsaw and "drag the teeth of that saw under the little chin; to feel the baby blood pump like oil in her hands; to hold her face so her head would stay on; to squeeze her so she could absorb, still, the death spasms that shot through that adored body, plump and sweet with life" (B, 251). There is no doubt about the deliberateness of her act or about her intent to kill.

Sethe's acts against her children are depicted as both a response to the Fugitive Slave Act (the "Misery") and as the direct result of the lack of legal protection for female slaves (B, 171). Like Harriet Jacobs, who sought to protect her daughter, Sethe "could never let it happen to her children" (B, 251). She has to protect her daughter from what Sethe saw perpetrated against herself and others:*

> Whites might dirty *her* all right, but not her best thing, her beautiful, magical best thing—the part of her that was clean. No undreamable dreams about whether the headless, feetless torso hanging in the tree with a sign on it was her husband or Paul A; whether the bubbling-hot girls in the colored-school fire set by patriots included her daughter; whether a gang of whites invaded her daughter's private parts, soiled her daughter's thighs and drew her out of the wagon. *She* might have to work in the slaughterhouse yard, but not her daughter. (B, 251)

The one life Sethe cannot give or guarantee her children is one of freedom. Sethe believes "that what she has done was right because it came from true love" (B, 251). In her judgment it is better to murder her daughter than to return to slavery, where the child might be physically and mentally abused. Unlike Margaret Garner, however, Sethe is not sent back into slavery. She spends some time in jail, and her case is big news in Cincinnati, but it is unclear what legal action is taken against Sethe.

---

* Sethe's extreme and controversial reaction to her experiences under slave law are also generally connected to the harm suffered by others at Sweet Home. The arrival of one of the "Sweet Home men," Paul D., eighteen years after Sethe fled, explains why Halle never joined Sethe and his children. Sethe is initially outraged when she learns that Halle apparently watched the schoolteacher's assault on her. Powerless to intervene, what he saw happening in the barn "broke him like a twig" (B, 68). The last time Paul D. saw Halle, he was sitting by the churn with butter all over his face, a broken man. With a bit in his mouth, Paul D. himself was unable to offer any solace to his friend (B, 69). After the schoolteacher sold him to a man named Brandywine, Paul D. suffered his own personal hell. Shackled to a coffle, Brandywine was leading Paul D. in a coffle with ten others through Kentucky into Virginia. Angered about what had happened to each of the other Sweet Home men, Paul D. lashed out, attempting to kill Brandywine (B, 106). Later in prison in Alfred, Georgia, Paul D. and the other prisoners were forced to fellate the guards in exchange for breakfast (B, 107–8, 111). A fugitive himself five times over, because of his dark skin and hair Paul D. was never able to escape successfully. By the time he shows up at Sethe's house, Paul D. has compartmentalized all of his bad memories in a "tobacco tin lodged in his chest" that "nothing in this world could pry" open (B, 113). Moreover, Paul D. recalls a "witless colored woman" that he saw "jailed and hanged for stealing ducks she believed were her own babies" (B, 66). As Paul D. thinks as he is talking to Sethe, "For a used-to-be slave woman to love anything that much was dangerous, especially if it was her children she had settled on to love" (B, 45). (In "Figurations of Rape and the Supernatural in *Beloved*," Pamela E. Barnett explores Paul D.'s experiences in depth.)

By giving Sethe such a self-righteous stance, Morrison begins to advance the argument that Sethe should, perhaps, not be held accountable for the murder. Sethe is ostensibly so scarred by the schoolteacher's reprehensible acts that she is justified in killing her daughter and badly injuring her sons. Like the Garner case, the abolitionists "managed to turn infanticide and the cry of savagery around, and build a further case for abolishing slavery" (*B*, 260). Morrison, however, stops just short of embracing this position. To fully exonerate Sethe from the crime would be tantamount to acknowledging that she has dominion over her children's bodies.[134] Indeed, it is this point that makes Sethe's acts so problematic. Like the masters who asserted ownership of their slaves, Sethe "sees her children as property."[135] Because she "does not differentiate her children from herself" Sethe believes that she has the right to murder them and "claims the right to *be* the primal mother."[136] In addition to having troubling social consequences, the act of killing one's child is simply too extreme to be left without any censure. When questioned about the ethics of Sethe's action, Morrison responded, "I got to a point where in asking myself who could judge Sethe adequately, since I couldn't, and nobody else that knew her could, really, I felt the only person who could judge her would be the daughter she killed."[137] Beloved's presence is far from supportive of her mother's decision. In fact, it appears as if Beloved is slowly killing Sethe, because as Beloved grew larger, Sethe grew smaller, as if Beloved were making Sethe pay for her actions. If Beloved were acting as Sethe's jury, a conviction would surely be forthcoming.

Moreover, Sethe's violence is not celebrated as "just" by the other characters in *Beloved.* Her damaging experiences are poignantly echoed by two other women in the text who have also suffered under slavery, yet they do not condone the murder.* Baby Suggs, Sethe's mother-in-law, was used as a breeder woman; she had eight children by six fathers (*B*, 23). Four were taken from her—including two girls "neither of whom had their adult teeth—and the other four became fugitives" (*B*, 5, 23). Baby Suggs "coupled" with a straw boss for four months "in exchange for keeping her third child, a boy, with her—

---

* A number of critics view Sethe as acting as a primal mother. Christian writes, "Sethe's killing...is not only the killing of that individual baby but also the collective anguish African women must have experienced when they realized their children were cut off forever" ("Fixing Methodologies," 369–70).

only to have him traded for lumber in the spring of the next year and to find herself pregnant" (*B*, 23). Abused and betrayed, she endured "sixty years of losing children to the people who chewed up her life and spit it out like a fishbone" (*B*, 177). At the end of her life, Baby Suggs claims that as each of her children died, she "felt each one go the very day and hour" (*B*, 8). Despite all of this, Baby Suggs, a holy voice in *Beloved*, "could not approve or condemn Sethe's rough choice"* (*B*, 180). Defeated by slavery, Baby Suggs's final words are, "Lay down your sword. This ain't a battle; it's a rout" (*B*, 244). The fact that Baby Suggs ultimately "descends from the legendary status that has defined her to become just another victim of slavery" is particularly "tragic because she clearly had the power not to adhere to such a fate."[138] Overwhelmed by the human toll of slavery, Baby Suggs still does not countenance her daughter-in-law's decision.

Likewise, Ella, a former slave, is also critical of Sethe. Ella "measured all atrocities against 'the lowest yet'"—her name for the father and son who repeatedly raped her (*B*, 256). These men "gave her a disgust for sex," and she is not able to find anything, no killing, kidnap, or rape, that compared to "the lowest yet." Ella may have "understood Sethe's rage in the shed," but she cannot comprehend "her reaction to it"; Ella thinks Sethe is "prideful, misdirected, and...too complicated (*B*, 256). When Sethe is released from jail, "Ella junked her and wouldn't give her the time of day" (*B* 257). This is a bit ironic coming from a woman who was herself directly responsible for her own child's death. Ella "had delivered, but refused to nurse, a hairy white thing, fathered by 'the lowest yet'" (*B*, 258–59). After five days, the infant starved to death. Because she, too, has killed an innocent child, Ella's stance against Sethe is problematic, tinged with hypocrisy. Perhaps it is for this reason that Ella ultimately endeavors to rescue Sethe from Beloved's presence. Even though "Sethe's crime was staggering and her pride outstripped even that," Ella "could not countenance the possibility of sin moving in on the house, unleashed and sassy" (*B*, 256). Ella, thus, becomes Sethe's ally in opposition to Beloved's menacing presence.

The law maintained the harsh world that was endured by Sethe, Baby Suggs, Ella, and the other women in *Beloved*. What is most

---

* Baby Suggs, who is referred to as "holy" in the text (*B*, 138), is a moral center of the narrative. See Krumholz, who argues that Baby Suggs "is the moral and spiritual backbone of *Beloved*" (399), and Ball (90–95).

important about the effect of the law is that it created a power structure in which both owners and slaves acted inhumanely. At the close of the novel, it would be easy just to scorn the schoolteacher for his brutality or to disdain Sethe for killing her daughter. Such an analysis is too simplistic and fails to take into account the overall perversion of human behavior under slavery. During the nineteenth century, many reprehensible acts went largely unpunished by the judicial system. Through *Beloved*, Morrison offers a productive forum to consider a sampling of such acts.*

Intermixed with jurisprudential considerations of legal liability and moral culpability, however, is a glimpse of the possibility of a more positive future through interracial compassion and individual power to overcome adversity. Like Dessa Rose, at one point in the novel, Sethe must rely on the kindness of a white woman to survive. During her twenty-eight days of "freedom" as a fugitive, Sethe briefly has an encounter with Amy, a white woman, whose homespun philosophy helps to form the basis for the importance of remembering the ills of the past to correct the future. Massaging Sethe's swollen and cut feet, Amy tells Sethe "It's gonna hurt, now...Anything dead coming back to life hurts" (*B*, 35). It is also Amy who tells Sethe that "Can't nothing heal without pain" (*B*, 78). It is Amy who delivers Sethe's daughter Denver outside of the context of slavery. As the surviving daughter, who is named in honor of Amy, Denver becomes a hopeful symbol for the future of race relations.

Amy's metaphorical statements also take on a larger meaning much later in the text in connection with the return of Sethe's slain daughter, Beloved. The manifestation of Beloved and Sethe's demise become a reminder that an unresolved past can become all consuming: "Like all ghosts in literature, she embodies a fearful claim of the past upon the present, the past's desire to be recognized by, and even possess the living."[139]

Although not so developed as the relationship between Dessa Rose and Rufel, Sethe's encounter with Amy also helps to ease the mental pain of slavery. This is a detour into the kind of humanity possible between the races—despite the law.† Moreover, Sethe tries to take

---

* In his review of *Beloved*, Stanley Crouch takes a much more cynical view of the novel, suggesting that Morrison lacks "the courage to face the ambiguities of the human soul, which transcend race" (Crouch, "Aunt Medea," 43).

† Regarding reading *Beloved* and other works by Morrison to understand the racial turmoil in the United States, see Philip M. Weinstein, who contends that "*Beloved*

Baby Suggs' advice "to lay it all down, sword and shield" (*B*, 173), to move beyond her bitterness about slavery.

Ultimately, however, it is Paul D. who gives Sethe the most powerful advice for moving ahead. With great compassion, he reminds her that, "You are your best thing, Sethe. You are" (*B*, 273). This concluding moment in the narrative exalts the internal strength that Sethe must have to live. It says to Sethe and to others who have endured oppression that they have not merely survived; they have *prevailed* and can continue to rise above adversity. Because she is on the threshold of a place of resolution for the wrongs done—by herself and others—in the past, Sethe embodies hope for a more just future.†

CONCLUSION

Dessa Rose and *Beloved* confront the laws of the past, raise questions about culpability, and conclude with a glimpse of what it will take for justice in the future. Cornell West's insights about *Beloved* also have resonances in *Dessa Rose:* "*Beloved* can be construed as bringing together the loving yet critical affirmation of black humanity found in the best of black nationalist movements, the perennial hope against hope for transracial coalition in progressive movements, and the painful struggle for self-affirming sanity in a history in which the nihilistic threat *seems* insurmountable."[140] Dessa Rose and Sethe bear physical and psychological scars of slavery but, more importantly, by the end of their stories they are black feminist pioneers. As described by bell hooks, they are "no longer victimized, no longer unrecognized, no longer afraid"; they are courageous.[141] An essential feature of these texts is the moral foundation they present through what Robin West calls "nonverbal interactions."[142] The lesson that *Dessa Rose* and *Beloved* teach is that "we should attend to those nontextual and nonverbal interactions and the communities they create" to understand human spirituality and, in turn, justice.[143] As Toni Morrison acknowledges,

---

conducts perhaps the most powerful investigation in American literature of the subjective response to slavery as an impersonal institution" (176–77).

† See Otten, *The Crime of Innocence in the Fiction of Toni Morrison*, 81–98. Otten discusses the moral ambiguity and racial consciousness in Morrison's work in the context of "the paradoxical theme of losing innocence to achieve 'higher innocence'" (81).

"The past, until you confront it, until you live through it, keeps coming back in other forms."[144]

A key part of that future for modern readers is the consideration of the way that current laws are executed. Some legal scholars argue that the civil rights laws now in place are adequate to redress racial discrimination. The federal and state laws that drew a stark line between the treatment of white and African Americans, laws which deeply affect the characters in *Dessa Rose and Beloved,* are no longer on the books. Individuals who are discriminated against ostensibly have civil legal recourse to redress their grievances.* Much of the problem that exists today, however, is getting individual states, judges, and juries to take seriously claims based on racial discrimination. By analyzing the past and projecting the end of their novels into the future, Williams and Morrison offer contemporary audiences a deeper understanding about how unjust laws in the nineteenth century affected not merely enslaved African-American women, but the entire fabric of society. To combat the roots of racism that descend deeply into the history of the United States, the end of each work offers hope for the future. That hope, however, is contingent on understanding the injustice of the past, respecting people as individuals, and working together. Each of these elements is crucial for justice, which should "bear the mark of immersion in our culture and of a learned sensitivity toward the communities that have created a distinctive culture"[145]—in short, a legal system that delegitimizes racism and promotes humanity.

---

* The most recent legislation, the Civil Rights Act of 1991, 105 Stat. 1071, amended the Civil Rights Act of 1964 to strengthen and improve federal civil rights laws to provide for damages in cases of intentional employment discrimination, and to clarify provisions regarding disparate impact actions. Because it was enacted after the publication of *Dessa Rose* and *Beloved,* it is not discussed in this book.

❧ Conclusion ☙

Beyond the Rule of Law

> Unjust laws exist: shall we be content to obey them, or shall we endeavor to amend them, and obey them until we have succeeded, or shall we transgress them at once?
> —Henry David Thoreau, "Civil Disobedience"

The introduction to this book begins with an epigraph from Plato's *Crito*. Unjustly condemned to death, Socrates refused to take action that would save his life. Socrates believed that strict obedience to the rule of law was essential for a stable society. Even though he may have been wronged, Socrates concluded that he must adhere to the laws and authority of the state. A very different philosophy is presented by the stories of Anne Hutchinson, Nelema, Magawisca, Eliza, Linda Brent, Dessa Rose, and Sethe. Because story telling is "a moral act drawing audiences into a moral universe,"[1] their narratives create an eloquent forum in which to explore the concept of "justice" in the American legal system. Struggling between the poles of their own individual liberty and the prescribed social order, each of these women ultimately relies on an inner sense of justice that challenges the code of law, thereby underscoring the injustice of those laws.

The transcripts of the proceedings against Anne Hutchinson evidence that she was perceived as a potent force in the Massachusetts Bay Colony. Hutchinson preached religious ideas that ran directly counter to those of the majority. Undeterred by formal pressure to recant her beliefs, Hutchinson maintained steadfast fidelity to religious beliefs. Her defiance of Protestant orthodoxy and her insistence that conduct was irrelevant to a determination of who is saved was considered to be a social anathema. Such religious views could lead to an abdication of social responsibility in favor of unbridled individualism. Led by Governor Winthrop, community leaders feared that Hutchinson had the potential to undermine any existing cohesiveness, which was already threatened by life in a difficult environment. Because they believed that the colony could not withstand the social consequences of Hutchinson's ideas, an evolving legal system was used to silence and banish her.

A similar lesson is learned in Sedgwick's *Hope Leslie*, where the legal system is used to condemn Nelema and Magawisca for their fidelity to their Native American values. The Pequot Indians' fierce resistance to the colonists, and the resulting fear they generated, shaped emerging colonial law. Because the colonists did not understand Nelema's behavior, she was perceived as demonic and was prosecuted as a witch-like menace to the community. By virtue of the fact that her father is a fierce Pequot leader, Magawisca is an easy target for a charge of treachery. Like Hutchinson, by refusing to renounce her beliefs and failing to embrace the colonists' religious views, Magawisca is condemned in a court of law. Many early colonial laws were designed to control and suppress expressions of individualism that were perceived as promoting dissension. Ironically, over a hundred years later, Hutchinson, Nelema and Magawisca were ultimately vindicated by the First Amendment's protection of the free exercise of religion and speech.

Unfortunately, however, when the U.S. Constitution and the Bill of Rights became law, they did not protect the rights of African Americans. Quite to the contrary, U.S. federal and state law provided institutional support that legitimized slavery. Instead of having the protection of the law, slaves such as Eliza, Linda, Dessa Rose, and Sethe were subject to the harsh legal reality that they were human chattel. There was no legal protection available to them or to their children against rape, sexual abuse, and violence. *Uncle Tom's Cabin* and *Incidents in the Life of a Slave Girl* present the stories of Eliza and Linda Brent as caring mothers who defy slave laws through nonviolent means. These texts were designed to emphasize the devastating effects of slavery on families and to arouse a call to action against slave laws, especially the fugitive slave acts.

As twentieth-century texts written after the Civil Rights Movement, *Dessa Rose* and *Beloved* have a different focus. Based on historical events, these novels present a more detailed psychological portrait of slavery. Like their nineteenth-century counterparts, Dessa Rose and Sethe act according to their own code against the oppression of slavery.

Even so, because their acts involve violence, their stories raise disquieting jurisprudential questions about the extent to which violence is an acceptable form of resistence to injustice. Ultimately, however, Williams and Morrison seem to offer these brutal depictions of slavery as a way of understanding the past and promoting racial justice in the present.

There was no justice under civil law for any of the women considered here. Each in her own way refused to renounce her convictions and to submit to rules that would deny her freedom of belief and personal liberty. Each name summons an image of internal fortitude, perseverance, and acts—some admirable, some objectionable—that are beyond the rule of law. They answered to an inner truth, an instinctive moral code. Their voices make "eloquent the need for human justice"[2] that was so lacking in their experience. Unlike Socrates, they refused to submit to the dictate of the law. Instead, like Henry David Thoreau, they defended the individual conscience against the expediency of the law; moral law is superior to civil law. The bold acts of Anne Hutchinson, Nelema, Magawisca, Eliza, Linda Brent, Dessa Rose, and Sethe remind readers of the necessity to look critically at the social forces underlying the law's call to order. All of these women assume a revolutionary stance advocating radical social change. "After all, *radical* simply means 'grasping things at the root'"[3] —and here, that root is the law.

❖ NOTES ❖

INTRODUCTION: IN DEFIANCE OF THE LAW

1. Leon A. Higginbotham, Jr., *In the Matter of Color: Race and the American Legal Process: The Colonial Period* (New York: Oxford University Press, 1978), 13. Lawrence M. Friedman elaborates on this notion of law as social control in *American Law: An Introduction*, rev. and updated ed. (New York: W.W. Norton & Co., 1998), 17–28.
2. Eugene D. Genovese, *Roll, Jordan, Roll: The World the Slaves Made* (New York: Pantheon, 1972), 27.
3. Thomas Paine, *Common Sense*, 1776, in *Thomas Paine Reader*, ed. Michael Foot and Isaac Kramnick (New York: Penguin, 1997), 92. For law and literature commentary on this quote, see Robert A. Ferguson, *Law and Letters in American Culture* (Cambridge: Harvard University Press, 1984), 11–33; Barry R. Schaller, *A Vision of American Law: Judging Law, Literature, and the Stories We Tell* (Westport, CT: Praeger, 1997), 147.
4. Paine, *Common Sense*, 70.
5. James Boyd White, *The Legal Imagination* (Chicago: University of Chicago Press, 1973). In subsequent works, White has explored issues regarding legal rhetoric; see, for example, *Heracles' Bow: Essays on the Rhetoric and Poetics of the Law* (Madison: University of Wisconsin Press, 1985) and *Acts of Hope: Creating Authority in Literature, Law, and Politics* (Chicago: University of Chicago Press, 1995).
6. See Paul J. Heald, *Guide to Law and Literature for Teachers, Students, and Researchers* (Durham, NC: Duke University Press, 1998). For an overview of the law and literature movement, see Gary Minda, *Postmodern Legal Movements: Law and Jurisprudence at Century's End* (New York: New York University Press, 1995), 149–66.
7. See, for example, Richard Posner, *Law and Literature: A Misunderstood Relation* (Cambridge: Harvard University Press,

1988); Robin West, *Narrative, Authority, & Law* (Ann Arbor: University of Michigan Press, 1993); Richard H. Weisberg, *Poethics and Other Strategies of Law and Literature* (New York: Columbia University Press, 1992) and *The Failure of the Word: The Lawyer as Protagonist in Modern Fiction* (New Haven: Yale University Press, 1984); Stanley Fish, *Doing What Comes Naturally: Change, Rhetoric, and the Practice of Theory in Literary and Legal Studies* (Durham, NC: Duke University Press, 1989).

8. Brook Thomas, *American Literary Realism and the Failed Promise of Contract* (Berkeley: University of California Press, 1997) and *Cross-Examinations in Law and Literature: Cooper, Hawthorne, Stowe, and Melville* (Cambridge: Cambridge University Press, 1987); Robert A. Ferguson, *Law and Letters.*

9. See, for example, Milner S. Ball, *The Word and the Law* (Chicago: University of Chicago Press, 1993); Wai Chee Dimock, *Residues of Justice: Law, Literature and Philosophy* (Berkeley: University of California Press, 1996); Ian Ward, *Law and Literature: Possibilities and Perspectives* (Cambridge: Cambridge University Press, 1995); Theodore Ziolkowski, *The Mirror of Justice: Literary Reflections of Legal Crisis* (Princeton: Princeton University Press, 1997); Schaller, *A Vision of American Law*; Martha Nussbaum, *Poetic Justice: The Literary Imagination and Public Life* (Boston: Beacon, 1996); Martha Grace Duncan, *Romantic Outlaws, Beloved Prisons: Unconscious Meanings of Crime and Punishment* (New York: New York University Press, 1996).

10. See, for example, Peter Brooks and Paul Gewirtz, eds., *Law's Stories: Narrative and Rhetoric in Law* (New Haven: Yale University Press, 1996); Bruce L. Rockwood, *Law and Literature Perspectives* (New York: Peter Lang, 1996); Martin L. Friedland, *Rough Justice: Essays on Crime in Literature* (Toronto: University of Toronto Press, 1991); Carl S. Smith, John P. McWilliams, Jr., and Maxwell Bloomfield, eds., *Law and American Literature: A Collection of Essays* (New York: Knopf, 1982).

11. Louis Filler, *Slavery in the United States* (New Brunswick: Transaction Publishers, 1998); Fred R. Shapiro and Jane Garry, eds., *Trial and Error: An Oxford Anthology of Legal Stories* (New York: Oxford University Press, 1998); Jacqueline St. Joan and Annette Bennington McElhiney, eds., *Beyond Portia: Women, Law, and Literature in the United States* (Boston: Northeastern University Press, 1997); Lenora Ledwon, ed., *Law and Literature:*

Text and Theory (New York: Garland, 1996); Martha Minow, ed., *Family Matters: Readings on Family Lives and the Law* (New York: New Press, 1993).

12. Maria L. Ontiveros, "Fictionalizing Harassment: Disclosing the Truth," 93 *Michigan Law Review* 1373 (1995); Susan Sage Heinzelman and Zipporah Batshaw Wiseman, eds., *Representing Women: Law, Literature, and Feminism* (Durham, NC: Duke University Press, 1994); Lisa Weil, "Virginia Woolf's 'To the Lighthouse': Toward an Integrated Jurisprudence," 6 *Yale Journal of Law & Feminism* 1 (1994); Marie Ashe, "'Bad Mothers,' 'Good Lawyers,' and 'Legal Ethics,'" 81 *Georgetown Law Journal*, 25–33 (1993); Emily Hartigan, "From Righteousness to Beauty: Reflections on Poethics and Justice as Translation," 67 *Tulsa Law Review* 455–505 (1992); Judy Scales-Trent, "Using Literature in Law School: The Importance of Reading and Telling Stories," *Berkeley Women's Law Journal* 90 (1992); Anita L. Morse, "Pandora's Box: An Essay Review of American Law and Literature on Prostitution," 4 *Wisconsin Women's Law Journal*, 21–62 (1988).
13. James Boyd White, "Phi Beta Kappa Lecture," 4 May 1998, University of Georgia, Athens, GA.
14. Richard Posner, *Law and Literature*, rev. and enlarged edition (Cambridge: Harvard University Press, 1998), 7.
15. Robert M. Cover, *Narrative, Violence, and the Law: The Essays of Robert Cover*, edited by Martha Minow, Micheal Ryan, and Austin Sarat (Ann Arbor: University of Michigan Press, 1992).
16. Robin West, *Narrative, Authority, and Law*, 3.
17. Catharine A. MacKinnon, "Law's Stories as Reality and Politics," *Law's Stories: Narrative and Rhetoric in the Law*, edited by Peter Brooks and Paul Gewirtz (New Haven: Yale University Press, 1996), 237.
18. Robert W. Gordon, "Critical Legal Histories," *Stanford Law Review* 36 (January 1984): 58. Like the law and literature movement, there is no consensus about what constitutes the critical legal studies movement. The following books and collections of essays also discuss the parameters of thought raised by critical legal scholars: James Boyle, ed., *Critical Legal Studies* (Aldershot, England: Dartmouth, 1992); Andrew Altman, *Critical Legal Studies: A Liberal Critique* (Princeton: Princeton University Press, 1989); Mark Kelman, *A Guide to Critical Legal*

Studies (Cambridge: Harvard University Press, 1987); Peter Fitzpatrick and Alan Hunt, eds., *Critical Legal Studies* (New York: Basil Blackwell, 1987).

19. John H. Wigmore, "A List of Legal Novels," 2 *University of Illinois Law Review* 547 (1908): 579. Wigmore was also an authority on evidence.
20. Hannah Arendt, *Crisis of the Republic* (New York: Harcourt Brace Jovanovich, Inc., 1969), 75.

PART I: TESTING THE BOUNDS OF COLONIAL LAW

1. Winthrop, "A Modell of Christian Charity," 283.
2. James G. Moseley, *John Winthrop's World: History as a Story; The Story as History* (Madison: University of Wisconsin Press, 1992).
3. Darrett B. Rutman, *Winthrop's Boston: Portrait of a Puritan Town 1630-1649* (Chapel Hill: University of North Carolina Press, 1965).
4. Winthrop, "A Modell of Christian Charity," 283.
5. Nathaniel B. Shurtleff, M.D., ed., *Records of the Governor and Company of the Massachusetts Bay in North East,* vol. I 1628–1641 (Boston: William White, 1853), 12 (hereafter *Mass. Bay Records*).
6. Amy Schrager Lang, *Prophetic Woman: Anne Hutchinson and the Problem of Dissent in the Literature of New England* (Berkeley: University of California Press, 1987), 17.
7. Perry Miller, ed., *The American Puritans: Their Prose and Poetry* (New York: Columbia University Press, 1956), 49.
8. Kai T. Erikson, *Wayward Puritans: A Study in the Sociology of Deviance* (New York: John Wiley and Sons, Inc., 1966), 4. Erikson explores this idea of deviance from a sociological perspective using the theories of Emile Durkheim.

CHAPTER 1: THE LAW OF DIVINE REVELATION

1. Emery Battis, *Saints and Sectaries: Anne Hutchinson and the Antinomian Controversy in the Massachusetts Bay Colony* (Chapel Hill: University North Carolina Press, 1962), 219; George L. Haskins, *Law and Authority in Early Massachusetts: A Study in Tradition and Design* (New York: Macmillian Co., 1960), 49.
2. Selma R. Williams, *Divine Rebel: The Life of Anne Marbury Hutchinson* (New York: Holt, Rinehart and Winston, 1981), 12.

3. William Dunlea, *Anne Hutchinson and the Puritans: An Early American Tragedy* (Pittsburgh: Dorrance Publishing Co., Inc., 1993), 1–4; Selma Williams, *Divine Rebel*, 9–23.
4. Francis Marbury, "The Conference Between Me and the Bishop of London," c. 1590, *Notes and Documents on Rev. Francis Marbury*, edited by Frederick L. Gay (Boston: Massachusetts Historical Society, 1915), 283, 287.
5. Battis, *Saints and Sectaries*, 8.
6. John Denison Champlin, "Hutchinson Ancestry and Descendents of William and Anne Hutchinson," *N.Y. Genealogical and Biographical Record* 45 (1914): 167–68.
7. William G. McLoughlin, "Anne Hutchinson Reconsidered," *Rhode Island History* 49.1 (February 1991): 16; Battis, *Saints and Sectaries*, 44, 49–50. A number of authors discuss Cotton's reputation in England, including Selma Williams in *Divine Rebel*, 48–49, and Emery Battis in *Saints and Sectaries*, 15.
8. Albert Bushnell Hart, ed., *Commonwealth History of Massachusetts*, vol. 1 (New York: The States History Co., 1927), 137.
9. Edmund S. Morgan, *The Puritan Dilemma: The Story of John Winthrop* (Boston: Little, Brown and Co., 1958), 136.
10. For a discussion about Cotton's decision, see Larzar Ziff, *The Career of John Cotton: Puritanism and the American Experience* (Princeton: Princeton University Press, 1962), 65–70.
11. Wellington Newcomb, "Anne Hutchinson Versus Massachusetts," *American Heritage* XXV.4 (June 1974): 12–13.
12. Edmund Morgan, *The Puritan Dilemma*, 134.
13. Selma Williams, *Divine Rebel*, 79–82.
14. James F. Cooper, Jr., "Anne Hutchinson and the 'Lay Rebellion' Against the Clergy," *The New England Quarterly* LXI:3 (September 1988), 382; Edmund Morgan, *The Puritan Dilemma*, chapter 10; John Winthrop, *The Journal of John Winthrop*, edited by Richard S. Dunn, James Savage, and Laetitia Yeandle (Cambridge: Belknap Press of Harvard University Press, 1996), 193 n. 21.
15. Hart, *Commonwealth History of Massachusetts*, 310.
16. Norman Pettit, *The Heart Prepared: Grace and Conversion in Puritan Spiritual Life* (New Haven: Yale University Press, 1966), 142; James Cooper, "Anne Hutchinson and the 'Lay Rebellion,'" 383.
17. Perry Miller, *The New England Mind: From Colony to Providence* (Cambridge: Harvard University Press, 1953), 58.

18. Newcomb, "Anne Hutchinson versus Massachusetts," 14.
19. Hart, *Commonwealth History of Massachusetts*, 137.
20. McLoughlin, "Anne Hutchinson Reconsidered," 17.
21. Ibid.
22. Miller, *The New England Mind*, 59; Hart, *Commonwealth History of Massachusetts*, 138.
23. Miller, *The New England Mind* 59.
24. Edmund Morgan, *The Puritan Dilemma*, 7–8.
25. McLoughlin, "Anne Hutchinson Reconsidered," 17.
26. Lyle Koehler, *A Search for Power: The 'Weaker Sex' in Seventeen-Century New England* (Urbana: University of Illinois Press, 1980), 221.
27. Selma Williams, *Divine Rebel*, 4.
28. Ibid., 122–24.
29. Ziff, *The Career of John Cotton*, 118.
30. Shurtleff, *Mass. Bay Records*, 189.
31. Edmund Morgan, *The Puritan Dilemma*, 143.
32. Shurtleff, *Mass. Bay Records*, 3–19. For commentary on the charter, see Mark DeWolfe Howe, ed., *Readings in American Legal History* (Cambridge, Harvard University Press, 1949), 100.
33. Shurtleff, *Mass. Bay Records*, 10–11.
34. Ibid., 12 and 16.
35. Peter Charles Hoffer, *Law and People in Colonial America* (Baltimore: Johns Hopkins University Press, 1992), 19.
36. Howe, *Readings*, 108.
37. Howe, *Readings*, 108.
38. Shurtleff, *Mass. Bay Records*, 163, and Howe, *Readings*, 108.
39. Shurtleff, *Mass. Bay Records*, 169, and Howe, *Readings*, 109.
40. Howe, *Readings*, 110.
41. Shurtleff, *Mass. Bay Records*, 196.
42. Battis, *Saints and Sectaries*, 157.
43. Howe, *Readings*, 161.
44. Winthrop, *Winthrop Papers*, 422.
45. Ibid.
46. Shurtleff, *Mass. Bay Records*, 202–03.
47. George L. Haskins, "Law and Colonial Society," *Essays in the History of Early American Law*, edited by David H. Flaherty (Chapel Hill: University of North Carolina Press, 1969), 48.
48. For an elaboration and commentary on the reliance of early American Massachusetts courts on the Bible, see Bradley

Chapin, *Criminal Justice in Colonial America, 1606-1660* (Athens: University of Georgia Press, 1893), 17-19; David Thomas Konig, *Law and Society in Puritan Massachusetts: Essex County, 1629-1692* (Chapel Hill: University of North Carolina Press, 1979), 30-31; Haskins, *Law and Authority in Early Massachusetts*, 141-62.

49. Haskins, "Law and Colonial Society," 50.
50. George Francis Dow, *Every Day Life in the Massachusetts Bay Colony* (New York: Benjamin Blom, 1967), 199.
51. John D. Cushing, *Massachusetts Province Laws 1692-1699* (Wilmington, DE: Michael Glazier, Inc., 1978), vii.
52. Haskins, "Law and Colonial Society," 48-49.
53. Regarding the development of law that ensued in Massachusetts Bay Colony and elsewhere in New England, see Julius Goebel, Jr., "King's Law and Local Custom in Seventeenth Century New England," *31 Columbia Law Review* 416 (1931). Goebel also elaborates on the Biblical nature of that law (432-33).
54. Shurtleff, *Mass. Bay Records*, 174; for commentary about Cotton's involvement, see Ziff, *The Career of John Cotton*, 104.
55. John Cotton, "How far Moses Judicialls bind Massachusetts (An Abstract; or, the Laws of New England)" in *Proceedings of the Massachusetts Historical Society*, 2nd series, vol. XIV (Boston: Massachusetts Historical Society, 1903), 280-85. For more detail about Cotton's code, see Stephen Botein, *Early American Law and Society* (New York: Knopf, 1983), 25; Ziff, *The Career of John Cotton*, 104; Haskins, *Law and Authority in Early Massachusetts*, 125-27, 265 n. 63; Charles M. Andrews, *The Colonial Period of American History*, vol. I (New Haven: Yale University Press, 1934), 454-57.
56. Cushing, *Massachusetts Province Laws*, vii; Haskins, *Law and Authority in Early Massachusetts*, 124-31.
57. Cushing, *Massachusetts Province Laws*, vii; Dow, *Everyday Life in Massachusetts Bay Colony*, 200.
58. Dow, *Everyday Life in Massachusetts Bay Colony*, 200.
59. For a general overview of the law in early New England and a fairly comprehensive series of bibliographic notes, see Richard J. Ross, "The Legal Past of Early New England: Notes for the Study of Law, Legal Culture, and Intellectual History," *William and Mary Quarterly*, 3rd series, L.1 (Jan. 1993): 28-41.

60. Jean Cameron, *Anne Hutchinson Guilty or Not? A Closer Look at Her 'Trials'* (New York: Peter Lang, 1994), 96.
61. Ziff, *The Career of John Cotton*, 131.
62. Miller, *The New England Mind*, 56.
63. Battis, *Saints and Sectaries*, 167.
64. Charles Francis Adams, ed., introduction to *Antinomianism in the Colony of Massachusetts Bay, 1636–1638* (Boston: The Prince Society, 1894), 100–18; Battis, *Saints and Sectaries*, 166–67.
65. Battis, *Saints and Sectaries*, 107.
66. John Stetson Barry, *The History of Massachusetts: The Colonial Period* (Boston: Phillips, Sampson and Company, 1855), 247; Charles Francis Adams, *Three Episodes of Massachusetts History*, Vol. 1 (Boston: Houghton, Mifflin and Company, 1892), 394–95.
67. Edmund Morgan, *The Puritan Dilemma*, 147–48.
68. Rutman, *Winthrop's Boston*, 117–18.
69. Mary Beth Norton, *Founding Mothers and Fathers: Gendered Power and the Forming of American Society* (New York: Alfred A. Knopf, 1996); Ben Barker-Benfield, "Anne Hutchinson and the Puritan Attitude Toward Women," *Feminist Studies* 1:2 (Fall 1992): 65–96; Koehler, *A Search for Power* and "The Case of the American Jezibels: Anne Hutchinson and Female Agitation During the Years of Antinomian Turmoil, 1636–1640," *William and Mary Quarterly* XXX1 (1974): 55–78; Lang, *Prophetic Woman*.
70. See, e.g., Marcy Moran Heidish, *Witnesses* (Boston: Houghton Mifflin Co., 1980); Winnifred King Rugg, *Unafraid: A Life of Anne Hutchinson* (Freeport, NY: Books for Libraries Press, 1930); Helen Augur, *An American Jezebel: The Life of Anne Hutchinson* (New York: Brentano's, 1930).
71. See, e.g., Dunlea, *Anne Hutchinson and the Puritans*; Ann Kibbey, *The Interpretation of Material Shapes in Puritanism: A Study of Rhetoric, Prejudice, and Violence* (Cambridge University Press: Cambridge, 1986); Marlene Stein Wortman, ed., *Women in American Law: From Colonial Times to the New Deal*, vol. 1 (New York: Holmes and Meier, Pub., Inc., 1985); Selma Williams, *Divine Rebel*; Patricia Caldwell, "The Antinomian Language Controversy," *Harvard Theological Review* 69.3–4 (July–October 1976): 345; Louise M. Young, "Women's Place in American Politics: The Historical Perspective," *Journal of Politics* 38.3 (August 1976): 295; Eleanor Flexner, *Century of Struggle: The*

Woman's Rights Movement in the United States, rev. ed. (Cambridge: Harvard University Press, 1975); Deborah Crawford, *Four Women in a Violent Time* (New York: Crown Publishers, 1970); Perry Miller, *Orthodoxy in Massachusetts 1630-1650* (Gloucester, MA: Peter Smith, 1965) and *The New England Mind*; Erikson, *Wayward Puritans*; Reginald Pelham Bolton, *A Woman Misunderstood: Anne, Wife of William Hutchinson* (New York: Schoen Printing Company, 1931).

72. Cameron offers the most comprehensive look at the legal proceedings in *Anne Hutchinson, Guilty or Not?* For cursory legal analysis, see also Koehler, *A Search for Power*, 221-27; Herbert L. Osgood, *The American Colonies in the Seventeenth Century*, vol. I (New York: Macmillan Co., 1904), 188-89; Battis, *Saints and Sectaries*, 209-31.
73. Nathaniel Hawthorne, "Mrs. Hutchinson," 1830, in *Writings of Nathaniel Hawthorne* (New York: Library of America, 1982), 22-23.
74. Ibid., 23.
75. Selma Williams, *Divine Rebel*, 133.
76. Osgood, *The American Colonies*, 189.
77. Ibid.
78. Haskins, *Law and Authority in Early Massachusetts*, 49-50.
79. Battis, *Saints and Sectaries*, 221.
80. Botein, *Early American Law and Society*, 31.
81. Shurtleff, *Mass. Bay Records*, 174-75.
82. Titus 2:3-5.
83. 1 Corinthians 14:34, 35; see David D. Hall, ed., *The Antinomian Controversy, 1636-1638: A Documentary History*, 2nd ed. (Durham: Duke University Press, 1990), 316.
84. Wortman, *Women in American Law*, 107.
85. Rutman, *Winthrop's Boston*, 125.
86. Ziff, *The Career of John Cotton*, 135.
87. Wortman, *Women in American Law*, 107.
88. Ann Fairfax Withington and Jack Schwartz, "The Political Trial of Anne Hutchinson," *The New England Quarterly* LI.2 (June 1978): 237-38.
89. Marilyn J. Westerkamp, "Puritan Patriarch, and the Problem of Revelation," *Journal of Interdisciplinary History* xxiii.3 (Winter 1993): 580.
90. Ibid., 571.

91. Pettit, *The Heart Prepared*, 153.
92. Edmund Morgan, *The Puritan Dilemma*, 148.
93. Shurtleff, *Mass. Bay Records*, 211.
94. Ibid., 212–13.
95. Ibid., 213.
96. J.F. Maclear, "Anne Hutchinson and the Moralist Heresy," *The New England Quarterly* LIV.1 (March 1981): 87. Note the discussion in Maclear and in Hall, *AC*, 350, that there is some controversy about the accuracy of the transcript. Caldwell presents an interesting argument that Anne Hutchinson was "more than an out-and-out liar" in her discussion about the roots of the controversy (345–67).
97. Johan Winsser, "Mary Dyer and the 'Monster' Story," *Quaker History* 79.1 (1990): 23. For more elaboration on Mary Dyer, see Valerie Pearl and Morris Pearl, eds., "Governor John Winthrop on the Birth of the Antinomians' 'Monster': The Earliest Reports to Reach England and the Making of a Myth," *Proceedings of the Massachusetts Historical Society*, vol. CH (Boston: The Society, 1991), 21–37; Crawford, *Four Women in a Violent Time*; Carol F. Karlsen, *The Devil in the Shape of a Woman: Witchcraft in Colonial New England* (New York: W. W. Norton, 1987).
98. Battis, *Saints and Sectaries*, 247.
99. See Battis, *Saints and Sectaries*, Appendix VII, "Dr. John Clarke's Description of Mrs. Hutchinson's Hydatidiform Mole," 347–48.
100. Kibbey, *Interpretation of Material Shapes*, 113.
101. Newcomb, "Anne Hutchinson versus Massachusetts," 81.

CHAPTER 2: THE LAW OF THE GREAT SPIRIT

1. Nina Baym, *Woman's Fiction: A Guide to Novels by and about Women in America 1820–70*, 2nd ed. (Urbana: University of Illinois Press, 1993), 53.
2. Dana Nelson, "Sympathy as Strategy in Sedgwick's *Hope Leslie*," *The Culture of Sentiment: Race, Gender and Sentimentality in Nineteenth-Century America*, edited by Shirley Samuels (New York: Oxford University Press, 1992), 194.
3. T. Gregory Garvey, "Risking Reprisal: Catharine Sedgwick's *Hope Leslie* and the Legitimation of Public Action by Women," *American Transcendental Quarterly* 8.4 (Dec. 1994): 290.

4. Philip Gould, "Catharine Sedgwick's 'Recital' of the Pequot War," *American Literature* 66.4 (December 1994): 63, 65.
5. Catharine Maria Sedgwick, "Slavery in New England," *Bentley's Miscellany* 34 (1853): 417.
6. Ibid., 417-24.
7. Garvey, "Risking Reprisal," 288.
8. In a number of works, Mary Kelley gives a good overview of Sedgwick's life and the influence of her family. See her Introduction to *The Power of Her Sympathy* (Boston: Massachusetts Historical Society, 1993), 3-41; "Negotiating a Self: The Autobiography and Journals of Catharine Maria Sedgwick," *The New England Quarterly* 66.3 (Spring 1993): 366-97; "Catharine Maria Sedgwick, 1789-1867," *Legacy* 6.2 (Fall 1989): 43-50.
9. Edward Halsey Foster, *Catharine Maria Sedgwick* (New York: Twayne Publishers, 1974), 24-25.
10. Catharine Maria Sedgewick, *Life and Letters*, edited by Mary E. Dewey (New York: Harper and Brothers, 1871), 26.
11. Edward Foster, *Catharine Maria Sedgwick*, 25.
12. Ibid., 27.
13. Ibid., 28.
14. Ibid., 29; Steven Mintz, *A Prison of Expectations: The Family in Victoria Culture* (New York: New York University Press, 1983), 45.
15. Sedgewick, *Life and Letters*, 46-47.
16. Suzanne Gossett and Barbara Ann Bardes. "Women and Political Power in the Rupublic: Two Early American Novels," *Legacy* 2.2 (1985): 25.
17. Edward Foster, *Catharine Maria Sedgwick*, 26.
18. Ibid.
19. Theodore Sedgwick to Catharine Maria Sedgwick, 23 April 1806, Sedgwick III, Massachusetts Historical Society, reprinted in Kelley, Introduction to *The Power of Her Sympathy*, 21.
20. Edward Foster, *Catharine Maria Sedgwick*, 29.
21. Richard E. Welch, "Mumbet and Judge Sedgwick: A Footnote to the Early History of Massachusetts Justice," *The Boston Bar Journal* VII (January 1964): 14, quoted in Edward Foster, *Catharine Maria Sedgwick*, 29. See also the summary of events in Sedgwick, *The Power of Her Sympathy*, 125-26, and Arthur Zilversmit's detailed description of the legal proceedings in "Quolk Walker, Mumbet, and the Abolition of Slavery in

Massachusetts," *William and Mary Quarterly*, 3rd ser., 25.4 (Oct. 1968): 619–22.

22. Zilversmit, "Quok Walker," 622. For an analysis of the *Jennison* case and related matters, see Elaine MacEacheren, "Emancipation of Slavery in Massachusetts: A Reexamination, 1770–1790," *Journal of Negro History* 55 (Oct. 1970): 289–306; John D. Cushing, "The Cushing Court and the Abolition of Slavery in Massachusetts: More Notes on the Quock Walker Case," *The American Journal of Legal History* 5 (1961):118–44; and William O'Brien, "Did the Jennison Case Outlaw Slavery in Massachusetts?" *William and Mary Quarterly*, 3rd ser., 17 (April 1960): 219–41.
23. Edward Foster, *Catharine Maria Sedgwick*, 28.
24. Sara Cabot Sedgwick and Christina Sedgwick Maraquand, *Stockbridge: 1739-1939: A Chronicle* (Great Barrington, MA: 1939), 172.
25. Edward Foster, *Catharine Maria Sedgwick*, 30–31.
26. Michael Davitt Bell, "History and Romance Conventions in Catharine Maria Sedgwick's *Hope Leslie*," *American Quarterly* 22.1 (Spring 1970): 214.
27. Mintz, *A Prison of Expectations*, 167.
28. Richard D. Birdsall, "William Collen Bryant and Catharine Sedgwick–Their Debt to Berkshire," *New England Quarterly* 28:1 (March 1955), 365.
29. Edward Foster, *Catharine Maria Sedgwick*, 22.
30. Quoted in Gossett and Bardes, "Women and Political Power," 25.
31. Letter from Catharine Maria Sedgwick to Eliza Pomeroy, 1 December 1822, Sedgwick IV, Massachusetts Historical Society, quoted in Kelley, introduction to *Power*, 23.
32. Letter from Catharine Maria Sedgwick to Orville Dewey, 12 June 1842, in *Life and Letters*, 281–82.
33. Kelley, introduction to *Power*, 24.
34. Francis Jennings, *The Invasion of America: Indians, Colonialism, and the Cost of Conquest* (Chapel Hill: Institute of Early American History and Culture, 1975), 202.
35. John Winthrop, *The History of New England from 1630 to 1649*, edited by James Savage (New York: Arno Press, 1972), 190.
36. Shurtleff, *Mass. Bay Records*, 187.
37. Ibid., 190.

38. Ibid., 192.
39. Ibid.
40. Ibid., 196.
41. Ibid.
42. Ibid., 196–97.
43. Ibid., 197.
44. Edward Foster, *Catharine Maria Sedgwick*, 74.
45. Alfred A. Cave, "Whoe Killed John Stone? A Note on the Origins of the Pequot War," *William and Mary Quarterly*, 3rd ser., 49.3 (July 1992): 509. For more background on the Pequot war, see Jennings, *The Invasion of America*, 202–27; Moseley, *John Winthrop's World*, 70–84; Yasuhide Kawashina, *Puritan Justice and the Indian: White Man's Law in Massachusetts, 1630–1763* (Middletown, CT: Wesleyan University Press, 1986); Edward Johnson, *Johnson's Wonder-Working Providence, 1628–1651*, edited by J. Franklin Jameson (New York: Barnes and Noble, 1910); Steven T. Katz, "The Pequot War Reconsidered," *New England Quarterly* 64.2 (June 1991): 206–24.
46. John Mason, *A Brief History of the Pequot War* (1736) (Ann Arbor: March of America Facsimile Series, 1966), 8, quoted in Jennings, *The Invasion of America*, 221.
47. John Underhill, *Newes From America; Or, A New Experimentall Discoverie of New England* (London, 1638), quoted in Jennings, *The Invasion of America*, 223.
48. William Bradford, *Of Plymouth Plantation, 1620–1641* (1856) (New York: Random House, 1981), 331.
49. Edward Johnson, *Wonder-Working Providence*, 170.
50. Shurtleff, *Mass. Bay Records*, 204.
51. Sedgwick, *Life and Letters*, 91.
52. Sandra A. Zagarell, "Expanding 'America': Lydia Sigourney's Sketch of Connecticut, Catharine Maria Sedgwick's *Hope Leslie*," *Tulsa Studies in Women's Literature* 6 (1987): 235.
53. Edward Foster, *Catharine Maria Sedgwick*, 77.
54. For a general discussion about the trials of Nelema and Magawisca, see Garvey, "Risking Reprisal," 292–95.
55. Baym, *Women's Fiction*, 47.
56. Gossett and Bardes, "Women and Political Power," 19.
57. See Bell, "History and Romance in *Hope Leslie*," 218; Garvey, "Risking Reprisal," 297–98; Gossett and Bardes, "Women and Political Power," 22–23.

58. Karlsen, *The Devil in the Shape of a Woman*, 2.
59. Ibid., 2.
60. Ibid., 9.
61. Edward Johnson, *Wonder-Working*, 72. For more on Eliot's narratives of attempts to convert the Indians, see *Collections of the Massachusetts Historical Society*, vol. IV (Cambridge: Charles Folsom, 1834).
62. Lauren Berlant, "Fantasies of Utopia in *The Blithedale Romance*." *American Literary History* 1.1 (Spring 1989): 45–46.

PART II: OVERCOMING SLAVE LAW

1. Higginbotham, *In the Matter of Color*, 14. On the lack of legal protection for black women, see Maime E. Locke, "From Three-Fifths to Zero: Implication of the Constitution for African-American Women, 1787–1870," rpt. in *Women and the American Legal Order,* edited by Karen J. Maschke (New York: Garland, 1997), 263–75.
2. Genovese, *Roll, Jordan, Roll,* 25. For a critical legal studies perspective on slavery, see Tushnet, *The American Law of Slavery.*
3. Hazel V. Carby and Ann Douglas both consider the disparity between white and black women in nineteenth-century America. See Hazel V. Carby, *Reconstructing Womanhood: The Emergence of the Afro-American Woman Novelist* (New York: Oxford University Press, 1987), 20–39; Ann Douglas, *The Feminization of American Culture* (New York: Alfred A. Knopf, 1977), 80–120.
4. Bethany Veney, "The Narrative of Bethany Veney, A Slave Woman, 1889" rpt. in *Collected Black Women's Narratives* (The Schomburg Library of Nineteenth-Century Biography of Writers) (New York: Oxford University Press, 1988), 26.
5. Judy Scales-Trent, "Black Women and the Constitution: Finding our Place, Asserting our Rights," 24 *Harvard Civil Rights-Civil Liberties Law Review* 9 (1989): 27; Higginbotham, *In the Matter of Color*, 43, 58, 251.
6. Dorothy E. Roberts, "Racism and Patriarchy in the Meaning of Motherhood," *Mothers in Law: Feminist Theory and the Legal Regulation of Motherhood,* edited by Martha Albertson Fireman and Isabel Karpin (New York: Columbia University Press, 1995), 230. For more regarding the characterization of slave women as "Jezebel" or "Mammy" see Deborah Gray White, *Ar'n't I a*

Woman? Female Slaves in the Plantation South (New York: W.W. Norton, 1985); Frances S. Foster, Changing Concepts of the Black Woman," *Journal of Black Studies* 3.4 (June 1973): 433–54.
7. Genovese, *Within the Plantation Household*, 292.
8. See Gerda Lerner, ed., "The Case of Margaret Garner," *Black Women in White America: A Documentary History* (New York: Vintage Books, 1972), 287.
9. Trudier Harris, *Exorcising Blackness: Historical and Literary Lynching and Burning Rituals* (Bloomington: Indiana University Press, 1984), x.
10. Angela Y. Davis, *Women, Race, and Class* (New York: Random House, 1981), 19.

CHAPTER 3: PREEMANCIPATION ACTIVISM

1. Bert James Loewenberg and Ruth Bogin, eds., *Black Women in Nineteenth-Century American Life: Their Words, Their Thoughts, Their Feelings* (University Park: Pennsylvania State University, 1976), 329. Judy Scales-Trent uses this quote in "Black Women and the Constitution," to emphasize the destructive power of the law (27, n. 81).
2. Angela Y. Davis, *Women, Race & Class*, 30.
3. Barbara Welter, "The Cult of True Womanhood: 1820–1860," *American Quarterly* XVIII.2 (Summer 1966): 152.
4. Ruth H. Bloch, "American Feminine Ideals in Transition: The Rise of the Moral Mother, 1785–1815," *Feminist Studies* 4.2 (June 1978): 101.
5. Claudia Tate, "Allegories of Black Female Desire; Or, Rereading Nineteenth-Century Sentimental Narratives of Black Female Autobiography," *Changing Our Own Words: Essays on Criticism, Theory, and Writing by Black Women*, edited by Cheryl A. Wall (New Brunswick, NJ: Rutgers University Press, 1989), 108.
6. Don E. Fehrenbacher, *The Dred Scott Case: Its Significance in American Law and Politics* (New York: Oxford University Press, 1978), 28–29.
7. Lawrence M. Friedman, *A History of American Law*, 2nd ed. (New York: Simon and Schuster, 1985), 87.
8. Robert A. Ferguson, *Law and Letters*, 11.
9. Friedman, *A History of American Law*, 112.

10. Robert M. Cover, *Justice Accused: Antislavery and the Judicial Process* (New Haven: Yale University Press, 1975), 16.
11. Sir William Blackstone, *Commentaries on the Laws of England*, Book 1, 1765 (London: Dawsons of Pall Mall, 1966), 134. For an analysis of the evolving concept of property in law, see Gregory S. Alexander, *Commodity and Propriety: Competing Visions of Property in American Legal Thought* (Chicago: University of Chicago Press, 1997).
12. Blackstone, *Commentaries on the Laws of England*, 2.
13. Friedman, *A History of American Law*, 86.
14. Ferguson, *Law and Letters*, 232. Regarding Thomas Jefferson's opposition to Blackstone's work as "superficial and anti-republican," see Julius S. Waterman, "Thomas Jefferson and Blackstone's *Commentaries*," *Illinois Law Review* xxvii (1933): 629–59.
15. Thomas Jefferson, "Autobiography" (1821), *Writings* (New York: Library of America, 1984), 22.
16. Higginbotham, *In the Matter of Color*, 6.
17. Derrick A. Bell, *Race, Racism and American Law*, 2nd ed. (Boston: Little Brown, 1980), 22.
18. Leon A. Higginbotham, Jr., *Shades of Freedom: Radical Politics and Presumptions of the American Legal Process* (New York: Oxford University Press, 1996), 68. For an excellent discussion about the "constitutional language of slavery," see pages 68–80.
19. Higginbotham, *Shades of Freedom*, 69. Mary Frances Berry likewise discusses these specific constitutional provisions that reinforced slavery in "Slavery, the Constitution, and the Founding Fathers: The African American Vision," *African Americans and the Living Constitution*, edited by John Hope Franklin and Genna Rea McNeil (Washington: Smithsonian Institution Press, 1995), 11–12. For an argument that the Constitution is essentially a pro-slavery document, see Madison, "The Constitution—A Pro-slavery Compact," 5–9.
20. Derrick Bell, *Race and Racism*, 23, citing the work of lawyer-historian Staughton Lynd. Michael L. Levine also details constitutional and federal law that recognized the legitimacy of slavery in *African Americans and Civil Rights: From 1619 to the Present* (Phoenix: Oryx Press, 1996), 51–56.

21. Quoted in Lerone Bennett, *Before the Mayflower: A History of the Negro in America, 1619-1964* (Baltimore: Penguin Books, 1964), 146.
22. For an excellent summary of relevant literature on slavery and natural law, see Cover, *Justice Accused,* 8-30.
23. Fehrenbacher, *The Dred Scott Case,* 40-41.
24. Fugitive Slave Law of 1793, 1 Stat. 302.
25. Franklin, "Race and the Constitution in the Nineteenth Century," 25.
26. Stanley W. Campbell, *The Slave Catchers: Enforcement of the Fugitive Slave Law, 1850-1860* (Chapel Hill: University North Carolina Press, 1968), 10; Virginia, *Acts of the General Assembly,* 43-44.
27. Don E. Fehrenbacher, *Slavery, Law, and Politics: The Dred Scott Case in Historical Perspective* (New York: Oxford University Press, 1981), 21. For a summary of the personal liberty laws see Marion Gleason McDougall, *Fugitive Slaves 1619-1865* (Boston: Ginn & Company, 1891).
28. *Prigg v. Pennsylvania,* 16 Peters 539 (1842). For an analysis of personal liberty laws and the *Prigg* decision, see Thomas D. Morris, *Free Men All: The Personal Liberty Laws of the North, 1780-1861* (Baltimore: Johns Hopkins University Press, 1974), 94-106.
29. *Prigg v. Pennsylvania,* 16 Peters at 611.
30. Fehrenbacher, *The Dred Scott Case,* 44.
31. Campbell, *The Slave Catchers,* 15. See pages 15-25 for an elaboration on the background and passage of the Fugitive Slave Act of 1850.
32. Ralph Waldo Emerson, "The Fugitive Slave Law" (1854), *The Selected Writings of Ralph Waldo Emerson,* edited by Brooks Atkinson (New York: The Modern Library, 1992), 784. For commentary about Emerson's address, see Gertrude R. Hughes, "'How came he there?' Self Reliance, Misalliance, and Emerson's Second Fugitive Slave Law Address," *ATQ* 52 (Fall 1981): 273-86.
33. Walt Whitman, "Song of Myself," *Leaves of Grass,* 1855, *Complete Poetry and Collected Prose* (New York: Library of America, 1982), 35-36.
34. Ibid., 65.
35. Fugitive Slave Act of 1850, 9 Stat. 462, §4. Regarding the effect of the law as expressed in narratives about various individuals,

see James Oliver Horton and Lois E. Horton, "A Federal Assault: African Americans and the Impact of the Fugitive Slave Law of 1850," *Slavery and the Law*, edited by Paul J. Finkelman (Madison, WI: Madison House, 1997), 143–60.
36. Fugitive Slave Act of 1850, §7.
37. Ibid.
38. Ibid., §6.
39. Franklin, "Race and the Constitution in the Nineteenth Century," 27.
40. Ibid.
41. *Somerset v. Stewart*, 98 Eng. Rep. 499, 510 (K.B. 1772).
42. Higginbotham, *Shades of Freedom*, 61. See pages 62–67 for an excellent and succinct summary of the facts of the *Dred Scott* case and its two predecessor cases: *Emmerson v. Harriet*, 11 Mo. 413 (1848) and *Scott v. Emerson*, 15 Mo. 576 (1852). See Fehrenbacher, *The Dred Scott Case*, pages 239–84 for an elaboration on the details of *Dred Scott*.
43. *Dred Scott v. Sandford*, 60 U.S. (19 How.) 393, 403 (1857).
44. Higginbotham, *In the Matter of Color*, 6.
45. See Fehrenbacher, *The Dred Scott Case*, 322–34 for an analysis of the nuances of the significance of each justice's vote on the various issues. See also Higginbotham, *Shades of Freedom*, 66–67, regarding public disagreement over the import of Justice Taney's opinion.
46. *Dred Scott v. Sandford*, 60 U.S. at 407.
47. Ibid. at 416–17.
48. Derick Bell, *Race, Racism and American Law*, 19.
49. J. H. Van Evrie, introduction to *The Dred Scott Decision* (New York: Van Evrie, Horton Co., 1859), ix.
50. Higginbotham, *Shades of Freedom*, 67.
51. For further elaboration on the historical basis of the slave laws, see Mark V. Tushnet, *The American Law of Slavery 1810–1860: Considerations of Humanity and Interest* (Princeton: Princeton University Press, 1981); Paul Finkelman, ed., *Slavery and the Law* (Madison, WI: Madison House, 1997); John P. Kaminski, ed., *A Necessary Evil? Slavery and the Debate Over the Constitution* (Madison, WI: Madison House, 1995); Don E. Fehrenbacher, "Slavery, the Framers, and the Constitution," *Slavery and Its Consequences: The Constitution, Equality, and Race*, edited by Robert A. Goldwin and Art Kaufman (Washington, DC: American

Enterprise Institute for Public Policy Research, 1988), 1–22; Kermit L. Hall, ed., *The Law of Slavery: Major Historical Interpretations* (New York: Garland, 1987).

52. Jeanne Boydston, Mary Kelly, and Anne Margolis, *The Limits of Sisterhood: The Beecher Sisters on Women's Rights and Woman's Sphere* (Chapel Hill: University of North Carolina Press, 1988), 155.

53. Boydston, Kelly, and Margolis, *The Limits of Sisterhood*, 155; Joan D. Hedrick, *Harriet Beecher Stowe: A Life* (New York: Oxford University Press, 1994), 189–93 and 434, n. 32.

54. Boydston, Kelly, and Margolis, *The Limits of Sisterhood*, 156; Charles Edward Stowe, *Life of Harriet Beecher Stowe* (Boston: Houghton Mifflin and Co., 1889), 145.

55. Elizabeth Ammons, "Stowe's Dream of the Mother-Savior: *Uncle Tom's Cabin* and American Women Writers Before the 1920s," *New Essays on Uncle Tom's Cabin*, edited by Eric Sundquist (Cambridge: Cambridge University Press, 1986), 159.

56. Although there are literally hundreds of critical works discussing various aspects of *UTC*, few focus on the legal aspects of the text. For a detailed discussion of slavery-related legal issues in *UTC* primarily focusing on the character of Tom, see Brook Thomas, *Cross-Examinations in Law and Literature: Cooper, Hawthorne, Stowe, and Melville* (Cambridge: Cambridge University Press, 1987), 113–37.

57. Lang, *Prophetic Woman*, 214.

58. Angela Y. Davis, *Women, Race & Class*, 27, 29. Cf. the uncritical celebration of Stowe's work by Reynolds, *Uncle Tom's Cabin and Mid-Nineteenth Century United State*.

59. Higginbotham, *Shades of Freedom*, 58.

60. James Baldwin, "Everybody's Protest Novel" (1949), rpt. in *The Norton Anthology of African American Literature*, edited by Henry Louis Gates, Jr., and Nellie Y. McKay (New York: W. W. Norton & Company, 1997), 1654–55.

61. Higginbotham, *Shades of Freedom*, 56.

62. Thomas considers Stowe's treatment of the North Carolina case *State v. Mann* and its influence on *UTC* in *Cross-Examinations*, 117–20.

63. Angela Y. Davis, *Women, Race & Class*, 27–28.

64. For a discussion about the story of Margaret Garner and *UTC* see Cynthia Griffin Wolff, "'Margaret Garner': A Cincinnati Story,"

Discovering Difference: Essays in American Culture, edited by Christoph K. Lohmann (Bloomington: Indiana University Press, 1993), 107–12.

65. See, e.g., Jean Fagan Yellin,"Written by Herself: Harriet Jacobs' Slave Narrative," *American Literature* 53 (Nov. 1981): 479–86; also her "Texts and Contexts in Harriet Jacobs' *Incidents in the Life of a Slave Girl: Written by Herself,*" *The Slave's Narrative*, edited by Charles T. Davis and Henry Louis Gates, Jr. (New York: Oxford University Press, 1985), 265; Introduction to *Incidents in the Life of a Slave Girl, Written by Herself* by Harriet Jacobs (Cambridge: Harvard University Press, 1987), xiii–xxxiv. Other recent critics support Yellin's research. In "Texts and Contexts" Yellin summarizes those who have questioned and those who have supported Jacobs's narrative (278, n. 2).
66. Berlant "The Queen of America," 549.
67. Krista Walter, "Surviving in the Garret: Harriet Jacobs and the Critique of Sentiment," *American Transcendental Quarterly*, 8.3 (September 1994): 194. For an analysis of the complex network of power relations in *Incidents* using the theories of Michel Foucault see Debra Humphreys, "Power and Resistance in Harriet Jacobs' *Incidents in the Life of a Slave Girl*," *Anxious Power: Reading, Writing, and Ambivalence in Narrative by Women*, edited by Carol J. Singley and Susan Elizabeth Sweeney (New York: SUNY Press, 1993), 143–55.
68. Braxton, Joanne M. *Harriet Jacobs'* Incidents in the Life of a Slave Girl: *The Re-Definition of the Slave Narrator Genre*, vol. 27 (1986): 379.
69. Janice B. Daniel, "A New Kind of Hero: Harriet Jacobs' *Incidents in the Life of a Slave Girl*," *The Southern Quarterly* 35.3 (Spring 1997): 7–12.
70. Harriet Jacobs to Amy Post, June 21st [1857], Isaac and Amy Post Family Papers (hereafter "IAPFP") #90 and *Black Abolitionist Papers* (hereafter *BAP*), 160676–78, rpt. in *I*, 242.
71. See, e.g., Valerie Smith, introduction to *Incidents in the Life of a Slave Girl* by Harriet Jacobs, edited by Henry Louis Gates, Jr. (New York: Oxford University Press, 1988), xxxvi. For a comparison of Jacobs's and Thoreau's acts of civil disobedience see Anita Goldman, "Harriet Jacobs, Henry Thoreau, and the Character of Disobedience," *Harriet Jacobs and Incidents in the Life of a Slave Girl: New Critical Essays*, edited by Deborah M. Garfield

and Rafia Zafar (Cambridge: Cambridge University Press, 1996), 233-50.
72. Winifred Morgan explores the complexity of Jacobs's relationship with her primarily white audience in "Gender-Related Difference in the Slave Narratives of Harriet Jacobs and Frederick Douglas," *American Studies* 35.2 (Fall 1994): 87-89.
73. Harriet Jacobs to Amy Post [1852?], IAPFP #84, *BAP* 16:0700-02, rpt. in *I*, 232.
74. Ibid.
75. Yellin, Introduction to *I*, xix; Harriet Jacobs to Amy Post, Feby 14th [1853], IAPFP #785; *BAP* 16:0710-11, rpt. in *I*, 233-34.
76. Jacobs to Post, April 4 [1853], IAPFP #788, *BAP* 16:0681-83, rpt. in *I*, 235.
77. Jacobs to Post, New Bedford, MA (Spring 1853?) n.d. #80, quoted in Yellin, "Texts and Contexts," 266.
78. Jacobs to Post, April 4 [1853], IAPFP #788, *BAP* 16:0681-83, rpt. in *I*, 235.
79. Ibid.; Jacobs to Post, October 9th [1853], IAPFP #85, *BAP* 16:0713-14, rpt. in *I*, 236.
80. Carolyn L. Karcher, *The First Woman in the Republic: A Cultural Biography of Lydia Maria Child* (Durham: Duke University Press, 1994), 435-37.
81. Ruth Bogan and Jean Fagan Yellin, Introduction to *The Abolitionist Sisterhood: Women's Political Culture in Antebellum America*, edited by Jean Fagan Yellin and John C. Van Jorne (Ithaca: Cornell University Press, 1994), 4-5.
82. *Proceedings of the Anti-Slavery Convention of American Women*, (New York, 1837), 7-9.
83. Bogan and Yellin, Introduction to *The Abolitionist Sisterhood*, 5.
84. *The State Records of North Carolina*, vol. XXIII - Laws 1715-1776. These laws were later replaced by the Acts of April 4, 1741, ch 24. For detailed background on North Carolina slave law, see Marvin L. Michael Kay and Lorin Lee Carey, *Slavery in North Carolina, 1748-1775* (Chapel Hill: University North Carolina Press, 1995), 61-69.
85. Acts of 1723, *Laws of the State of North Carolina*. Levine makes reference to this law in his discussion about North Carolina slave law in *African Americans and Civil Rights*, 25.
86. Acts of 1729, chapter V, sec. viii, 52.
87. Acts of 1741, chapters XXVIII, XL and LVI, 90, 93, 95.

88. Acts of 1741, ch. XLVIII, 94.
89. Acts of 1741, ch. L, 94.
90. Acts of 1753, ch. IV–VI, 153.
91. Act of 1774, ch. XXXI, 274.
92. *State v. Mann*, 13 N.C. Reports 263, 266 (1829)
93. Ibid., 264 and 266. For commentary about Judge Ruffin, see Tushnet, *The American Law of Slavery*, 54–65, and Cover, *Justice Accused*, 77–78.
94. *State v. Mann*, 13 N.C. Reports at 268.
95. Friedman, *A History of American Law*, 86.
96. *State v. Will*, 18 N.C. Reports 121 (1834)
97. Ibid., 165.
98. Ibid., 171.
99. Jean Yellin, Introduction to *I*, xv.
100. Genovese, *Roll, Jordan, Roll*, 33. Regarding the effects of the rape of black slave women, see Darlene Clark Hine, "Rape and the Inner Lives of Black Women in the Middle West: Preliminary Thoughts on the Culture of Dissemblance," *Signs* 14.4 (Summer 1989): 912–20.
101. *Revised Code of North Carolina*, Chapter 107, Section 45, 573.
102. Angela Y. Davis, *Women, Race & Class*, 7.
103. Ibid., 23–24. Catherine Clinton focuses on the complexity of sexual exploitation of slave women in "Caught in the Web of the Big House: Women and Slavery," *The Web of Southern Social Relations: Women, Family, and Education*, edited by Walter J. Fraser, Jr., R. Frank Saunders, Jr., and Jon L. Wakelyn (Athens: University of Georgia Press, 1985), 19–34.
104. For a discussion about the tensions between the sexual abuse that Jacobs literally describes and metaphorically suggests, see Anne B. Dalton, "The Devil and the Virgin: Writing Sexual Abuse in *Incidents in the Life of a Slave Girl*," in *Violence, Silence, and Anger: Women's Writing as Transgression*, edited by Deidre Lashgari (Charlottesville: University of Virginia Press, 1995), 38–61.
105. For a discussion about slave women and their relationships with their mistresses who were angry over their husbands' fornications, see Jacqueline Jones, *Labor of Love, Labor of Sorrow: Black Women, Work, and the Family from Slavery to the Present* (New York: Basic Books, 1985).
106. Act of 1787, chapter VI, section III, 610.
107. Ibid.

108. Donald B. Gibson, "Harriet Jacobs, Frederick Douglas, and the Slavery Debate: Bondage, Family, and the Discourse of Domesticity," *Harriet Jacobs and Incidents in the Life of a Slave Girl: New Critical Essays*, edited by Deborah M. Garfield and Rafia Zafar (Cambridge: Cambridge University Press, 1996), 166.
109. Nellie Y. McKay, "The Girls Who Became the Women: Childhood Memories in the Autobiographies of Harriet Jacobs, Mary Church Terrell, and Anne Moody," *Tradition and the Talents of Women*, edited by Florence Howe (Urbana: University of Illinois Press, 1991), 120–21.

CHAPTER 4:   PERSPECTIVES AFTER CIVIL RIGHTS

1. Julius Lester, "James Baldwin—Reflections of a Maverick," *New York Times Book Review*, 27 May 1994, 1, 22–24, rpt. in *Conversations with James Baldwin*, edited by Fred L. Standley and Louis H. Pratt (Jackson: University of Mississippi Press, 1989), 226.
2. Toni Morrison discusses how she gains access to the interior life of her characters in "The Site of Memory," *Inventing the Truth: The Art of Craft of Memoir*, rev. and expanded 2nd ed., edited by William Zinsser (Boston: Houghton Mifflin Company, 1995), 91–92.
3. Angela Y. Davis, *Women, Race & Class*, 29. Davies, "Mother Right/Write Revisited," 56. Anne E. Goldman argues that in "recounting their histories and reclaiming them" Dessa Rose and Sethe "pose a different dialectic than the one produced and enforced by racist exploitation"("'I Made the Ink,'" 328). Regarding names in *Dessa Rose* and *Beloved* and their power to "disrupt and revise the Master narrative," see McKibble, "'These are the facts of the darky's history,'" 223–35.
4. Ibid.
5. Herbert Aptheker, Preface to *American Negro Slave Revolts* (New York: International Publishers, 1969), 4.
6. Sherley Anne Williams, *Give Birth to Brightness: A Thematic Study in Neo-Black Literature* (New York: Dial Press, 1972), 57–58.
7. Kenneth M. Stampp, *The Peculiar Institutes: Slavery in the Ante-Bellum South* (New York: Knopf, 1956).
8. Richard Wright, *Native Son* (1940) (New York: Harper Perennial, 1993), 460.
9. Ibid., 461.

10. Baldwin, "Everybody's Protest Novel," 1658.
11. Ann E. Trapasso, "Returning to the Site of Violence: The Restructuring of Slavery's Legacy in Sherley Anne Williams's *Dessa Rose*," *Violence, Silence, and Anger: Women's Writing as Transgression*, edited by Deirdre Lashgari (Charlottesville: University Press of Virginia, 1995), 229. See also Christian, "'Somebody Forgot to Tell Somebody Something,'" 341.
12. Caroline Rody, "Toni Morrison's *Beloved*: History, 'Rememory,' and a 'Clamor for a Kiss,'" *American Literary History* 7.1 (Spring 1995): 99.
13. Farah Jasimine Griffin, "Textual Healing: Claiming Black Women's Bodies, the Erotic and Resistance in Contemporary Novels of Slavery," *Callaloo* 19.2 (1996): 521. In her analysis, Griffin historicizes the social constructions of standards of beauty for black women.
14. Rebecca Ferguson, "History, Memory and Language in Toni Morrison's *Beloved*," *Feminist Criticism: Theory and Practice*, edited by Susan Sellers (Toronto: University of Toronto Press, 1991), 109.
15. In the chapter "On Being the Subject of Property," law professor Patricia J. Williams considers the importance of this issue of reclaiming heritage in connection with her own family's history with slavery (*The Alchemy of Race and Rights*, Cambridge: Harvard University Press, 1991), 216–36.
16. Helen Lock, "'Building up from Fragments': The Oral Memory Process in Some Recent African-American Written Narratives," *College Literature* 22.3 (Oct. 1995): 118.
17. Donna Haisty Winchell, "Cries of Outrage: Three Novelists' Use of History," *Mississippi Quarterly* XLIX: 4 (Fall 1996): 741.
18. Mae G. Henderson, "The Stories of O(Dessa): Stories of Complicity and Resistance," *Female Subjects in Black and White: Race, Psychoanalysis, Feminism*, edited by Elizabeth Abel, Barbara Christian, and Helene Moglen (Berkeley: University of California Press, 1997), 289.
19. Emancipation Proclamation, 12 Stat. 1269. (All "Stat." cites refer to the series of volumes known as *The Statutes at Large, Treaties and Proclamations of the United States of America*.)
20. Higginbotham, *Shades of Freedom*, 73.
21. An Act to Repeal the Fugitive Slave Act of 1850, 13 Stat. 200.
22. *U.S. Constitution*, Amendment XIII (1865).

23. Ibid. For a general discussion about the shortcomings of the Thirteenth Amendment, see Higginbotham, *Shades of Freedom*, 73–75; Derrick Bell, *Race, Racism and American Law*, 30–33.
24. Civil Rights Act of 1866, 14 Stat. 27, § 1. The modern counterpart to the 1866 and 1870 Acts is 42 U.S.C. §1981, *et seq.*
25. Civil Rights Act of 1866, 14 Stat. 27, § 1.
26. *U.S. Constitution*, Amendment XIV (1868).
27. *U.S. Constitution*, Amendment XV (1870).
28. For a discussion about the historical political powerlessness of black women, see Scales-Trent, "Black Women and the Constitution," 9–44.
29. Civil Rights Act of 1871, 16 Stat. 433. Regarding interpretations of the 1871 Act, see *Collins v. Hardyman*, 341 U.S. 651 (1951) and *Griffin v. Breckenridge*, 403 U.S. 88 (1971).
30. Civil Rights Act of 1875, 18 Stat. 335.
31. Franklin, "Race and the Constitution in the Nineteenth Century," 29.
32. *Civil Rights Cases*, 109 U.S. 3, 25 (1883).
33. *Civil Rights Cases*, 109 U.S. at 36.
34. *Plessy v. Ferguson*, 163 U.S. 537 (1896).
35. Ibid. at 551.
36. *Plessy v. Ferguson*, 163 U.S. at 540, 552.
37. Ibid. at 559, 560, and 562.
38. *Brown v. Board of Education of Topeka*, 347 U.S. 483 (1954).
39. Ibid. at 495.
40. Ibid.
41. Civil Rights Act of 1957, 71 Stat. 634.
42. Civil Rights Act of 1960, 74 Stat. 86.
43. Civil Rights Act of 1894, 78 Stat. 241.
44. Ralph C. Chandler, Richard A. Enslen, and Peter G. Renstrom, eds., *Constitutional Law Deskbook: Individual Rights* (Rochester, NY: Lawyers Co-Operative Publishing Co., 1987), 481.
45. Levine, *African Americans and Civil Rights*, 285–87.
46. *Regents of the University of California v. Bakke*, 438 U.S. 265 (1978).
47. Christopher Lehmann-Haupt, "Books of the Times; Friendship in Chains," *New York Times*, 12 July 1986, sec. 1, 12.
48. Sherley Anne Williams, "Meditations on History," *Midnight Birds*, edited by Mary Helen Washington (New York: Doubleday, 1980), 200–48. Williams discusses the evolution of *Dessa Rose* from "Meditations on History" in "The Lion's History:

The Ghetto Writes B[l]ack," *Soundings* 76.2-3 (Summer/Fall 1993): 249-58.

49. Albert E. Stone, *The Return of Nat Turner*, 380. Stone argues that *Dessa Rose* is a "purposeful black feminist reply to Styron's novel" (367). Suzan Harrison argues this point regarding *Dessa Rose*, William Styron's *Confessions of Nat Turner*, and Melton McLaurin's historical study, *Celia, a Slave* (New York: Avon, 1991) by considering each as a *failed* slave narrative ("Mastering Narratives/Subverting Masters: Rhetorics of Race in *The Confessions of Nat Turner, Dessa Rose* and *Celia, a Slave*," *Southern Quarterly* 35.3 (Spring 1997): 24. Using the theory of Bakhtin, Nicole R. King also explores the connections between *Dessa Rose* and *Celia, A Slave* ("Meditations and Mediations: Issues of History and Fiction in *Dessa Rose*," *Soundings* 76.2-3 (Summer/Fall 1993): 351-68. For more commentary regarding the treatment of history in both *Dessa Rose* and *Beloved*, as well as *The Confessions of Nat Turner*, see John C. Inscoe, "Slave Rebellion in the First Person: The Literary 'Confessions' of Nat Turner and *Dessa Rose*," *The Virginia Magazine of History and Biography* 97.4 (October 1989): 419-36.
50. Winchell, "Cries of Outrage," 733-34.
51. Sherley Anne Williams, interview in Tate, *Black Women Writers*, 207; Author's Note, *DR*, ix.
52. For an overview of these historical incidents, see Mary Kemp Davis, "Everybody Knows Her Name: The Recovery of the Past in Sherley Anne Williams' *Dessa Rose*," *Callahoo* 12.3 (Summer 1989): 545-46.
53. Angela Y. Davis, "Reflections on the Black Woman's Role in the Community of Slaves," *The Black Scholar* 3.4 (December 1971): 11.
54. Aptheker, *Slave Revolts*, 287.
55. Ibid.; Aptheker, "Affray and Murder," *Columbian Centinel*, 22 August 1829, qtd. in David Walker's "Appeal to the Colored Citizens of the World" (1829-1830), rpt. in Aptheker *One Continual Cry*, 86.
56. "Affray and Murder," rpt. in Aptheker, *One Continual Cry*, 87.
57. Aptheker, *Slave Revolts*, 287.
58. Ibid.
59. Portsmouth, Virginia *Times* and Richmond, Virginia *Enquirer*, 28 January 1830, qtd. in Aptheker, *Slave Revolts*, 287.

60. Aptheker, *Slave Revolts,* 289.
61. Ibid.
62. David Bradley, "On the Lam from Race and Gender," *New York Times Book Review,* 3 August 1986, 7.
63. Laws of the State of Alabama, Slaves, and Free Persons of Color, §4.
64. Laws of the State of Alabama, Patrols, §1.
65. Ibid., §2.
66. Ashraf H. A. Rushdy, "Reading Mammy: The Subject of Relation in Sherley Anne Williams' *Dessa Rose,*" *African American Review* 27.3 (1993): 365. Regarding Nehemiah and his controversial treatment of Dessa Rose, see Mae G. Henderson, "Speaking in Tongues: Dialogics, Dialectics, and the Tradition of the Black Woman Writer's Literary Tradition," *Changing Our Own Words: Essays on Criticism, Theory, and Writing by Black Women,* edited by Cheryl A. Wall (New Brunswick: Rutgers University Press, 1989), 119–38; Winchell, "Cries of Outrage," 735; Inscoe, "Slave Rebellion," 425–36; Marta E. Sánchez, "The Estrangement Effect in Sherley Anne William's *Dessa Rose,*" *Genders* 15 (Winter 1992): 25–37.
67. Nehemiah Adams, *A South-Side View of Slavery; Three Months at the South in 1855* (Boston: T. R. Marvin, 1855), 207. At the American Literature Association Conference on American Literature (May 1998), Keith Williams explored this connection in his paper "The (Un)spoken History: Sherley Anne Williams' *Dessa Rose* and the Production Narrative."
68. Laws of the State of Alabama, Slaves, and Free Persons of Color, §4.
69. Laws of the State of Alabama, Penal Code, Ch. XV, §2.
70. Ibid., §1.
71. Laws of the State of Alabama, Slaves and Free Persons of Color, §14.
72. Laws of the State of Alabama, Patrols, §2.
73. Laws of the State of Alabama, Penal Code, Ch. III, §20.
74. Nancy Porter, "Women's Interracial Friendships and Visions of Community in Meridian, The Salt Eaters, and Dessa Rose," in *Tradition and the Talents of Women,* edited by Florence Howe (Urbana: University of Illinois Press, 1991), 252.
75. Laws of the State of Alabama, Penal Code, Ch. IV, §14.

76. Mary Condé, "Some African-American Fictional Responses to *Gone with the Wind,*" *The Yearbook of English Studies* 26 (1996): 215.
77. Melissa Walker, *Down from the Mountaintop: Black Women's Novels in the Wake of the Civil Rights Movement, 1966-1989* (New Haven: Yale University Press, 1991), 32-33.
78. Deborah E. McDowell, "Negotiating Between Tenses: Witnessing Slavery after Freedom—Dessa Rose," *Slavery and the Literary Imagination,* edited by Deborah E. McDowell and Arnold Rampersad (Baltimore: Johns Hopkins University Press, 1989), 161. For a discussion about how Williams "reinvents" slavery, see Jane Mathison-Fife, "*Dessa Rose*: A Critique of the Received History of Slavery," *Kentucky Philological Review* 8 (1993): 43-52.
79. Toni Morrison, "Rootedness: The Ancestor as Foundation," *Black Women Writers (1950-1980): A Critical Evaluation* (Garden City, NY: Anchor Press/Doubleday, 1984), 344.
80. Barbara Christian, "Fixing Methodologies: *Beloved,*" *Female Subjects in Black and White: Race, Psychoanalysis, Feminism,* edited by Elizabeth Abel, Barbara Christian, and Helene Moglen (Berkeley: University of California Press, 1997), 364.
81. Helene Moglen, "Redeeming History: Toni Morrison's *Beloved,*" *Female Subjects in Black and White: Race, Psychoanalysis, Feminism,* edited by Elizabeth Abel, Barbara Christian and Helene Moglen (Berkeley: University of California Press, 1997), 206.
82. Morrison, "The Site of Memory," 86.
83. A number of critics endeavor to draw parallels between *Beloved* and works by other authors, including Condé, "Some African-American Fictional Responses to *Gone with the Wind*"; Charles Lewis, "The Ironic Romance of New Historicism: *The Scarlet Letter* and *Beloved* Standing Side by Side," *Arizona Quarterly* 51.1 (Spring 1995), 33-60; Caroline M. Woidat, "Talking Back to Schoolteacher: Morrison's Confrontation with Hawthorne in *Beloved,*" *Modern Fiction Studies* 39.3&4 (Fall/Winter 1993): 527-43. Regarding the literary connections between *Beloved* and *Uncle Tom's Cabin,* see also Nancy Armstrong, "Why Daughters Die: The Racial Logic of American Sentimentalism," *Yale Journal of Criticism* 7.2 (Fall 1994): 1-24; John N. Duvall, "Authentic Ghost Stories: *Uncle Tom's Cabin, Absolom, Absolom!,* and *Beloved, The Faulkner Journal* 4.1-2 (1988): 83-97. Discussing the intertextuality between *Beloved* and the literary tradition of slave

narratives, Waxman argues that "Morrison reconstructs the history of slavery from a gendered African-American perspective" (57–83). Askeland contends that Morrison's *Beloved* "sets itself up as a remodeling of *Uncle Tom's Cabin*" that examines domestic ideology and "revises it in a way that avoids reification of a patriarchal power structure" (787).
84. Eileen T. Bender, "Repossessing *Uncle Tom's Cabin*: Toni Morrison's *Beloved,*" *Cultural Power/Cultural Literacy*, edited by Bonnie Braendlin (Tallahassee, FL: Florida State University Press, 1991), 139.
85. Ibid.
86. Ibid.
87. Deborah Guth, "A Blessing and a Burden: The Relation to the Past in *Sula, Song of Solomon* and *Beloved,*" *Modern Fiction Studies* 39.3&4 (Fall/Winter 1993): 575.
88. Harold Bloom, Introduction to *Modern Critical Views: Toni Morrison* (New York: Chelsea House, 1990), 2.
89. Morrison, "The Site of Memory," 91, 92. Linda Anderson argues that in "*Beloved* there is no authoritative version of history, no single 'truth'" ("The Re-imagining of History in Contemporary Women's Fiction," 138. Ashraf Rushdy writes, "In shared experience, memory is healing, as everyone in Morrison's narratives discovers" ("Rememory," 321–22). For more regarding Morrison's effective use of "rememory" to encourage healing, see Cynthia S. Hamilton, "Revisions, Rememories and Exorcisms: Toni Morrison and the Slave Narrative," *Journal of American Studies* 30.1 (April 1996): 429–45.; Madelyn Jablon, "Rememory, Dream Memory, and Revision in Toni Morrison's *Beloved* and Alice Walker's *The Temple of My Familiar,*" *CLA Journal* 37:2 (Dec. 1993): 136–44; Marianne Hirsch, "Maternity and Rememory: Toni Morrison's *Beloved,*" *Representations of Motherhood*, edited by Donna Basin, Margaret Honey, and Meryle Mahrer Kaplan (New Haven: Yale University Press, 1994), 92–110; Ashraf Rushdy, "Rememory: Primal Scenes and Constructions in Toni Morrison's Novels," *Contemporary Literature* 31.3 (1990): 59–77; Susan Bowers, "*Beloved* and the New Apocalypse," *The Journal of Ethnic Studies* 18:1 (Spring 1990), 59–77.
90. Toni Morrison, interview with Toni Morrison, *MacNeil/Lehrer Newshour*, PBS. WOSU, Columbus, Ohio, 29 September 1987,

qtd. in Otten, Terry. "Horrific Love in Toni Morrison's Fiction," *Modern Fiction Studies* 39.3&4 (Fall/Winter 1993): 657. For similar comments by Morrison, see Mervyn Rothstein, "Morrison Defends Women," *New York Times*, 26 August 1987.
91. Bill Cosby, introduction to *The Black Book*, edited by Middleton Harris (New York: Random House, 1973), i. For an excellent account of Margaret Garner's story see Wolff, "'Margaret Garner': A Cincinnati Story." For a discussion of intertextuality between *Beloved* and slave narratives, including the story of Margaret Garner, see Marilyn Sanders Mobley, "A Different Remembering: Memory, History and Meaning in Toni Morrison's *Beloved*," *Toni Morrison: Modern Critical Views*, edited by Harold Bloom (New York: Chelsea House Publishers, 1990).
92. Gloria Naylor and Toni Morrison, "A Conversation," *The Southern Review* 21.3 (July 1985): 583.
93. Ibid.
94. Ibid., 583–84.
95. Ibid., 584.
96. Levi Coffin, *Reminiscences* (Cincinnati, OH: Western Tract Society, 1876). For more commentary about Margaret Garner, see Angela Y. Davis, *Women, Race & Class*, 21–22, 29.
97. Coffin, *Reminiscences*, 559–60.
98. Ibid., 563.
99. Fugitive Slave Act of 1850, §§ 1–4; Ibid., 560.
100. Coffin, *Reminiscences*, 560.
101. Fugitive Slave Act of 1850, § 6; Ibid., 561.
102. Ibid., 561–62.
103. Fugitive Slave Act of 1850, § 6.
104. *The Cincinnati Daily Enquirer*, 12 February 1856, qtd. in Wolff, "Margaret Garner," 115.
105. Coffin, *Reminiscences*, 560.
106. Ibid., 566.
107. Leslie Wheeler, editorial notes to Introduction to *Loving Warriors: Selected Letters of Lucy Stone and Henry B. Blackwell, 1853 to 1893* (New York: Dial Press, 1981), 143, and Lucy Stone's February 3, 1856 letter, 155.
108. Wolff, "Margaret Garner," 117.
109. *The Cincinnati Daily Gazette*, 14 February 1856, qtd. in Wolff, "Margaret Garner,"117.
110. Wheeler, *Loving Warriors*, 143.

111. Coffin, *Reminiscences*, 567.
112. Marsha Darling, "In the Realm of Responsibility: A Conversation with Toni Morrison," *The Women's Review of Books* 5 (March 1988), rpt. in *Conversations with Toni Morrison*, edited by Danielle Taylor-Guthrie (Jackson: University of Mississippi Press, 1994), 248.
113. Ibid.
114. "A Constitution or Form of Government for the State of Kentucky," *The State Law of Kentucky*, edited by William Littell (series is known as *"Littell's Laws,"*) I:21.
115. *Littell's Laws*, I:32.
116. Ibid.
117. Ivan E. McDougle, *Slavery in Kentucky: 1792-1865* (1918), (Westport, CT: Negro University Press, 1970), 43.
118. Act of February 8, 1798, *Littell's Laws*, II.5-6 (1810).
119. *Littell's Laws*, II.113. Chapter CXLIV of the 1798 Act also provided for special courts to hear trials involving slaves (*Littell's Laws*, II.215-16).
120. *Littell's Laws*, II.113.
121. Ibid.
122. *Littell's Laws*, II.120 and Act of November 26, 1800, *Littell's Laws*, II.374.
123. Act of January 25, 1811, *Littell's Laws*, IV.223-24 (1814).
124. *Littell's Laws*, IV.224.
125. KY Rev. Stat., Ch. XCIII, Art. I, §2.
126. Ibid., Art. I, §§1 and 3.
127. Ibid., Art. III, VII and VIII.
128. Ibid., Art. IV, §2.
129. Ibid., Art. IV, §3.
130. Ibid., Art. III, §1.
131. Ibid., Art. III, §12.
132. For an in-depth analysis of issues of rape in *Beloved*, see Pamela E. Barnett, "Figurations of Rape and the Supernatural in *Beloved*," *PMLA* 112.3 (May 1997).
133. Fugitive Slave Act of 1850 and KY Rev. Stat., Ch. XCIII, Art. VI.
134. Lori Askeland poses a series of provocative questions about this troubling matter in "Remodeling the Model Home in *Uncle Tom's Cabin* and *Beloved*," *American Literature* 64.4 (Dec. 1992): 797-98.

135. Wilfred Samuels and Clenora Hudson-Weems, *Toni Morrison* (Boston: Twayne, 1990), 106.
136. Moglen, "Redeeming History," 210. On the primal mother, see also Jean Wyatt, "Giving Body to the Word: The Maternal Symbolic in Toni Morrison's *Beloved,*" *PMLA* 108.3 (May 1993): 474. 484; Barbara Hill Rigney, "'A Story to Pass On': Ghosts and the Significance of History in Toni Morrison's *Beloved,*" in *Haunting the House of Fiction: Feminist Perspectives on Ghost Stories by American Women,* edited by Lynette Carpenter and Wendy K. Kolmar (Knoxville: University of Tennessee Press, 1991), 229–35. Drucilla Cornell analyzes Sethe's acts as a retelling of the Medea myth in *Beyond Accommodation,* 194.
137. Darling, "In the Realm of Responsibility," 248.
138. Trudier Harris, *Fiction and Folklore: The Novels of Toni Morrison* (Knoxville: University of Tennessee Press, 1991), 175.
139. Rody, "Toni Morrison's *Beloved,*"104.
140. Cornell West, *Race Matters* (New York: Vintage Books, 1993), 30.
141. bell hooks, "Sexism and the Black Female Slave Experience," *Ain't I a Woman: Black Women and Feminism* (Boston: South End Press, 1981), 196.
142. Robin West, *Caring for Justice* (New York: New York University Press, 1997), 198.
143. Ibid.
144. Morrison, qtd. in Gail Caldwell, "Author Toni Morrison Discusses Her Latest Novel *Beloved,*" *Boston Globe,* 6 October 1987: 67–68, rpt. in Taylor-Guthrie, *Conversations,* 241.
145. Robin West, *Caring for Justice,* 189. West's jurisprudential ideas draw on the work of James Boyd White and Martha Nussbaum.

CONCLUSION: BEYOND THE RULE OF LAW

1. Jo Anne Pagano, "Relating to One's Students: Identity, Morality, Stories and Questions," *Journal of Moral Education* 20.3 (1991): 260.
2. Dorothy Allison, *Skin: Talking About Sex, Class & Literature* (Ithaca, NY: Firebrand Books, 1994), 165.
3. Angela Y. Davis, *Women, Culture, and Politics,* 14.

❧ Bibliography ❦

Adams, Charles Francis. *Three Episodes of Massachusetts History.* Vol. 1. Boston: Houghton, Mifflin and Company, 1892.

———, ed. Introduction to *Antinomianism in the Colony of Massachusetts Bay, 1636–1638.* Boston: The Prince Society, 1894.

Adams, Nehemiah. *A South-Side View of Slavery; Three Months at the South in 1855.* Boston: T. R. Marvin, 1855.

Alexander, Gregory S. *Commodity and Propriety: Competing Visions of Property in American Legal Thought.* Chicago: University of Chicago Press, 1997.

Allen, David Grayson. *In English Ways: The Movement of Societies and the Transferal of English Local Law and Custom to Massachusetts Bay in the Seventeenth Century.* Chapel Hill: University North Carolina Press, 1981.

Allison, Dorothy. *Skin: Talking about Sex, Class & Literature.* Ithaca, NY: Firebrand Books, 1994.

Altman, Andrew. *Critical Legal Studies: A Liberal Critique.* Princeton: Princeton University Press, 1989.

Ammons, Elizabeth. "Stowe's Dream of the Mother-Savior: *Uncle Tom's Cabin* and American Women Writers Before the 1920s." In *New Essays on Uncle Tom's Cabin*, edited by Eric Sundquist. Cambridge: Cambridge University Press, 1986.

Anderson, Linda. "The Re-Imagining of History in Contemporary Women's Fiction." In *Plotting Change: Contemporary Women's Fiction*, edited by Linda Anderson. London: Edward Arnold, 1990.

Andrews, Charles M. *The Colonial Period of American History*. Vol. I. New Haven: Yale University Press, 1934.

Andrews, William L. "The Charging Moral Discourse of Nineteenth-Century African-American Women's Autobiography: Harriet Jacobs and Elizabeth Keckley." In *De/Colonizing the Subject: The Politics of Gender in Women's Autobiography*. Minneapolis: University of Minnesota Press, 1992.

Aptheker, Herbert. *American Negro Slave Revolts*. New York: International Publishers, 1969.

———, ed. *David Walker's Appeal to the Colored Citizens of the World (1829-1830)*. New York: Humanities Press, 1965.

Arendt, Hannah. *Crisis of the Republic*. New York: Harcourt Brace Jovanovich, Inc., 1969.

Armstrong, Nancy. "Why Daughters Die: The Racial Logic of American Sentimentalism." *Yale Journal of Criticism* 7.2 (Fall 1994): 1-24.

Ashe, Marie. "'Bad Mothers,' 'Good Lawyers,' and 'Legal Ethics,'" 81 *Georgetown Law Journal*, 25-33 (1993).

Askeland, Lori. "Remodeling the Model Home in *Uncle Tom's Cabin* and *Beloved*." *American Literature* 64.4 (Dec. 1992): 785-805.

Augur, Helen. *An American Jezebel: The Life of Anne Hutchinson*. New York: Brentano's, 1930.

Babbitt, Susan E. "Identity, Knowledge, and Toni Morrison's *Beloved*: Questions about Understanding Racism." *Hypatia* 9.3 (Summer 1994): 1-18.

Baldwin, James. "Everybody's Protest Novel." 1949. Rpt. in *The Norton Anthology of African American Literature*, edited by Henry Louis Gates, Jr. and Nellie Y. McKay. New York: W. W. Norton & Company, 1997.

Ball, Milner S. *The Word and the Law.* Chicago: University of Chicago Press, 1993.

Barbeito, Patricia Felisa. "'Making Generations' in Jacobs, Larsen, and Hurston: A Genealogy of Black Women's Writing." *American Literature* 70.2 (June 1998): 365-95.

Bardes, Barbara, and Suzanne Gossett. "Women and Political Power in the Republic: Two Early American Novels." *Legacy* 2.2 (1985): 13-30.

Barker-Benfield, Ben. "Anne Hutchinson and the Puritan Attitude toward Women." *Feminist Studies* 1.2 (Fall 1992): 65-96.

Barnett, Pamela E. "Figurations of Rape and the Supernatural in *Beloved.*" *PMLA* 112.3 (May 1997): 418-27.

Barry, John Stetson. *The History of Massachusetts. The Colonial Period.* Boston: Phillips, Sampson and Company, 1855.

Battis, Emery. *Saints and Sectaries: Anne Hutchinson and the Antinomian Controversy in the Massachusetts Bay Colony.* Chapel Hill: University North Carolina Press, 1962.

Bauermeister, Erica R. "*The Lamplighter, The Wide, Wide World* and *Hope Leslie*: Reconsidering the Recipes for Nineteenth-Century American Women's Novels." *Legacy* 8.1 (Spring 1991): 17-28.

Baym, Nina. *Woman's Fiction: A Guide to Novels by and about Women in America 1820-70.* 2nd ed. Urbana: University of Illinois Press, 1993.

Bell, Derrick A. *Race, Racism and American Law.* 2nd ed. Boston: Little Brown, 1980.

Bell, Michael Davitt. "History and Romance Conventions in Catharine Maria Sedgwick's *Hope Leslie.*" *American Quarterly* 22.1 (Spring 1970): 213-21.

Bender, Eileen T. "Repossessing *Uncle Tom's Cabin*: Toni Morrison's *Beloved.*" In *Cultural Power/Cultural Literacy*, edited by Bonnie Braendlin. Tallahassee: Florida State University Press, 1991.

Bennett, Lerone. *Before the Mayflower: A History of the Negro in America, 1619-1964*. Baltimore: Penguin Books, 1964.

Berlant, Lauren. "Fantasies of Utopia in *The Blithedale Romance.*" *American Literary History* 1.1 (Spring 1989): 30–62.

———. "The Queen of America Goes to Washington City: Harriet Jacobs, Frances Harper and Anita Hill." *American Literature* 65.3 (September 1993): 549–574.

Berry, Mary Frances. "Slavery, the Constitution, and the Founding Fathers: The African American Vision." In *African Americans and the Living Constitution*, edited by John Hope Franklin and Genna Rea McNeil. Washington: Smithsonian Institution Press, 1995.

Birdsall, Richard D. "William Collen Bryant and Catharine Sedgwick—Their Debt to Berkshire." *New England Quarterly* 28.1 (March 1955): 349–71.

Blackstone, Sir William. *Commentaries on the Laws of England*, Book 1, 1765. London: Dawsons of Pall Mall, 1966.

Blassingame, John W. *The Slave Community: Plantation Life in the Antebellum South*. New York: Oxford University Press, 1979.

Bloch, Ruth H. "American Feminine Ideals in Transition: The Rise of the Moral Mother, 1785–1815." *Feminist Studies* 4.2 (June 1978): 101–26.

Bloom, Harold. Introduction to *Modern Critical Views: Toni Morrison*. New York: Chelsea House, 1990.

Bogan, Ruth, and Jean Fagan Yellin. Introduction to *The Abolitionist Sisterhood: Women's Political Culture in Antebellum America*, edited by Jean Fagan Yellin and John C. Van Jorne. Ithaca: Cornell University Press, 1994.

Bolton, Reginald Pelham. *A Woman Misunderstood: Anne, Wife of William Hutchinson.* New York: Schoen Printing Company.

Botein, Stephen. *Early American Law and Society.* New York: Knopf, 1983.

Bowers, Susan. "*Beloved* and the New Apocalypse." *The Journal of Ethnic Studies* 18.1 (Spring 1990): 59–77.

Boydston, Jeanne, Mary Kelly, and Anne Margolis. *The Limits of Sisterhood: The Beecher Sisters on Women's Rights and Woman's Sphere.* Chapel Hill: University of North Carolina Press, 1988.

Boyle, James, ed. *Critical Legal Studies.* Aldershot, England: Dartmouth, 1992.

Bradford, William. *Of Plymouth Plantation, 1620–1641.* 1856. New York: Random House, 1981.

Bradley, David. "On the Lam from Race and Gender." *New York Times Book Review,* 3 August 1986, 7.

Braxton, Joanne M. "Harriet Jacobs's *Incidents in the Life of a Slave Girl*: The Re-Definition of the Slave Narrator Genre." *Massachusetts Review.* Vol. 27 (1986): 379–87.

Brooks, Gladys. *Three Wise Virgins.* New York: E.P. Dutton, 1957.

Brooks, Peter, and Paul Gewirtz, eds. *Law's Stories: Narrative and Rhetoric in Law.* New Haven: Yale University Press, 1996.

Buell, Lawrence. *New England Literary Culture: From Revolution through Renaissance.* Cambridge: Cambridge University Press, 1986.

Burnham, Michelle. "Loopholes of Resistance: Harriet Jacobs' Slave Narrator and the Critique of Agency in Foucault." *Arizona Quarterly* 49.2 (Summer 1993): 53–73.

Caldwell, Patricia. "The Antinomian Language Controversy." *Harvard Theological Review* 69.3–4 (July-October 1976): 345.

Cameron, Jean. *Anne Hutchinson Guilty or Not? A Closer Look at Her 'Trials'.* New York: Peter Lang, 1994.

Campbell, Stanley W. *The Slave Catchers: Enforcement of the Fugitive Slave Law, 1850-1860.* Chapel Hill: University North Carolina Press, 1968.

Carby, Hazel V. *Reconstructing Womanhood: The Emergence of the Afro-American Woman Novelist.* New York: Oxford University Press, 1987.

Castiglia, Christopher. "In Praise of Extra-Vagant Women: *Hope Leslie* and the Captivity Romance." *Legacy* 6.2 (Fall 1989): 3-16.

Catterall, Helen Tunnicliff. *Judicial Cases Concerning American Slavery and the Negro.* Vol. I-II. Baltimore, MD: The Lord Baltimore Press, 1926.

Cave, Alfred A. "Whoe Killed John Stone? A Note on the Origins of the Pequot War." *William and Mary Quarterly.* 3rd series 49.3 (July 1992): 509-21.

Champlin, John Denison. "Hutchinson Ancestry and Descendents of William and Anne Hutchinson." *N.Y. Genealogical and Biographical Record*, 45 (1914): 167-68.

Chandler, Ralph C., Richard A. Enslen, and Peter G. Renstrom, eds. *Constitutional Law Deskbook: Individual Rights.* Rochester, NY: Lawyers Co-Operative Publishing Co., 1987.

Channing, William E. *Slavery.* Boston: James Monroe and Co., 1835.

Chapin, Bradley. *Criminal Justice in Colonial America, 1606-1660.* Athens: University of Georgia Press, 1893.

Chatee, Zechariah, Jr. *Free Speech in the United States.* Cambridge: Harvard University Press, 1946.

Christian, Barbara. "Fixing Methodologies: *Beloved.*" In *Female Subjects in Black and White: Race, Psychoanalysis, Feminism,* edited by

Elizabeth Abel, Barbara Christian, and Helene Moglen. Berkeley: University of California Press, 1997, 363–70.

——. "'Somebody Forgot to Tell Somebody Something': African-American Women's Historical Novels." In *Wild Women in the Whirlwind: Afro-American Culture and the Contemporary Literary Renaissance*, edited by Joanne Braxton and Andree Nicola McLaughlin. New Brunswick, NJ: Rutgers University Press, 1990: 326–41.

Clinton, Catherine. "Caught in the Web of the Big House: Women and Slavery." In *The Web of Southern Social Relations: Women, Family, and Education*, edited by Walter J. Fraser, Jr., R. Frank Saunders, Jr., and Jon L. Wakelyn. Athens: University Georgia Press, 1985.

Cluskey, M.W, ed. *Speeches, Messages, and Other Writings of the Honorable Albert G. Brown*. Philadelphia: J.B. Smith & Co., 1859.

Coffin, Levi. *Reminiscences*. Cincinnati, OH: Western Tract Society, 1876.

Collections of the Massachusetts Historical Society. Vol. IV. Cambridge: Charles Folsom, 1834.

Condé, Mary. "Some African-American Fictional Responses to *Gone with the Wind*." *The Yearbook of English Studies* 26 (1996): 208–17.

Cooper, Anna Julia. "Statement to the Congress of Representative Women, 1893." In *Black Women in Nineteenth-Century American Life: Their Words, Their Thoughts, Their Feelings*, edited by Bert J. Loewenberg and Ruth Bogan. University Park: Pennsylvania State University Press, 1990.

Cooper, James F., Jr. "Anne Hutchinson and the 'Lay Rebellion' Against the Clergy." *The New England Quarterly* LXI.3 (September 1988): 381–397.

Coquillette, Daniel R., ed. *Law in Colonial Massachusetts 1630–1800*. Boston: The Colonial Society of Massachusetts, 1984.

Cornell, Drucilla. *Beyond Accommodation: Ethical Feminism, Deconstruction, and the Law.* New York: Routledge, 1991.

Cosby, Bill. Introduction to *The Black Book*, edited by Middleton Harris. New York: Random House, 1973.

Cotton, John. "How far Moses Judicialls bind Massachusetts (An Abstract; or, the Laws of New England." In *Proceedings of the Massachusetts Historical Society.* 2nd series. Vol. XIV. Boston: Massachusetts Historical Society, 1903.

Cover, Robert M. *Narrative, Violence, and the Law: The Essays of Robert Cover*, edited by Martha Minow, Micheal Ryan, and Austin Sarat, Ann Arbor: University of Michigan Press, 1992.

——. *Justice Accused: Antislavery and the Judicial Process.* New Haven: Yale University Press, 1975.

Crawford, Deborah. *Four Women in a Violent Time.* New York: Crown Publishers, 1970.

Crouch, Stanley. "Aunt Medea." *The New Republic* 197.16 (October 19, 1987): 43.

Cushing, John D. *Massachusetts Province Laws 1692–1699.* Wilmington, DE: Michael Glazier, Inc., 1978.

——. "The Cushing Court and the Abolition of Slavery in Massachusetts: More Notes on the Quock Walker Case." *The American Journal of Legal History* 5 (1961): 118–44.

Dalton, Anne B. "The Devil and the Virgin: Writing Sexual Abuse in *Incidents in the Life of a Slave Girl.*" In *Violence, Silence, and Anger: Women's Writing as Transgression*, edited by Deidre Lashgari. Charlottesville: University of Virginia Press, 1995.

Daniel, Janice B. "A New Kind of Hero: Harriet Jacobs' *Incidents in the Life of a Slave Girl.*" *The Southern Quarterly* 35.3 (Spring 1997): 7–12.

Darling, Marsha. "In the Realm of Responsibility: A Conversation with Toni Morrison," *The Women's Review of Books* 5 (March 1988). Rpt. in *Conversations with Toni Morrison*, edited by Danielle Taylor-Guthrie. Jackson: University of Mississippi Press, 1994.

Davies, Carole Boyce. *Mother Right/Write Revisited:* Beloved *and* Dessa Rose *and the Construction of Motherhood in Black Women's Fiction*. In *Narrating Mothers: Theorizing Maternal Subjectivities*, edited by Brenda O. Daly and Maureen T. Reddy. Knoxville: University of Tennessee Press, 1991.

Davis, Angela Y. *Women, Culture, and Politics*. New York: Random House, 1984.

——. *Women, Race and Class*. New York: Random House, 1981.

——. "Reflections on the Black Woman's Role in the Community of Slaves." *The Black Scholar* 3.4 (December 1971): 2–15.

Davis, Mary Kemp. "Everybody Knows Her Name: The Recovery of the Past in Sherley Anne Williams' *Dessa Rose*." *Callahoo* 12.3 (Summer 1989): 544–58.

Dimock, Wai Chee. *Residues of Justice: Law, Literature and Philosophy*. Berkeley: University of California Press, 1996.

Douglas, Ann. *The Feminization of American Culture*. New York: Alfred A. Knopf, 1977.

Dow, George Francis. *Every Day Life in the Massachusetts Bay Colony*. New York: Benjamin Blom, 1967.

Duncan, Martha Grace. *Romantic Outlaws, Beloved Prisons: Unconscious Meanings of Crime and Punishment*. New York: New York University Press, 1996.

Dunlea, William. *Anne Hutchinson and the Puritans: An Early American Tragedy*. Pittsburgh: Dorrance Publishing Co., Inc., 1993.

Durkheim, Emile. *The Rules of Society and Method.* 8th ed. Translated by Sarah A. Solovay and John H. Mueller, edited by George E.G. Catlin. New York: The Free Press, 1938.

Duvall, John N. "Authentic Ghost Stories: *Uncle Tom's Cabin, Absolom, Absolom!,* and *Beloved. The Faulkner Journal* 4.1-2 (1988): 83-97.

Emerson, Ralph Waldo. "The Fugitive Slave Law." Originally delivered 1854. In *The Selected Writings of Ralph Waldo Emerson,* edited by Brooks Atkinson. New York: The Modern Library, 1992.

Erikson, Kai T. *Wayward Puritans: A Study in the Sociology of Deviance.* New York: John Wiley and Sons, Inc., 1966.

Fehrenbacher, Don E. "Slavery, the Framers, and the Constitution." In *Slavery and Its Consequences: The Constitution, Equality, and Race,* edited by Robert A. Goldwin and Art Kaufman. Washington, DC: American Enterprise Institute for Public Policy Research, 1988.

———. *Slavery, Law, and Politics: The Dred Scott Case in Historical Perspective.* New York: Oxford University Press, 1981.

———. *The Dred Scott Case: Its Significance in American Law and Politics.* New York: Oxford University Press, 1978.

Ferguson, Rebecca. "History, Memory and Language in Toni Morrison's *Beloved.*" In *Feminist Criticism: Theory and Practice,* edited by Susan Sellers. Toronto: University of Toronto Press, 1991.

Ferguson, Robert. *Law and Letters in American Culture.* Cambridge: Harvard University Press, 1984.

Ferreira, Patricia. "What's Wrong with Miss Anne: Whiteness, Women, and Power in *Meridian* and *Dessa Rose.*" *SAGE* VIII.1 (Summer 1991): 15-20.

Fetterley, Judith. "'My Sister! My Sister!' The Rhetoric of Catharine Sedgwick's *Hope Leslie*. *American Literature* 70.3 (September 1998): 491–516.

Filler, Louis. *Slavery in the United States*. New Brunswick: Transaction Publishers, 1998.

Finkelman, Paul, ed. *Slavery and the Law*. Madison, WI: Madison House, 1997.

Fish, Stanley. *Doing What Comes Naturally: Change, Rhetoric, and the Practice of Theory in Literary and Legal Studies*. Durham: Duke University Press, 1989.

Fitzpatrick, Peter, and Alan Hunt, eds. *Critical Legal Studies*. New York: Basil Blackwell, 1987.

Flexner, Eleanor. *Century of Struggle: The Woman's Rights Movement in the United States*. Rev. ed. Cambridge: Harvard University Press, 1975.

Foster, Charles H. *The Rungless Ladder: Harriet Beecher Stowe and New England Puritanism*. Durham: Duke University Press, 1954.

Foster, Edward Halsey. *Catharine Maria Sedgwick*. New York: Twayne Publishers, 1974.

Foster, Frances Smith. *Witnessing Slavery: The Development of Antebellum Slave Narratives*. Madison: University of Wisconsin Press, 1979.

———. "Changing Concepts of the Black Woman." *Journal of Black Studies* 3.4 (June 1973): 433–54.

Fox-Genovese, Elizabeth. *Within the Plantation Household: Black and White Women of the Old South*. Chapel Hill: University North Carolina Press, 1988.

Franklin, John Hope, and Genna Rae McNeil. *African Americans and the Living Constitution*. Washington: Smithsonian Institute Press, 1995.

Friedland, Martin L. *Rough Justice: Essays on Crime in Literature.* Toronto: University of Toronto Press, 1991.

Friedman, Lawrence M. *American Law: An Introduction.* Rev. and updated ed. New York: W.W. Norton & Co., 1998.

——. *A History of American Law.* 2nd ed. New York: Simon and Schuster, 1985.

Garvey, T. Gregory. "Risking Reprisal: Catharine Sedgwick's *Hope Leslie* and the Legitimation of Public Action by Women." *American Transcendental Quarterly* 8.4 (Dec. 1994): 287–98.

Gay, Frederick L. *Rev. Francis Marbury,* Proceedings October, 1914–June 1915. *Massachusetts History Society.* Vol. XLV, 111. Boston: 1915.

Genovese, Eugene D. *Roll, Jordan, Roll: The World the Slaves Made.* New York: Pantheon, 1972.

Gerson, Noel B. *Harriet Beecher Stowe: A Biography.* New York: Praeger Publishers, 1976.

Gibson, Donald B. "Harriet Jacobs, Frederick Douglass, and the Slavery Debate: Bondage, Family, and the Discourse of Domesticity." In *Harriet Jacobs and Incidents in the Life of a Slave Girl: New Critical Essays,* edited by Deborah M. Garfield and Rafia Zafar. Cambridge: Cambridge University Press, 1996.

Goebel, Julius, Jr. "King's Law and Local Custom in Seventeenth Century New England," 31 *Columbia Law Review* 416 (1931).

Goldman, Anita. "Harriet Jacobs, Henry Thoreau, and the Character of Disobedience." In *Harriet Jacobs and Incidents in the Life of a Slave Girl: New Critical Essays,* edited by Deborah M. Garfield and Rafia Zafar. Cambridge: Cambridge University Press, 1996.

Goldman, Anne E. "'I Made the Ink': (Literary) Production and Reproduction in *Dessa Rose* and *Beloved.*" *Feminist Studies* 16.2 (Summer 1990): 313–30.

Gordon, Robert W. "Critical Legal Histories." *Stanford Law Review* 36 (January 1984): 58.

Gossett, Suzanne, and Barbara Ann Bardes. "Women and Political Power in the Rupublic: Two Early American Novels." *Legacy* 2.2 (1985): 13–30.

Gould, Philip. "Catharine Sedgwick's 'Recital' of the Pequot War." *American Literature* 66.4 (December 1994): 641–62.

Griffin, Farah Jasmine. "Textual Healing: Claiming Black Women's Bodies, the Erotic and Resistance in Contemporary Novels of Slavery." *Callaloo* 19.2 (1996): 519–36.

Guth, Deborah. "A Blessing and a Burden: The Relation to the Past in *Sula, Song of Solomon* and *Beloved,*" *Modern Fiction Studies* 39.3&4 (Fall/Winter 1993): 575–96.

Gutman, Herbert G. *The Black Family in Slavery and Freedom 1750–1925*. New York: Vintage, 1976.

Hall, David D., ed. *The Antinomian Controversy, 1636–1638: A Documentary History*. 2nd ed. Durham: Duke University Press, 1990.

Hall, Kermit L., ed. *The Law of Slavery: Major Historical Interpretations*. New York: Garland, 1987.

Hamilton, Cynthia S. "Revisions, Rememories and Exorcisms: Toni Morrison and the Slave Narrative." *Journal of American Studies* 30.1 (April 1996): 429–45.

Harris, Trudier. *Fiction and Folklore: The Novels of Toni Morrison*. Knoxville: University of Tennessee Press, 1991.

———. *Exorcising Blackness: Historical and Literary Lynching and Burning Rituals*. Bloomington: Indiana University Press 1984.

Harrison, Suzan. "Mastering Narratives/Subverting Masters: Rhetorics of Race in *The Confessions of Nat Turner, Dessa Rose* and *Celia, A Slave." Southern Quarterly* 35.3 (Spring 1997): 13–28.

Hart, Albert Bushnell, ed. *Commonwealth History of Massachusetts.* Vol. 1. New York: The States History Co., 1927.

Hartigan, Emily. "From Righteousness to Beauty: Reflections on Poethics and Justice as Translation," 67 *Tulsa Law Review* 455–505 (1992).

Haskins, George L. "Law and Colonial Society." In *Essays in the History of Early American Law,* edited by David H. Flaherty. Chapel Hill: University of North Carolina Press, 1969.

———. *Law and Authority in Early Massachusetts: A Study in Tradition and Design.* New York: Macmillian Co., 1960.

Hawthorne, Nathaniel. "Mrs. Hutchinson," 1830. In *Writings of Nathaniel Hawthorne.* New York: Library of America, 1982.

Heald, Paul J. *Guide to Law and Literature for Teachers, Students, and Researchers.* Durham, NC: Carolina Academic Press, 1998.

Hedrick, Joan D. *Harriet Beecher Stowe: A Life.* New York: Oxford University Press, 1994.

Heidish, Marcy Moran. *Witnesses.* Boston: Houghton Mifflin Co., 1980.

Heinzelman, Susan Sage, and Zipporah Batshaw Wiseman, eds. *Representing Women: Law, Literature, and Feminism.* Durham: Duke University Press, 1994.

Henderson, Mae G. "The Stories of O(Dessa): Stories of Complicity and Resistance." In *Female Subjects in Black and White: Race, Psychoanalysis, Feminism,* edited by Elizabeth Abel, Barbara Christian, and Helene Moglen. Berkeley: University of California Press, 1997.

———. "Speaking in Tongues: Dialogics, Dialectics, and the Tradition of the Black Woman Writer's Literary Tradition." In *Changing*

Our Own Words: Essays on Criticism, Theory, and Writing By Black Women, edited by Cheryl A. Wall. New Brunswick: Rutgers University Press, 1989.

Higginbotham, A. Leon, Jr. *In the Matter of Color: Race and the American Legal Process: The Colonial Period.* New York: Oxford University Press, 1978.

———. *Shades of Freedom: Radical Politics and Presumptions of the American Legal Process.* New York: Oxford University Press, 1996.

Hine, Darlene Clark. "Rape and the Inner Lives of Black Women in the Middle West: Preliminary Thoughts on the Culture of Dissemblance." *Signs* 14.4 (Summer 1989): 912–20.

Hirsch, Marianne. "Maternity and Rememory: Toni Morrison's *Beloved.*" In *Representations of Motherhood,* edited by Donna Basin, Margaret Honey, and Meryle Mahrer Kaplan. New Haven: Yale University Press, 1994.

Hoffer, Peter Charles. *Law and People in Colonial America.* Baltimore: Johns Hopkins University Press, 1992.

hooks, bell. "Sexism and the Black Female Slave Experience." *Ain't I a Woman: Black Women and Feminism.* Boston: South End Press, 1981.

Horton, James Oliver, and Lois E. Horton. "A Federal Assault: African Americans and the Impact of the Fugitive Slave Law of 1850." In *Slavery and the Law,* edited by Paul J. Finkelman. Madison, WI: Madison House, 1997.

Howe, Mark DeWolfe, ed. *Readings in American Legal History.* Cambridge, Harvard University Press, 1949.

Hughes, Gertrude R. "'How came he there?' Self Reliance, Misalliance, and Emerson's Second Fugitive Slave Law Address." *ATQ* 52 (Fall 1981): 273–86.

———. "Christian Revolution: Harriet Beecher Stowe's Response to Slavery and the Civil War." *New England Quarterly* XLVII.4 (December 1974): 535-49.

Hull, N.E.H. *Female Felons: Women and Serious Crime in Colonial Massachusetts.* Urbana: University of Illinois Press, 1987.

Humphreys, Debra. "Power and Resistance in Harriet Jacobs' *Incidents in the Life of a Slave Girl.*" In *Anxious Power: Reading, Writing, and Ambivalence in Narrative by Women,* edited by Carol J. Singley and Susan Elizabeth Sweeney. New York: SUNY Press, 1993.

Hutchinson, Thomas. *The History of the Colony and Province of Massachusetts-Bay,* edited by Lawrence Shaw Mayo. Cambridge: Harvard University Press, 1936.

Inscoe, John C. "Slave Rebellion in the First Person: The Literary 'Confessions' of Nat Turner and *Dessa Rose.*" *The Virginia Magazine of History and Biography* 97.4 (October 1989): 419-36.

Jablon, Madelyn. "Rememory, Dream Memory, and Revision in Toni Morrison's *Beloved* and Alice Walker's *The Temple of My Familiar.*" *CLA Journal* 37.2 (Dec. 1993): 136-44.

Jacobs, Harriet. *Incidents in the Life of a Slave Girl: Written by Herself,* edited by Jean Fagin Yellin. 1861. Cambridge: Harvard University Press, 1987.

———. Correspondence. *Black Abolitionist Papers.* New York: Microfilming Corporation of America, 1981-1983; Ann Arbor: University Microfilms International, 1984.

Jefferson, Thomas. *Autobiography.* In *Writings.* 1821. New York: Library of America, 1984.

Jennings, Francis. *The Invasion of America: Indians, Colonialism, and the Cost of Conquest.* Chapel Hill: Institute of Early American History and Culture, 1975.

Johnson, Edward. *Johnson's Wonder-Working Providence, 1628-1651*, edited by J. Franklin Jameson. New York: Barnes and Noble, 1910.

Jones, Jacqueline. *Labor of Love, Labor of Sorrow: Black Women, Work, and the Family from Slavery to the Present.* New York: Basic Books, 1985.

Kaminski, John P., ed. *A Necessary Evil? Slavery and the Debate Over the Constitution.* Madison, WI: Madison House, 1995.

Kammen, Michael. Introduction to *The Origins of the American Constitution: A Documentary History.* New York: Penguin, 1986.

Karcher, Carolyn L. *The First Woman in the Republic: A Cultural Biography of Lydia Maria Child.* Durham: Duke University Press, 1994.

Karlsen, Carol F. *The Devil in the Shape of a Woman: Witchcraft in Colonial New England.* New York: W. W. Norton, 1987.

Katz, Stanley N. "Looking Backward: The Early History of American Law," 33 *University of Chicago Law Review* 867 (1966).

Katz, Steven T. "The Pequot War Reconsidered." *New England Quarterly 64.2* (June 1991): 206-24.

Kawashina, Yasuhide. *Puritan Justice and the Indian: White Man's Law in Massachusetts, 1630-1763.* Middletown, CT: Wesleyan University Press, 1986.

Kay, Marvin L. Michael, and Lorin Lee Carey. *Slavery in North Carolina, 1748-1775.* Chapel Hill: University North Carolina Press, 1995.

Kekeh, Andrée-Anne. "Sherley Anne Williams' *Dessa Rose*: History and the Disruptive Power of Memory." In *History and Memory in African-American Culture,* edited by Genevieve Fabre and Robert O'Meally. New York: Oxford University Press, 1994.

Kelley, Mary. Introduction to *Power of Her Sympathy*. Boston: Massachusetts Historical Society, 1993.

———. "Negotiating a Self: The Autobiography and Journals of Catharine Maria Sedgwick." *The New England Quarterly* 66.3 (Spring 1993): 366–97.

———. "Catharine Maria Sedgwick, 1789–1867." *Legacy* 6.2 (Fall 1989): 43–50.

Kelman, Mark. *A Guide to Critical Legal Studies*. Cambridge: Harvard University Press, 1987.

Kibbey, Ann. *The Interpretation of Material Shapes in Puritanism: A Study of Rhetoric, Prejudice, and Violence*. Cambridge University Press: Cambridge, 1986.

King, Nicole R. "Meditations and Mediations: Issues of History and Fiction in *Dessa Rose*." *Soundings* 76.2–3 (Summer/Fall 1993): 351–68.

Koehler, Lyle. *A Search for Power: The 'Weaker Sex' in Seventeenth-Century New England*. Urbana: University of Illinois Press, 1980.

———. "The Case of the American Jezibels: Anne Hutchinson and Female Agitation During the Years of Antinomian Turmoil, 1636–1640." *William and Mary Quarterly* XXX.1 (1974): 55–78.

Konig, David Thomas. *Law and Society in Puritan Massachusetts: Essex County, 1629–1692*. Chapel Hill: University of North Carolina Press, 1979.

Krumholz, Linda. "The Ghosts of Slavery: Historical Recovery in Toni Morrison's *Beloved*." *African American Record* 26.3 (Fall 1992): 395–408.

Lang, Amy Schrager. *Prophetic Woman: Anne Hutchinson and the Problem of Dissent in the Literature of New England*. Berkeley: University of California Press, 1987.

Ledwon, Lenora, ed. *Law and Literature: Text and Theory.* New York: Garland, 1996.

Lehmann-Haupt, Christopher. "Books of the Times; Friendship in Chains." *New York Times,* 12 July 1986, sec. 1, p. 12.

Lerner, Gerda, ed. 'The Case of Margaret Garner," *Black Women in White America: A Documentary History.* New York: Vintage Books, 1972.

Lester, Julius. "James Baldwin—Reflections of a Maverick." *New York Times Book Review,* 27 May 1994, 1, 22-24. Rpt. in *Conversations with James Baldwin,* edited by Fred L. Standley and Louis H. Pratt. Jackson: University Press of Mississippi, 1989.

Levine, Michael L. *African Americans and Civil Rights: From 1619 to the Present.* Phoenix: Oryx Press, 1996.

Lewis, Charles. "The Ironic Romance of New Historicism: *The Scarlet Letter* and *Beloved* Standing Side by Side." *Arizona Quarterly* 51.1 (Spring 1995): 33-60.

Lock, Helen. "'Building up from Fragments': The Oral Memory Process in Some Recent African-American Written Narratives." *College Literature* 22.3 (Oct. 1995): 109-20.

Locke, John. "Of Slavery," *Second Treatise of Government* (1690), edited by C.B. Macphearson. Indianapolis: Hackett Publishing Company, 1980.

Locke, Mamie E. *From Three-Fifths to Zero: Implication of the Constitution for African-American Women, 1787-1870.* Rpt. in *Women and the American Legal Order,* edited by Karen J. Maschke. New York: Garland, 1997.

Loewenberg, Bert James, and Ruth Bogin, eds. *Black Women in Nineteenth-Century American Life: Their Words, Their Thoughts, Their Feelings.* University Park: Pennsylvania State University, 1976.

Lovell, Thomas B. "By Dint of Labor and Economy: Harriet Jacobs, Harriet Wilson, and the Salutary View of Wage Labor." *Arizona Quarterly* 52.3 (Autumn 1996): 1.

MacEacheren, Elaine. "Emancipation of Slavery in Massachusetts: A Reexamination, 1770-1790." *Journal of Negro History* 55 (Oct. 1970): 289-306.

MacKinnon, Catharine A. "Law's Stories as Reality and Politics." In *Law's Stories: Narrative and Rhetoric in the Law*, edited by Peter Brooks and Paul Gewirtz. New Haven: Yale University Press, 1996.

Maclear, J.F. "Anne Hutchinson and the Moralist Heresy." *The New England Quarterly* LIV.1 (March 1981): 74-103.

Maida, Particia. "*Kindred* and *Dessa Rose*: Two Novels That Reinvent Slavery." *CEAMagazine* 4.1 (1991): 43-52.

Marbury, Francis. "The Conference Between Me and the Bishop of London." (c. 1590). In *Notes and Documents on Rev. Francis Marbury*, edited by Frederick L. Gay. Boston: Massachusetts Historical Society, 1915.

Mason, John. *A Brief History of the Pequot War* (1736). Ann Arbor: March of America Facsilime Series, 1966.

Mathison-Fife, Jane. "*Dessa Rose*: A Critique of the Received History of Slavery." *Kentucky Philological Review* 8 (1993): 29-33.

McDougall, Marion Gleason. *Fugitive Slaves 1619-1865*. Boston: Ginn & Company, 1891.

McDougle, Ivan E. *Slavery in Kentucky: 1792-1865* (1918). Westport, CT: Negro University Press, 1970.

McDowell, Deborah E. "Negotiating Between Tenses: Witnessing Slavery after Freedom—Dessa Rose." In *Slavery and the Literary Imagination*, edited by Deborah E. McDowell and Arnold Rampersad. Baltimore: Johns Hopkins University Press, 1989.

McKay, Nellie Y. "The Girls Who Became the Women: Childhood Memories in the Autobiographies of Harriet Jacobs, Mary Church Terrell, and Anne Moody." In *Tradition and the Talents of Women*, edited by Florence Howe. Urbana: University of Illinois Press, 1991.

McKible, Adam. "'These are the facts of the darky's history': Thinking History and Reading names in Four African American Tests." *African American Review* 28.2 (1994): 223–35.

McLaurin, Melton A. *Celia, a Slave*. New York: Avon, 1991.

McLoughlin, William G. "Anne Hutchinson Reconsidered." *Rhode Island History* 49.1 (February 1991): 13.

Miller, Perry. *Orthodoxy in Massachusetts 1630–1650*. Gloucester, MA: Peter Smith, 1965.

———. *The New England Mind: From Colony to Providence*. Cambridge: Harvard University Press, 1953.

———, ed. *The American Puritans: Their Prose and Poetry*. New York: Columbia University Press, 1956.

Minda, Gary. *Postmodern Legal Movements: Law and Jurisprudence at Century's End*. New York: New York University Press, 1995.

Minow, Martha, ed. *Family Matters: Readings on Family Lives and the Law*. New York: New Press, 1993.

Mintz, Steven. *A Prison of Expectations: The Family in Victorian Culture*. New York: New York University Press, 1983.

Mobley, Marilyn Sanders. "A Different Remembering: Memory, History and Meaning in Toni Morrison's *Beloved*." In *Toni Morrison: Modern Critical Views*, edited by Harold Bloom. New York: Chelsea House Publishers, 1990.

Moglen, Helene, "Redeeming History: Toni Morrison's *Beloved.*" In *Female Subjects in Black and White: Race, Psychoanalysis, Feminism*, edited by Elizabeth Abel, Barbara Christian, and

Helene Moglen. Berkeley: University of California Press, 1997.

Moody, Joycelyn K. "Ripping Away the Veil of Slavery: Literacy, Communal Love, and Self-Esteem in Three Slave Women's Narratives." *Black American Literature Forum* 24.4 (Winter 1990): 633–48.

Morgan, Edmund S. *The Puritan Dilemma: The Story of John Winthrop*. Boston: Little, Brown and Co., 1958.

Morgan, Winifred. "Gender-Related Difference in the Slave Narratives of Harriet Jacobs and Frederick Douglass," *American Studies* 35.2 (Fall 1994): 73–94.

Morris, Thomas D. *Free Men All: The Personal Liberty Laws of the North, 1780–1861*. Baltimore: Johns Hopkins University Press, 1974.

Morrison, Toni. "The Site of Memory." In *Inventing the Truth: The Art of Craft of Memoir*. Rev. and expanded. 2nd ed., edited by William Zinsser. Boston: Houghton Mifflin Company, 1995.

———. *Beloved*. New York: Plume/Putnam Penguin, 1987.

———. "Rootedness: The Ancestor as Foundation." In *Black Women Writers (1950–1980): A Critical Evaluation*. Garden City, NY: Anchor Press/Doubleday, 1984.

Morse, Anita L. "Pandora's Box: An Essay Review of American Law and Literature on Prostitution," 4 *Wisconsin Women's Law Journal* 21–62 (1988).

Moseley, James G. *John Winthrop's World: History as a Story; The Story as History*. Madison: University of Wisconsin Press, 1992.

Naylor, Gloria and Toni Morrison, "A Conversation." *The Southern Review* 21.3 (July 1985): 567–93.

Nelson, Dana. "Sympathy as Strategy in Sedgwick's *Hope Leslie*." In *The Culture of Sentiment: Race, Gender and Sentimentality in*

Nineteenth-Century America, edited by Shirley Samuels. New York: Oxford University Press, 1992.

Newcomb, Wellington. "Anne Hutchinson Versus Massachusetts," *American Heritage* XXV.4 (June 1974): 12–81.

Norton, Mary Beth. *Founding Mothers and Fathers: Gendered Power and the Forming of American Society*. New York: Alfred A. Knopf, 1996.

Nussbaum, Martha. *Poetic Justice: The Literary Imagination and Public Life*. Boston: Beacon, 1996.

O'Brien, William. "Did the Jennison Case Outlaw Slavery in Massachusetts." *William and Mary Quarterly*, 3rd ser., 17 (April 1960): 219–41.

Ontiveros, Maria L. "Fictionalizing Harassment: Disclosing the Truth," 93 *Michigan Law Review* 1373 (1995).

Osgood, Herbert L. *The American Colonies in the Seventeenth Century*. Vol. I. New York: Macmillan Co., 1904.

Otten, Terry. "Horrific Love in Toni Morrison's Fiction," *Modern Fiction Studies* 39.3&4 (Fall/Winter 1993): 655–67.

Paine, Thomas. "Common Sense" (1776). In *Thomas Paine Reader*, edited by Michael Foot and Isaac Kramnick. New York: Penguin, 1997.

Pagano, Jo Anne. "Relating to One's Students: Identity, Morality, Stories and Questions." *Journal of Moral Education* 20.3 (1991): 257–66.

Pearl, Valerie, and Morris Pearl, eds. " Governor John Winthrop on the Birth of the Antinomians' 'Monster': The Earliest Reports to Reach England and the Making of a Myth." In *Proceedings of the Massachusetts Historical Society*. Vol. CH. Boston: The Society, 1991.

Pettit, Norman. *The Heart Prepared: Grace and Conversion in Puritan Spiritual Life.* New Haven: Yale University Press, 1966.

Plato. *The Last Days of Socrates: Euthyphro/The Apology/Crito/Phaedo,* translated by Hugh Tredennick and Harold Tarrant. New York: Penguin, 1993.

Porter, Nancy. "Women's Interracial Friendships and Visions of Community in Meridian, The Salt Eaters, and Dessa Rose." In *Tradition and the Talents of Women,* edited by Florence Howe. Urbana: University of Illinois Press, 1991, 251-67.

Porterfield, Amanda. *Female Piety in Puritan New England: The Emergence of Religious Humanism.* New York: Oxford University Press, 1992.

Posner, Richard. *Law and Literature.* Rev. and enlarged edition. Cambridge: Harvard University Press, 1998.

———. *Law and Literature: A Misunderstood Relation.* Cambridge: Harvard University Press, 1988.

Proceedings of the Anti-Slavery Convention of American Women. New York, 1837.

Reed, Kenneth T. "Thoreauvian Echo in *Uncle Tom's Cabin?*" *American Transcendental Quarterly* 11.1 (Summer 1971): 37-38.

Rigney, Barbara Hill. "'A Story to Pass On': Ghosts and the Significance of History in Toni Morrison's *Beloved.*" In *Haunting the House of Fiction: Feminist Perspectives on Ghost Stories by American Women,* edited by Lynette Carpenter and Wendy K. Kolmar. Knoxville: University of Tennessee Press, 1991.

Roberts, Dorothy E. "Racism and Patriarchy in the Meaning of Motherhood." In *Mothers in Law: Feminist Theory and the Legal Regulation of Motherhood,* edited by Martha Albertson Fireman and Isabel Karpin. New York: Columbia University Press, 1995.

Rockwood, Bruce L. "Retakings: Perspectives on the Nature of Property and Politics from the Law and Literature of Slavery." *Law and the Conflict of Ideologies: Nineth Round Table on Law and Seniotics*, edited by Roberta Kevelson. New York: Peter Lang, 1996.

———, ed. *Law and Literature Perspectives*. New York: Peter Lang, 1996.

Rody, Caroline. "Toni Morrison's *Beloved*: History, 'Rememory,' and a 'Clamor for a Kiss.'" *American Literary History* 7.1 (Spring 1995): 92–119.

Romero, Lora. *Home Fronts: Domesticity and Its Critics in the Antebellum United States*. Durham: Duke University Press, 1997.

Ross, Richard J. "The Legal Past of Early New England: Notes for the Study of Law, Legal Culture, and Intellectual History." *William and Mary Quarterly*, 3rd series, L.1 (Jan. 1993): 28–41.

Rothstein, Mervyn. "Morrison Defends Women." *New York Times*, 26 August 1987.

Rugg, Winnifred King. *Unafraid: A Life of Anne Hutchinson*. Freeport, NY: Books for Libraries Press, 1930.

Rugoff, Milton. *The Beechers: An American Family in the Nineteenth Century*. New York: Harper & Row, Publishers, 1981.

Rushdy, Ashraf H. A. "Reading Mammy: The Subject of Relation in Sherley Anne Williams' *Dessa Rose*." *African American Review* 27.3 (1993): 365–89.

———. "Rememory: Primal Scenes and Constructions in Toni Morrison's Novels." *Contemporary Literature* 31.3 (1990).

Rutman, Darrett B. *Winthrop's Boston: Portrait of A Puritan Town 1630–1649*. Chapel Hill: University of North Carolina Press, 1965.

St. Joan, Jacqueline, and Annette Bennington McElhiney, eds. *Beyond Portia: Women, Law, and Literature in the United States*. Boston: Northeastern University Press, 1997.

Samuels, Wilfred, and Clenora Hudson-Weems. *Toni Morrison.* Boston: Twayne, 1990.

Sánchez, Marta E. "The Estrangement Effect in Sherley Anne William's *Dessa Rose*." *Genders* 15 (Winter 1992): 21–36.

Scales-Trent, Judy. "Using Literature in Law School: The Importance of Reading and Telling Stories." *Berkeley Women's Law Journal* 90 (1992).

———."Black Women and the Constitution: Finding our Place, Asserting our Rights." 24 *Harvard Civil Rights-Civil Liberties Law Review* 9 (1989).

Schaller, Barry R. *A Vision of American Law: Judging Law, Literature, and the Stories We Tell.* Westport, CT: Praeger, 1997.

Sedgwick, Catharine Maria. *Hope Leslie*, edited by Mary Kelly. (1827). New Brunswick, NJ: Rutgers University Press, 1987.

———. "Slavery in New England." *Bentley's Miscellany* 34 (1853): 417–24.

———. *Life and Letters*, edited by Mary E. Dewey. New York: Harper and Brothers, 1871.

———. *The Power of Her Sympathy: The Autobiography and Journal of Catharine Maria Sedgwick*, edited by Mary Kelley. Boston: Massachusetts History Society, 1993.

Sedgwick, Sara Cabot, and Christina Sedgwick Maraquand. *Stockbridge: 1739–1939: A Chronicle.* Great Barrington, MA: 1939.

Shapiro, Fred R., and Jane Garry, eds. *Trial and Error: An Oxford Anthology of Legal Stories.* New York: Oxford University Press, 1998.

Shurtleff, Nathaniel B., ed. *Records of the Governor and Company of the Massachusetts Bay in North East.* Vol. I. 1628–1641. Boston: William White, 1853.

Singley, Carol J. "Catharine Maria Sedgwick's Hope Leslie: Radical Frontier Romance." In *The (Other) American Traditions: Nineteenth-Century Women Writers*, edited by Joyce W. Warren. New Brunswick, NJ: Rutgers University Press3.

Smith, Carl S., John P. McWilliams, Jr., and Maxwell Bloomfield, eds. *Law and American Literature: A Collection of Essays*. New York: Knopf, 1982.

Smith, Valerie. Introduction to *Incidents in the Life of a Slave Girl* by Harriet Jacobs, edited by Henry Louis Gates, Jr. New York: Oxford University Press, 1988.

Smith-Wright, Geraldine. "A Response to Williams." *Soundings* 76.2-3 (Summer/Fall 1993): 261-63.

Stampp, Kenneth M. *The Peculiar Institution: Slavery in the Ante-Bellum South*. New York: Knopf, 1956.

Standley, Fred L. and Louis H. Pratt, eds. *Conversations with James Baldwin*. Jackson: University of Mississippi Press, 1989.

Stone, Albert E. *The Return of Nat Turner: History, Literature, and Cultural Politics in Sixties America*. Athens: University of Georgia Press, 1992.

Stowe, Charles Edward. *Life of Harriet Beecher Stowe*. Boston: Houghton Mifflin and Co., 1889.

Stowe, Harriet Beecher. *A Key to Uncle Tom's Cabin: Presenting the Original Facts and Documents Upon Which the Story Is Founded*. London: Thomas Bosworth, 1853.

———. *Uncle Tom's Cabin, Or, Life Among the Lowly*. 1852. New York: Viking Penguin, 1986.

Tate, Claudia. "Allegories of Black Female Desire; Or, Rereading Nineteenth-Century Sentimental Narratives of Black Female Autobiography." In *Changing Our Own Words: Essays on Criticism, Theory, and Writing By Black Women*, edited by Cheryl A. Wall. New Brunswick, NJ: Rutgers University Press, 1989.

Taylor, Susie King. *Reminiscences of My Life in Camp With the 33rd United States Colored Troops Late 1st S.C. Volunteers*, 1902. Rpt. in *Collected Black Women's Narratives*. The Schomburg Library of Nineteenth-Century Black Women Writers. New York: Oxford University Press, 1988.

Thomas, Brook. *American Literary Realism and the Failed Promise of Contract*. Berkeley: University of California Press, 1997.

———. *Cross-Examinations in Law and Literature: Cooper, Hawthorne, Stowe, and Melville*. Cambridge: Cambridge University Press, 1987.

Thoreau, Henry David. *Walden and Civil Disobedience*, edited by Michael Mayer. New York: Penguin, 1983.

Tobin, Elizabeth. "Imagining the Mother's Text: Toni Morrison's *Beloved* and Contemporary Law." In *Beyond Portia: Women, Law, and Literature in the United States*, edited by Jacqueline St. Joan and Annette Bennington McElhiney. Boston: Northeastern University Press, 1997.

Trapasso, Ann E. "Returning to the Site of Violence: The Restructuring of Slavery's Legacy in Sherley Anne Williams's *Dessa Rose*." In *Violence, Silence, and Anger: Women's Writing as Transgression*, edited by Deirdre Lashgari. Charlottesville: University Press of Virginia, 1995.

Truth, Sojourner. *Narrative of Sojourner Truth: A Bondswoman of Olden Time*, compiled by Olive Gilbert. 1878. New York: Arno, 1968.

Tushnet, Mark V. *The American Law of Slavery 1810–1860: Considerations of Humanity and Interest*. Princeton: Princeton University Press, 1981.

Ulrich, Laurel Thatcher. *Good Wives: Image and Reality in the Lives of Women in Northern New England 1650–1750*. New York: Alfred A. Knopf, 1982.

Underhill. *Newes from America; Or, A Nwe Experimentall Discoverie of New England.* London, 1638.

Van Evrie, J. H. Introduction to *The Dred Scott Decision.* New York: Van Evrie, Horton Co., 1859.

Veney, Bethany. *The Narrative of Bethany Veney, A Slave Woman,* 1889. Rpt. in *Collected Black Women's Narratives.* The Schomburg Library of Nineteenth-Century Biography of Writers. New York: Oxford University Press, 1988.

Vermillion, Mary. "Reembodying the Self: Representations of Rape in *Incidents in the Life of a Slave Girl* and *I Know Why the Caged Bird Sings.*" *Biography: An Interdisciplinary Quarterly* 15.3 (Summer 1992): 243–60.

Walker, Melissa. *Down from the Mountaintop: Black Women's Novels in the Wake of the Civil Rights Movement, 1966–1989.* New Haven: Yale University Press, 1991.

Walter, Krista. "Surviving in the Garret: Harriet Jacobs and the Critique of Sentiment." *American Transcendental Quarterly* 8.3 (September 1994): 189–210.

Ward, Ian. *Law and Literature: Possibilities and Perspectives.* Cambridge: Cambridge University Press, 1995.

Waterman, Julius S. "Thomas Jefferson and Blackstone's *Commentaries,*" *Illinois Law Review* xxvii (1933): 629–59.

Watson, Alan. *Slave Law in the Americas.* Athens: University of Georgia Press, 1989.

Waxman, Barbara Frey. "Changing History through a Gendered Perspective: A Postmodern Feminist Reading of Morrison's *Beloved.*" In *Multicultural Literatures Through Feminist/Poststructuralist Lenses,* edited by Barbara Frey Waxman. Knoxville, University of Tennessee Press, 1993.

Weil, Lisa. "Virginia Woolf's 'To the Lighthouse': Toward an Integrated Jurisprudence," 6 *Yale Journal of Law & Feminism* 1 (1994).

Weinstein, Philip M. *What Else But Love? The Ordeal of Race in Faulkner and Morrison.* New York: Columbia University Press, 1996.

Weisberg, Richard H. *Poethics and Other Strategies of Law and Literature.* New York: Columbia University Press, 1992.

———. *The Failure of the Word: The Lawyer as Protagonist in Modern Fiction.* New Haven: Yale University Press, 1984.

Welch, Jr., Richard E. *Theodore Sedgwick, Federalist: A Political Portrait.* Middletown, CT: Wesleyan University Press, 1965.

———. "Mumbet and Judge Sedgwick: A Footnote to the Early History of Massachusetts Justice," *The Boston Bar Journal* VII (Jan. 1964).

Welter, Barbara, "The Cult of True Womanhood: 1820–1860." *American Quarterly* XVIII.2 (Summer 1966): 151–74.

West, Cornel. *Race Matters.* New York: Vintage Books, 1993.

West, Hollie I. "James Baldwin: No Gain for Race Relations," *The Miami Herald* 16 April 1979, D1. Rpt. in *Conversations with James Baldwin*, edited by Fred L. Standley and Louis H. Pratt. Jackson: University of Mississippi Press, 1989.

West, Robin. *Caring for Justice.* New York: New York University Press, 1997.

———. *Narrative, Authority, and Law.* Ann Arbor: University of Michigan Press, 1993.

Westerkamp, Marilyn J. "Puritan Patriarch, and the Problem of Revelation," *Journal of Interdisciplinary History* xxiii.3 (Winter 1993): 571–95.

Wheeler, Leslie, ed. Introduction to *Loving Warriors: Selected Letters of Lucy Stone and Henry B. Blackwell, 1853 to 1893.* New York: Dial Press, 1981.

White, Deborah Gray. *Ar'n't I a Woman? Female Slaves in the Plantation South.* New York: W.W. Norton, 1985.

White, James Boyd. "Phi Beta Kappa Lecture." 4 May 1998. University of Georgia, Athens, GA.

———. *Acts of Hope: Creating Authority in Literature, Law, and Politics.* Chicago: University of Chicago Press, 1995.

———. *Heracles' Bow: Essays on the Rhetoric and Poetics of the Law.* Madison: University of Wisconsin Press, 1985.

———. *The Legal Imagination.* Chicago: University of Chicago Press, 1973.

Whitman, Walt. "Song of Myself." *Leaves of Grass.* In *Complete Poetry and Collected Prose.* 1855. New York: Library of America, 1982.

Wigmore, John H. "A List of Legal Novels," 2 *University of Illinois Law Review* 547 (1908).

Williams, John. *The Redeemed Captive, Returning to Zion,* 1707. Rpt. in *Narratives of North America Indian Captivities.* Vol. 5, edited by Wilcomb E. Washburn. New York: Garland, 1978.

Williams, Keith. "The (Un)spoken History: Sherley Anne Williams' *Dessa Rose* and the Production Narrative." Paper presented at the American Literature Association Conference, San Diego, CA, 1998.

Williams, Patricia. *The Alchemy of Race and Rights.* Cambridge: Harvard University Press, 1991.

Williams, Selma R. *Divine Rebel: The Life of Anne Marbury Hutchinson.* New York: Holt, Rinehart and Winston, 1981.

Williams, Sherley Anne. "The Lion's History: The Ghetto Writes B[l]ack." *Soundings* 76.2-3 (Summer/Fall 1993): 245-60.

———. *Dessa Rose.* New York: Berkley Books, 1986.

———. Interview with Sherley Anne Williams. *Black Women Writers at Work*, edited by Clauldia Tate. New York: Continuum, 1983.

———. "Meditations on History." In *Midnight Birds*, edited by Mary Helen Washington. New York: Doubleday, 1980.

———. *Give Birth to Brightness: A Thematic Study in Neo-Black Literature.* New York: Dial Press, 1972.

Winchell, Donna Haisty. "Cries of Outrage: Three Novelists' Use of History." *Mississippi Quarterly* XLIX. 4 (Fall, 1996): 727–41.

Winsser, Johan. "Mary Dyer and the 'Monster' Story." *Quaker History* 79.1 (1990): 20–34.

Winthrop, John. *The Journal of John Winthrop*, edited by Richard S. Dunn, James Savage, and Laetitia Yeandle. Cambridge: Belknap Press of Harvard University Press, 1996.

———. *Winthrop Papers.* Vols. 2 & 3, edited by Arthur Meier Schlesinger. Boston: Massachusetts Historical Society, 1931 and 1943.

———. *The History of New England from 1630 to 1649*, edited by James Savage. New York: Arno Press, 1972.

Withington, Ann Fairfax, and Jack Schwartz. "The Political Trial of Anne Hutchinson," *The New England Quarterly* LI.2 (June 1978): 226–40.

Woidat, Caroline M. "Talking Back to Schoolteacher: Morrison's Confrontation With Hawthorne in *Beloved*." *Modern Fiction Studies* 39.3&4 (Fall/Winter 1993): 527–43.

Wolff, Cynthia Griffin. "'Masculinity' in Uncle Tom's Cabin." *American Quarterly* 47.4 (Dec. 1995).

———."'Margaret Garner': A Cincinnati Story." In *Discovering Difference: Essays in American Culture*, edited by Christoph K. Lohmann. Bloomington: Indiana University Press, 1993.

Wortman, Marlene Stein, ed. *Women in American Law: From Colonial Times to the New Deal.* Vol. 1. New York: Holmes and Meier, Pub., Inc., 1985.

Wright, Richard. *Native Son.* 1940. New York: Harper Perennial, 1993.

Wyatt, Jean. "Giving Body to the Word: The Maternal Symbolic in Toni Morrison's *Beloved.*" *PMLA* 108.3 (May 1993): 474.

Yellin, Jean Fagan. Introduction to *Incidents in the Life of a Slave Girl, Written by Herself* by Harriet Jacobs. Cambridge: Harvard University Press, 1987.

―――. "Texts and Contexts in Harriet Jacobs' *Incidents in the Life of a Slave Girl: Written by Herself*." In *The Slave's Narrative*, edited by Charles T. Davis and Henry Louis Gates, Jr. New York: Oxford University Press, 1985.

―――. "Written by Herself: Harriet Jacobs' Slave Narrative." *American Literature* 53 (Nov. 1981): 479–86.

Young, Louise M. "Women's Place in American Politics: The Historical Perspective." *Journal of Politics* 38.3 (August 1976): 295.

Zagarell, Sandra A. "Expanding 'America': Lydia Sigourney's Sketch of Connecticut, Catharine Maria Sedgwick's *Hope Leslie.*" *Tulsa Studies in Women's Literature* 6 (1987): 225–45.

Ziff, Larzar. *Puritanism in America: New Culture in a New World.* New York: Viking Press, 1973.

―――. *The Career of John Cotton: Puritanism and the American Experience.* Princeton: Princeton University Press, 1962.

Zilversmit, Arthur. "Quolk Walker, Mumbet, and the Abolition of Slavery in Massachusetts." *William and Mary Quarterly* 3rd ser., 25.4 (Oct. 1968): 614–24.

Ziolkowski, Theodore. *The Mirror of Justice: Literary Reflections of Legal Crisis.* Princeton: Princeton University Press, 1997.

Case Law

Brown v. Board of Education of Topeka, 347 U.S. 483 (1954).

Civil Rights Cases, 109 U.S. 3 (1883)

Collins v. Hardyman, 341 U.S. 651 (1951).

Dred Scott v. Sandford, 60 U.S. 393 (1857).

Emmerson v. Harriet, 11 Mo. 413 (1848).

Griffin v. Breckenridge, 403 U.S. 88 (1971).

Plessy v. Ferguson, 163 U.S. 537 (1896).

Prigg v. Pennsylvania, 16 Peters 539 (1842).

Regents of the University of California v. Bakke, 483 U.S. 265 (1978).

Scott v. Emerson, 15 mo. 576 (1852).

Somerset v. Stewart, 98 Eng. Rep. 499 (K.B. 1772).

State v. Mann, 13 N.C. Reports 263 (1829).

State v. Will, 18 N.C. Reports 121 (1834).

Statutory Law

Federal

The Fugitive Slave Act of 1793, 1 Stat. 302.

The Fugitive Slave Act of 1850, 9 Stat. 462.

Emancipation Proclamation, 12 Stat. 1269.

An Act to Repeal the Fugitive Slave Act, 13 Stat. 200.

Civil Rights Act of 1866, 14 Stat. 27.

Civil Rights Act of 1871, 16 Stat. 433.

Civil Rights Act of 1875, 18 Stat. 335.

Civil Rights Act of 1957, 71 Stat. 634.

Civil Rights Act of 1960, 74 Stat. 86.

Civil Rights Act of 1964, 78 Stat. 241.

Civil Rights Act of 1991, 105 Stat. 1071.

ALABAMA

Laws of the State of Alabama. Tuscaloosa: Marmaduke J. Slade, 1843.

KENTUCKY

The Statute Law of Kentucky, edited by William Littell (Frankfort, KY: William Hunter, 1809.

Kentucky Revised Statutes. Frankfort, KY: A.G. Hodges, 1852.

NORTH CAROLINA

The State Records of North Carolina. Vol. XXIII, Laws 1715–1776, edited by Walter Clark. Goldsboro, NC: Nash Brothers, 1904.

Laws of the State of North Carolina, Acts of 1723, 1729, 1741, 1753, 1774, 1787, edited by James Iredell. Edenton: Hodge & Wills, 1791.

Revised Code of North Carolina. Boston: Little, Brown and Company, 1855.

VIRGINIA

Virginia, *Acts of the General Assembly, Passed 1855–1856.* Richmond: William F. Richie, 1856.

Index

1870 Enforcement Act 121

A

Adams, Charles Francis 26
Anti-Slavery Convention of American Women 101
Antinomian Controversy 13, 18

B

Barry, John Stetson 26
Bill of Rights 156
Blackstone, William 85
Body of Liberties 23
Boyd, James White 1
Bradstreet, Simon 32
Brown, Albert Gallatin 112
Brown v. Board of Education 122

C

Child, L. Maria 101
Civil Disobedience 2, 98, 100, 114, 132
Civil Rights Act
  of 1866 120
  of 1871 121
  of 1875 121
  of 1957 123
  of 1964 123
Civil Rights Cases 121
Coddington, William 40
Colburn, William 41
Congress of Representative Women 83
Constitution, U.S. 2, 30, 48, 51, 52, 84, 85, 86, 87, 88, 90, 91, 92, 121, 122, 123, 124, 139, 140, 156
  Fifteenth Amendment to 121
  Thirteenth Amendment to 120
Cotton, John 1, 10, 16–17, 39
  A Conference Mr. John Cotton Held at Boston with the Elders of New-England 25
  An Abstract; or, the Lawes of New England 23
Cult of Motherhood 83. *See also* Motherhood
Cult of True Womanhood 80. *See also* Cult of Motherhood

D

Dred Scott v. Sandford 90
Dudley, Thomas 32
Dyer, Mary 43

E

Eliot, John 36
Emancipation Proclamation 119
Emerson, Ralph Waldo 89

F

Ferguson, Robert 1
Fish, Stanley 1
Freeman, Elizabeth 49, 52, 58, 68. *See also* Mumbet
  Brom and Bett v. Ashley 52
Fugitive Slave Act
  of 1793 119
  of 1850 90, 119

Fugitive Slave Laws 52, 87–89, 102, 112, 138

G

Garner, Margaret 137–40

H

Hawkins, Jane 44
Hutchinson, Anne 1–2, 47, 49, 155
  beliefs and teaching 10, 14, 17–18. *See also* Antinomian Controversy
  influence of Calvin on 17. *See also* Cotton, John
  early life and family 15–20, 22, 42
  ecclesiastical trial 43
  examination before the general court 25–27, 42–44
  day one 27–37
  day two 37–42
  life in exile 44
  meeting of the synod 23–25
Hutchinson, Thomas 25

J

Jacobs, Harriet 2, 80, 81, 83, 84, 99, 100–2, 105, 106, 108–16, 118, 119, 135, 136, 147
Jennison, William 42

L

Law and Literature Scholarship 1
Lincoln, Abraham 118

M

Mason, James 89
Massachusetts Bay Colony 9–11, 16, 155
  early laws and court system 14, 20–23

Missouri Compromise 89
Morrison, Toni 2, 81, 82, 115–19, 135–37, 140, 143, 144, 150–53, 157, 187
Motherhood 83, 84, 93, 95, 99, 100, 116. *See also* Cult of Motherhood
Mumbet 49, 58. *See also* Freeman, Elizabeth

N

Native Americans. *See* Pequot Indians

P

Paine, Thomas 1
Pequot Indians 2, 9, 21, 11, 47–49, 54–57, 59, 61–63, 68, 69, 75, 156
  war with Puritans 54–61
Peter, Hugh 34, 43
Plato 1
Plessy v. Ferguson 122
Post, Amy 101
Prigg v. Pennsylvania 88
Puritans 9, 10, 14, 16, 48, 57, 63, 74

R

Regents of the University of California v. Bakke 123

S

Sedgwick, Catharine Maria 2
  Calvinist influence on 53–54
  early life and family 50–54
Slave Law
  effect on families 95–100
  in Alabama 126–37
  in Kentucky 140–42
  in North Carolina 102–05
Somerset v. Stewart 90

State v. Mann 104
State v. Will 104
Stowe, Harriet Beecher 2, 81, 83, 84,
    92–101, 114–16, 118, 119, 136
  Key to Uncle Tom's Cabin 93–96,
    98, 101, 123
Symmes, Zechariah 36

T

Taney, Roger B. 91
Truth, Sojourner 80, 87

V

Veney, Bethany 80

W

Ward, Nathaniel 36
Webster, Daniel 89
Weld, Joseph 43
Weld, Thomas 26, 43
Westminster Confession 37
Wheelwright, John 17–20
Whitman, Walt 89
Wigmore, John H. 1
Williams, Sherley Anne 2, 61, 81, 82,
    115–19, 124–27, 129, 135, 153,
    157
Winthrop, John 9, 16–20
  A Modell of Christian Charity 9, 25
  as governor of Massachusetts Bay
    21–23, 47
  Higginson, John, letter from 9
  in *Hope Leslie* 47, 55–56, 59, 62,
    69–74

MODERN AMERICAN LITERATURE
New Approaches

Yoshinobu Hakutani, General Editor

The books in this series deal with many of the major writers known as American realists, modernists, and post-modernists from 1880 to the present. This category of writers will also include less known ethnic and minority writers, a majority of whom are African American, some are Native American, Mexican American, Japanese American, Chinese American, and others. The series might also include studies on well-known contemporary writers, such as James Dickey, Allen Ginsberg, Gary Snyder, John Barth, John Updike, and Joyce Carol Oates. In general, the series will reflect new critical approaches such as deconstructionism, new historicism, psychoanalytical criticism, gender criticism/feminism, and cultural criticism.

For additional information about this series or for the submission of manuscripts, please contact:

>Peter Lang Publishing
>P.O. Box 1246
>Bel Air, MD 21014-1246

To order other books in this series, please contact our Customer Service Department at:

>800-770-LANG (within the U.S.)
>(212) 647-7706 (outside the U.S.)
>(212) 647-7707 FAX

Or browse online by series at:

>www.peterlangusa.com